Facework

Facework

Bridging Theory and Practice

Kathy Domenici
Stephen W. Littlejohn

University of New Mexico and Domenici Littlejohn, Inc.

SAGE Publications
Thousand Oaks ▪ London ▪ New Delhi

For information:

Sage Publications, Inc.
2455 Teller Road
Thousand Oaks, California 91320
E-mail: order@sagepub.com

Sage Publications Ltd.
1 Oliver's Yard
55 City Road
London EC1Y 1SP
United Kingdom

Sage Publications India Pvt. Ltd.
B-42, Panchsheel Enclave
Post Box 4109
New Delhi 110 017 India

Printed in the United States of America.

Library of Congress Cataloging-in-Publication Data

Domenici, Kathy.
Facework : bridging theory and practice / Kathy Domenici, Stephen W. Littlejohn.
        p. cm.
Includes bibliographical references and index.
ISBN 1-4129-1404-3 (cloth) — ISBN 1-4129-1405-1 (pbk.)
   1. Interpersonal relations. 2. Interpersonal communication.
3. Self-presentation. 4. Social interaction. 5. Conflict management.
I. Littlejohn, Stephen W. II. Title.
HM1106.D66 2006
302.5—dc22

                                                              2005034858

This book is printed on acid-free paper.

06   07   08   09   10   10 9 8 7 6 5 4 3 2 1

Acquiring Editor:	Todd R. Armstrong
Editorial Assistant:	Camille Herrera
Project Editor:	Astrid Virding
Copyeditor:	Kris Bergstad
Typesetter:	C&M Digitals (P) Ltd.
Cover Designer:	Michelle Lee Kenny
Cover Artist:	Mary DeLave (www.MaryDeLave.com)

Contents

Preface

Originating in Chinese culture, the metaphor of face was made popular in the United States by sociologist Erving Goffman in his work on self-presentation in the 1950s and 1960s. Since then, substantial research has been conducted on face, especially in communication. Extending this work, we define facework as a set of coordinated practices in which communicators build, maintain, protect, or threaten personal dignity, honor, and respect. In this book, we aim to provide students with (1) knowledge about facework produced in the academic literature, (2) a practical theory for understanding and acting in real-world situations, and (3) useful examples and insights for building skills. The book presents both a theoretical and a practical introduction to the topic.

Facework is most often studied as a secondary goal of interaction. In our scholarship and practice, however, we have come to believe that facework has implications far beyond the individual. Following the work in our previous books, we take a systemic approach to highlight the importance of facework as a key to the management of difference on all levels.

Facework: Bridging Theory and Practice introduces a new approach that identifies facework as the key to effective communication in many aspects of life. Face is an ongoing accomplishment within the conversations and episodes of group life, in relationships, organizations, communities, nations, and international relations. For us, facework is a much more profound form of communication than simple techniques of "saving face." It is the hard work of face over time that does honor to individuals and communities and thereby builds effective relationships, establishes a basis for trust, and generates empowerment in systems of all kinds, from families to workplaces, economic partnerships, and international relations.

Facework is an integral part of the process by which we construct meaning through communication. As shown by the numerous cases featured in our book, facework is a central process in the social construction of both identity and community that has implications not just for individuals in the immediate situation, but for entire systems as well.

Facework, then, is more than "making people feel good about themselves" or maintaining cultural norms. It requires constant vigilance and demands simultaneous and sometimes paradoxical effort on a number of levels. It is sometimes tough, and communicators do not always "feel good" about what is happening in the immediate moment. Instead, they are conscious of the need to build ultimate honor and personal identity within larger systems over time. Good facework, then, may mean working through hard places to achieve a better sense of purpose, worth, and dignity for everyone.

Our approach reflects a communication perspective. Having been educated in the discipline of communication, we honor human interaction as central to all aspects of life. We see communication as more than the transfer of information and influence. Communication is the very medium in which human beings construct their social worlds.

The authors and Sage gratefully acknowledge the following reviewers: Liliana Castañeda Rossman, California State University, San Marcos; John Oetzel, University of New Mexico; and Deborah A. Cai, University of Maryland.

Introduction

There are solutions to the major problems of our time, some of them even simple. This profound statement from Fritjof Capra (1996, p. 4) gives us hope and makes us curious. Capra sees that most of our world's problems are just different facets of a single crisis, which is a crisis of perception. He asks us to consider a radical shift in our perceptions, our thinking, and our values. Our friends at the Public Conversations Project (2003) have a button that says, "Shifts Happen." A shift may be as radical as a change of paradigm in thinking or it may be as seemingly simple as a shift in the traditional questions we ask when confronted with difference. We want to try to rise to that challenge and offer this book as a "shifting tool." Facework offers people an opportunity to ask questions that shift from a limited worldview with scarce resources for change, to one of a complex network of relationships that embody a multitude of options for life's challenges.

You may look out your window and see a tree in the front yard. You can look at a couple of branches, you can look at a few leaves, or you can look at the whole tree, or even the group of trees that constitute the small grove. You perceive that a new season is approaching by the buds or the falling leaves. You perceive the geographical area in which you are standing, as you note the type of tree in your line of sight. Capra says that what we call a tree depends on our perceptions:

> When we see a network of relationships among leaves, twigs, branches, and a trunk, we call it a tree. When we draw a picture of a tree, most of us will not draw the roots. Yet the roots of a tree are often as expansive as the parts we see. In a forest, the roots of all trees are interconnected and form a dense underground network in which there are no precise boundaries between individual trees. (1996, p. 40)

Here we want to scope out to the larger dimension of the system and scope in to narrower parts of the relationships when appropriate. These shifts can be powerful moments, enough to finally bring an organization, community, or individual to the acknowledgment of its complex nature. Once we know about the interconnected network of roots under the forest, we will not forget to include that dimension in our quest for creating a future or a solution for the trees, whether for a single tree or for the system of forests throughout the world. Through the theory offered in this book, we invite the use of deliberate and purposeful pauses in life to consider shifting. The purpose for the shifts is to check on our perceptions and ask ourselves about the world being created by our communication.

Communication creates, rather than relays, our realities. If this assertion is true, then people have even greater responsibility as communicators, for they are now builders rather than just transmitters. Using the metaphor of face, this book explores the ways in which we establish and manage identity through communication. We label these processes collectively as *facework*. We are offering a practical theory as the source for the opportunity to make principled decisions and shifts in perception. In this book, we develop a method to make principled decisions when communicating with others. Facework theory should help people shift the questions they ask of themselves, of others, and of the systems within which they interact.

We like to think of communicators who follow a principled, theory-driven practice as "artisans." Like those skilled in painting, music, writing, and sculpture, these individuals are creative, but their work is also practical and functional. They are skilled craftspersons who use materials to produce useful and needed items. They look at what is desired or required in the moment and, using practical theory, make something that can be tested and proven through practice. Bricklayers, coppersmiths, masons, tanners, and weavers are considered artisans. Of course, there is a significant artistic quality to their work. Artisans know when it is appropriate to bring out their artistic talents and when they need to work hard to produce the essential material that is needed, using the practical skills they possess.

We are convinced that good communicators are artisans. We introduce some of the artisans we have come to know, and we share some of their facework practice and examples throughout the book. President Jimmy Carter is such a person, and we would like to start by telling a story about him.

In 1991, Jean-Bertrand Aristide was elected president of Haiti, in that country's first free and fair election in its history. Barely 7 months later, his opponents, including the military leaders he had appointed, overthrew President Aristide. For 3 years, General Raoul Cedras, the leader of the coup, ruled the country, along with Emile Jonassaint, who served temporarily as president. Cedras was accused by the United States of being an evil dictator, killer, and human rights violator, while the elected president, Aristide, lived in exile in the United States.

On September 17, 1994, at the invitation of President Bill Clinton, a group of negotiators traveled to Haiti. Former President Jimmy Carter, Senator Sam Nunn, and General Colin Powell were assembled on the brink of a planned U.S. invasion of Haiti to restore the shattered country to its elected president and ease the strife and violence. Several hours of negotiation produced deadlock. The key issue was whether General Cedras and his aides would leave the country and return the power to the elected president. At that moment, Cedras was not willing to resign until the following year and then with many accompanying stipulations.

Imagine Yannick Cedras, wife of General Cedras, standing with her husband in their living room in Port-au-Prince, Haiti, talking to the Carter-Nunn-Powell negotiating team. She had been awake all night preparing for the visit of the Americans and felt confident and motivated to make a fervent plea for acknowledgment of the grandeur and significance of Haiti. She spoke of Haiti's history, that it is the oldest black republic on earth. Mrs. Cedras expressed her disgust at the poverty in Haiti, and how the resulting strife was debilitating. She ended her speech with an explanation of the pride of the people of Haiti. She said that there was no way that foreign invaders could come into their country without Haitian citizens offering their lives in defense. The previous night she had brought her three children together to pledge to die together before being taken from their home. In essence, she told the Americans, "We will die for our country before fleeing in the face of your invasion."

This impassioned entreaty was followed by many moments of uncomfortable and poignant silence. The historic discussion and steps that followed were to lead to a peaceful and bloodless resolution to a crisis that had both civil and international implications. Carter and the American team offered a brave and unprecedented communication approach at a tense and significant time in the international relations of the world. Carter "managed face" in a way that helped *that situation* to move forward without aggression or hostilities.

Carter appealed to Cedras's honor and dignity, reminding him that this U.S. negotiation team was there in good faith. Carter relayed that the Carter-Nunn-Powell team was sincerely interested in discovering Cedras's hopes and plans for his people. The team members indicated that they were not interested in repeating the label heard back in the

United States, "Cedras is a thug," but wanted to honor Cedras's interest in working out a difficult situation. Those first hours of tense and seemingly fruitless negotiations ended at three o'clock in the morning. The mood indicated that further negotiations were pointless. As the group was disbanding, feeling exhausted and discouraged, Carter continued to display human interest in Cedras.

Carter engaged Cedras in a more personal conversation about his family and their common challenge of being busy fathers. Cedras shared that he had not been home for several days and had missed the birthday of his youngest son. Carter replied that he, also, was frustrated about having a busy schedule that prohibited him from attending many family gatherings. The following day, the team met at Cedras's family home. Carter gave a birthday present to the Cedras's youngest son and was introduced to the other children. After a personal and family-oriented discussion, Mrs. Cedras excused her children and began her powerful speech to the men. The crucial decision that followed the living room conversation is still not understood completely. Cedras agreed to meet within the next hour back at headquarters to try once again to reach an agreement. Both sides of the negotiation felt renewed confidence and safety in resuming talks. The irony of the following hours is that just as talks began again, the news was relayed that the 30,000 U.S. troops had begun boarding planes to begin the attack, hoping to force the exile of the military leaders.

Chaos ensued and everyone in the room experienced agony. The Haiti group was surprised and felt cheated, and rushed to marshal its troops. The U.S. team was also surprised and became desperate. Carter asked, in that rushed moment, to bring the issue to Acting President Jonassaint, so that the civilian leader could assist with the final decision. Cedras and his group apparently were able to remember the trust and honor that had so far been bestowed on them, and consented to this last request, even in this moment of seeming betrayal! The group met with the stately, aged Jonassaint, who was also universally ridiculed in America. Cedras and his military associates listened respectfully as Carter laid out the situation before Jonassaint, everyone aware that the invasion had already been launched. In a show of personal courage, Jonassaint decided, "Haiti chooses peace, not war." Everyone in the room reached agreement and the resolution was faxed to Washington. Clinton ordered the U.S. planes and paratroopers to return to their base. The elected leaders returned to Haiti the following month, after Cedras and his family moved to Panama.

Senator Sam Nunn later described the 2-day negotiation, remembering how General Powell and President Carter appealed to the Haitians' sense of honor, their sense of dignity, their sense of obligation, their sense of wanting to protect their country. Many people still ask the question, "How did Carter trust the word of these unsavory characters?" Setting that question aside, the bottom line in this situation is that there was no bloodshed. The legitimate president of Haiti was restored; the human rights violations stopped, and Haiti had a better chance to become an emerging democracy. Many reporters and scholars report that the respect and honor with which Carter and his team conducted their communication with the leaders in Haiti gave each negotiator the freedom to consider a wider range of options for agreement, and a trust of the negotiation process that may not have occurred with U.S. military intervention.

That living room conversation with the Cedras family took place in a time of tense, desperate, and seemingly hopeless negotiations. President Carter spoke eloquently and passionately that morning. He pointed out the difference between waging war and waging peace. Carter proposed that waging peace is a much more difficult road because it is more uncertain, continuing, and complex. With Carter's consistent promise and model of treating Cedras and all his military leaders with respect, no matter what their decision, the leaders felt safe enough to continue negotiating for a way out of the political nightmare they were caught in. Cedras was one of the many world leaders that the United States had labeled "evil," or, as in Cedras's case, as a "thug." Following one of the *Principles of Peacemaking*, Carter (1998) modeled his aim to be willing to deal with the key people in any dispute, even if they have been isolated or condemned by other parties or organizations. He saw his relationship with Cedras as two men seeking a way out of an intricate military and political situation. In Carter's international negotiations, his choice to communicate respectfully and honestly is not based on hopes of trying to redeem the leaders; he merely hopes to change their approach to the problem. For those interested in waging peace, we may want to remember this episode in Haiti when President Jimmy Carter told General Raoul Cedras, "I did not come here to call you a thug."

SIDEBAR I.1   Pause

Some may conjecture that it is dangerous to negotiate with evil persons. Does "building bridges of understanding" with dictators such as Raoul Cedras or Saddam Hussein mock our attempts at democracy? Does it threaten the civilized world to bargain with military strongmen who hold vast records of human rights violations? How far should these negotiators go in developing and signing agreements with illegal leaders?

As mediators and communication scholars, we have studied this U.S./Haiti international conflict management episode because it is one that offers powerful dimensions for study and practice. With almost 40 years of combined experience in managing conflict at multiple levels, we have been active in trying to identify some of the most significant and promising threads from the work of successful practitioners. Whether looking at the *personal* level, where individual communication interactions produce certain results, or at the *relationship* level, where many conversations can be occurring at once, or at the larger *systems* level, where multiple social worlds are collaborating and competing to create forward movement, we are beginning to see some common theory, skills, and methods in the productive management of difference.

In the Haiti example, we have been intrigued by the various contexts, or *scopes of action*, where facework was manifested. This book will offer and explore four scopes of action for the utilization of face management skills and methods: *act, conversation, episode*, and *lifescript*. First we look at the speech act itself. On the personal level, Carter and Cedras were successful by simply continuing the conversation at hand. So many international diplomatic efforts do not get that far, with breakdowns in communication occurring immediately. By offering a single message, or speech *act*, "I am not here to call you a thug," Carter was saying, "I am interested in continuing this conversation, and I want it to begin with the assumption that I am here out of respect." Here we saw facework manifested in the act.

Carter knew that this situation would most likely consist of lengthy negotiations and difficult choices and options for both sides. His statement to Cedras had an impact on the whole opening trust-building session. When Carter said, "I am not here to call you a thug," he was also beginning a series of statements to alert Cedras to the tone of the *conversation* at hand, creating a context where the negotiators could establish some safety and comfort. This series of interactions probably had multiple goals, but offered facework as the basis for moving forward. In this context we saw facework at the conversation level.

The entire intervention by Carter and his team had broader implications than the immediate conversation. President Clinton sent them with loftier aims than building the trust of military leaders in Haiti. The episode they were developing was one in which many connected events were coming into play. The American troops were poised for a difficult invasion. The Haitian people knew their country was once again hovering on the brink of change, after 3 years with a brutal military leader. The elected Haitian president was in exile in the United States, and the temporary president was not even immediately involved in the negotiations. Many other national and international situations had bearing on this intervention. Those interconnected events constituted a facework *episode*. When Carter stated to Cedras, "I did not come here to call you a thug," he was making a much larger statement that touched on various other short- and long-term concerns. At the episodic level, facework can carry many risks. By offering that statement, Carter risked losing the appreciation of the Haitian people, who were still reeling from years of cruelty. Carter took a further risk by insinuating his difference in opinion with his home country and its description of Cedras. It was also a major risk to begin authentic negotiations with the illegal leader of the country, even intending to craft a signed agreement at some point. Despite these risks, the facework affected the subsequent interactions in a way that prevented bloodshed, helping Haiti to begin reconstructing its democracy. Here we see a focus on facework at the episode level.

Carter's statement, "I did not come here to call you a thug," exemplified an aspect of the overriding mission of his life, waging peace. He sees that peacemaking is not easy, that it is definitely much more difficult than waging war. He encourages others to follow his example, stating, "We must not relax in our efforts to ease the pain and suffering caused by conflict and to help the world's people secure their safety, health, and freedoms" (Carter, 1993, p. xiv). Carter believes that the rewards of waging peace cannot be measured in ordinary terms and that it will bring us many shared blessings. By entering conflict situations with the intent to show honor, dignity, and respect in his interactions, Carter models a concept of facework that is central to waging peace.

Carter (1998) answers the critical voices that challenge him, "How can you negotiate with and respect oppressors?" Knowing the risks and challenges associated with this moral stance, Carter replies,

> This [positive change] can only be done if we are willing to communicate with the people in power, no matter how unsavory they may be. Only our willingness to have dialogue enables us to find room for compromises that can save lives, and in some cases, induce the dictators to change their ways. (p. 145)

Carter has experience under his belt with leaders branded as "evil" who turn out to be willing to work seriously for the sake of peace. With this guiding vision in his life, Carter communicates from the level of his *lifescript*.

We offer this book as a contribution to the efforts of peacemaking, to constructive communication, and to the search for methods of interaction that deliberately see both the parts and the whole. Such communication may occur at the personal level, where we direct our focus to a human being who will benefit from a face-saving comment. It may occur at the relationship level, where our efforts are not only directed at the individual but are intended to affect the relationship in some way. They may also be directed at the system level, where we aim to touch the broader levels of our world, where families, workplaces, industries, and countries intersect.

PART I

The Social Construction of Face

1

Identity and Facework

A Theoretical Perspective

Seventy years ago, the great sociologist George Herbert Mead (1934) taught that mind, self, and society are outcomes of symbolic interaction. How we think about the world, including our views of ourselves, is always created in everyday talk. Identity is never pre-formed, but is constantly being made in human interaction in a process that our colleague Barnett Pearce (1994) refers to as *making social worlds.*

We once went to a graduation party, where we met a relative of the graduate. This man, intoxicated, told us that he was carrying a gun; that he needed it to defend his friends; that several people he knew had been shot; and that when it was time for him to die, he hoped it would be in a gunfight. To say that we made a hasty departure would be an understatement, but this incident did give us reason to think about the social worlds in which people live and the kinds of identities they create within these worlds. Here was a world in which dignity and honor was established by loyalty, where the group itself gained position through prevailing in violent conflict, where the larger community was defined as a battleground, and where individuals were judged, at least in part, by how well they defended a certain code of honor, even their willingness to die for it. How do such identities arise?

3

❖ ACCOMPLISHING IDENTITY

As we make judgments and decisions in the actual situations of life, we have a sense of agency or purpose, and we act to meet our goals. As we talked to the man at the party, we understood what he said in a certain way. We assigned meaning to his statement, made a judgment about its implications, and responded in a very particular way. At this moment, we were acting within what Pearce (1994) calls the *first-person perspective,* viewing the situation through our own eyes. In this perspective, we experienced ourselves as actors within the situation, but other times we experience ourselves not just as actors, but also as objects. Let's see how that happens.

When we interact with other people, we see ourselves reflected back to us in their reactions—like a "looking glass self" (Cooley, 1902). In other words, people's reactions over time create a generalized meaning that we come to recognize. Interaction leaves an impression that builds up to provide a sense of personal identity. When we become conscious of our identity, we are taking what Pearce (1994) calls the *third-person perspective,* looking at ourselves as an object. Thus, there are two senses of self, which Mead calls the "I" and the "me." When we are in the first-person perspective (the "I"), we are busy deciding what to do; when we are in the third-person perspective, we step back to reflect on ourselves from some distance (the "me"). Who I am from a third-person perspective certainly influences what I think and do within the first-person perspective; and, reciprocally, what I think and do influences who I am from a third-person perspective.

Robyn Penman (1994) writes:

> The nature of our self-identity and the constancy of it are a function of the communicative practices in which we are situated. If, for example, our practices are constant, then so too will the self-identity we avow. And if our practices are varied and complex then so too will be our self-identity. (p. 21)

The identities you co-construct with your mother, your best friend, and your rabbi are not the same, because these relational contexts are different. You are always re-making yourself in interaction with others. In other words, identity is a social accomplishment, always re-negotiated in the discourse of everyday life (Tracy & Trethewey, 2005). Your identities have implications beyond specific relationships, however, as relationships connect to one another within larger communities.

SIDEBAR 1.1   Who Am I?

On a piece of paper or computer, make a list of 20 answers to the question, "Who am I?" Work quickly, making the list as fast as you can.

After you have completed the list, look back at what you wrote. These first thoughts are good indicators of some of the things that are most important to you. You can tell a lot about yourself by the kinds of things you include in the list. You might, for example, put down a lot of affiliations, like "I am a Baptist . . . student . . . union member . . . American," and so forth. Or perhaps you wrote qualities like, "I am smart . . . hard worker . . . sometimes depressed." Another possibility are roles such as, "I am a mother . . . manager . . . designer . . . city council member." You may have written down a mix of things.

Now identify the relationships and communities that seem to be reflected in your list and write these down. For example, if you wrote "student," you might find that the college is an important social group. If you wrote "Christian," you might find that your church is important. Someone who listed "mother" might say that family is important.

Ask now, "In what groups do I show these qualities? Who sees me this way? How do I show this when I am with others?" As you work through this exercise, become conscious of your identities—personal, relational, and community.

Source: Adapted from Kuhn & McPartland (1954).

Perhaps Rom Harré (1984) was the first to make a distinction between the social construction of the *person* and that of the *self.* Personhood is the concept of the human being shared widely within a community, while the self is one individual's personal view of how he or she fits into that ideal. Another way of saying this is that the group has a "theory" of personhood, and you have a "theory" of what kind of person you are. The social construction of identity, then, consists of both shared and personal images—an idea of *persons-in-general* and *I myself as a person.* You cannot separate your self-identity from your relationships and the larger communities of which you are a part.

Take body and dress as a case in point. How do you dress? How do you dress in different situations? When would an outfit that is quite comfortable in one situation be embarrassing in another? What parts of your body are you shy about exposing? What parts don't matter? Are you always comfortable exposing the top of your head in public? Are you never comfortable doing so? Are you usually comfortable exposing your legs? Your feet? The bottom of your feet? These are all issues for some persons in certain cultures. Body issues are only one of many aspects of identity that are defined and governed through socially constructed categories of personhood, and your sense of *self* is always framed by some larger relational or community context.

People can have a continuum of identities, but we want to make this concept easier to talk about by focusing on three points, or "ranges," on this continuum. These we will call personal identity, relational identity, and community identity (Hecht, 1993; Hecht, Collier, & Ribeau, 1993; Hecht, Jackson, & Ribeau, 2003; Jung & Hecht, 2004). *Personal identity* involves the individual—self and other (Who am I, and who are you?). *Relational identity* consists of expectations negotiated within a very small group, usually two individuals (Who are we together?). *Community identity* is something larger—groups, organizations, cultures, and systems of all types (Who are we all?). These are not discrete points, but are woven together, as illustrated by Figure 1.1. Our intent is just to introduce these three levels here, as we will return to them in much more detail later in this chapter and throughout the book.

Identity and the Lifescript

Each of us possesses a dynamic and changing lifescript that guides our personal, relational, and community identities. The lifescript is a

Figure 1.1   Identities

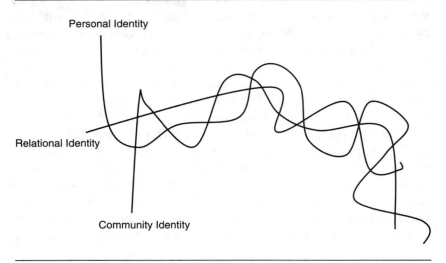

Personal Identity

Relational Identity

Community Identity

roadmap for how to live a life and how to respond to the constantly changing landscapes in which we exist. We like to use the term *moral order* to capture the assumptions that drive the lifescript (Pearce, 1989, p. 104). The moral order is a socially constructed set of understandings we carry with us from situation to situation. It is *moral* because it guides our sense of right and wrong, good and bad. It is an *order* because it is reflected in a patterned set of personal actions. The moral order is a tradition of thought worked out over time within a community. It is normally implicit and sub-conscious, but it is powerful in driving human action. The moral order guides our sense of how the world is divided up into categories; it establishes the place of humanity in the larger scheme of the universe; it delineates individual rights, roles, and responsibilities; it provides a set of values for characterizing the worlds of people and of things; it creates a logic of relations among things, or a sense of how things work together; and the moral order provides notions of how groups and individuals should act or respond to the conditions of life (Pearce & Littlejohn, 1997).

If you believe that human life is intricately connected to a larger ecology or spirituality of nature, your lifescript will take a different shape than if you believe that humans are separate and have dominion over the earth. Your lifescript will present a certain narrative if you believe that God has a plan for each person and a different narrative if you believe that people control their own destiny. You will tend to respond one way if you think that earthly life is only a stage in ongoing eternal life, and you will behave another way if you think that human beings are merely biological animals that exist only between birth and death.

We do not mean to imply here that one's lifescript is constant and consistent. If the individual is the unique merger of his or her social worlds, each of those worlds contributes to this sense of reality. Most people today do experience paradox and contradiction. We live in many social worlds, so the lifescript may contain numerous avenues for meaning and action. At any given time, a relatively coherent order may prevail, but as we live through life, our lifescript will shift, and we will not always know clearly how to act because of the inevitable contradictions we face.

Therefore, we do have moments of confusion, times when we are unsure about how to interpret events, how to act in those events, and how to respond to the messages of others. Other times, we may feel quite sure about what is going on and show a strong sense of how to behave. In general, however, individuals work out a way to feel that they are living in a coherent life. They tell stories that will demonstrate to others (and to themselves) that they are not reduced to a string of random acts, but that they are guided by a relatively coherent sense of identity.

SIDEBAR 1.2   Your Moral Order

Pick up a copy of a recent newspaper and scan the various headlines. Pick out three or four of the current controversial issues explored in these articles and read them. For each issue, ask yourself:

1. What do I believe about this issue?
2. What am I unsure about in considering this issue?
3. How have my beliefs changed over time about this issue?
4. If I had a chance to act on this issue in some way, what would I do?
5. What do the answers to Items 1–4 above tell me about my moral order?

The Coherent Identity

The sociologist Erving Goffman (1959) was firm in the belief that no one has a single, unified self. People often think that if they are honest, they will come in touch with who they "really" are. We agree with Goffman that this is a mistake. Because your sense of self-identity is always being constructed in relationship to others, you have many "selves" (Tracy & Trethewey, 2005). Because you are a member of many communities, you are influenced by numerous ideas of personhood. We also believe with Goffman that your identity is always made in how you present yourself, how you act within the situations in which you live and work.

Sometimes, you may experience a contradiction, or gap, among various identities. This can happen, for example, when your preferred personal identity conflicts with an important relational identity (Jung & Hecht, 2004). For example, you may pride yourself on your personal independence while finding yourself quite dependent on another person in a relationship that is very important to you.

Although moments of contradiction are challenging, you do organize your many portrayals into a picture or idea of your identity at any given time in your life. You may not "perform" all aspects of this coherent self at all times, but it lies there in your consciousness as an overall context or picture of who you think you are. Others also see patterns in your behavior that make it possible for them to identify you as a coherent being. This is what Mead meant by the "generalized other," or the "me." Indeed, a coherent sense of self is vital to mental health, as it gives our lives meaning. Identity confusion, which we all experience from time to time, can be a problem; when it persists, such confusion can become a mental health issue as well.

Coherence does not necessarily imply consistency. We often have a complex sense of identity. You might, for example, define yourself as a "complicated, adaptable, growing person." With this definition, you would eschew consistency and value diversity in your own behavior. You might pride yourself on thinking through each situation. Others, who tell you that you are amazingly complex and unpredictable, would actually reinforce this view. In this scenario, behavioral diversity is not a source of confusion, but achieves clarity.

Sarah Tracy and Angela Trethewey (2005) refer to one's coherent identity as a *crystallized self*. It focuses a diversity of resources that we can use in answering questions of identity. Like a crystal, the self

> is multidimensional—the more facets, the more beautiful and complex. Certainly crystals may feel solid, stable, and fixed, but just as crystals have differing forms depending upon whether they grow rapidly or slowly, under constant or fluctuating conditions, or from highly variable or remarkably uniform fluids or gasses, crystallized selves have different shapes depending on the various discourses through which they are constructed and constrained. (p. 186)

The coherent self—whether simple or complex—serves as a foundation or anchor for making decisions about how to act with other people, a standard with which to evaluate one's own behavior, and a baseline from which to grow and change. Over time, of course, self-identity shifts as we encounter new situations, new conversation partners, and new challenges. You probably would not want to be the same person when you are 60 that you were when you were 20, though there may be aspects of identity that you would like to retain. Reflect on the question: How am I different now than I was 5 years ago, 10 years ago, 20 years ago? No matter how you change, however, you usually want to present yourself to others as a person worthy of respect.

Dignity, Honor, and Respect

All of us want to believe that we are fulfilling the values of those communities and cultures most important to us. Achieving this affords dignity. We want to believe that other people see our positive role in society and share this value. Achieving this affords honor. We all want to believe that others admire us in some way for our individual and/or collective contributions, which affords respect. All mentally healthy people want to present themselves in these ways. No matter what else we may wish to convey, we also want to enact positive values, and we want others to recognize that we are doing so.

Honor depends upon the community and relationship in which the judgment is made. Pressed to justify their actions, even the most nefarious characters will frame their behavior in terms of some moral order in which the behavior is viewed as honorable:

"He may be a thief, but at least he is honest about it."

"They may have killed millions of people, but they were doing it in the name of progress."

"Some collateral damage is to be expected when evil-doers must be defeated."

Most of us are not evil and just want to do the right thing every day, even when it is not always clear what the right thing is. We want to be treated by others with respect, and we want to treat other people the same way. We often fail at this, but the ideal is there.

❖ THE METAPHOR OF FACE

The human face is so important in personal expression that it has become a symbol of close personal interaction. We use expressions such as "face to face," "face time," "in your face," and "saving face." In other words, the metaphor of face is powerful in bringing many aspects of personal communication to the fore. Within the metaphor, face is equated to your public identity—the "you" presented to others.

We use the metaphor of face to designate the universal desire to present oneself with dignity and honor. The idea of face probably originated in China, where it referred to respectability in terms of character and success (Ho, 1976; Hu, 1944). It involved a kind of reciprocated respect or deference. Erving Goffman (1967), who wrote extensively about the presentation of self, popularized the concept of face in the United States. Goffman showed how face can be "lost," "maintained," "protected," or "enhanced." These outcomes are accomplished through the work of communication, or facework. We define *facework* as *a set of coordinated practices in which communicators build, maintain, protect, or threaten personal dignity, honor, and respect.* Constructive facework is a vital aspect of all interpersonal communication. If we do it well, we build relationships, we reinforce our own competence as communicators, and we make interaction more rewarding and less distressing (Cupach & Metts, 1994, pp. 15–16). We teach our children how to do good facework from the time they can put a sentence together: Be polite, answer people when they talk to you, be respectful, present yourself well, and be kind. As fundamental as it is, facework remains one of the most challenging aspects of communication well into adulthood, especially in complex, systemic situations.

An important part of your lifescript, then, involves face—how you want to be seen by others, how you want others to treat you, and how you treat others. Indeed, facework itself is the never-ending process of presenting self to others and acting toward others in the ongoing narrative of life. How we do this is very much part and parcel of the moral order, which is why different communities, especially cultural communities, do facework differently.

SIDEBAR 1.3   In Your Face

As communication scholars, we have long been enthralled with all the nuances of sports activities and the "talk" on and off the court. Whether it is the grunts and groans of football (each with its unique meaning) or the deep conversations that long-distance running affords, many people enjoy special communication interactions while getting exercise. Of particular interest is the "language" of street basketball. Especially enjoyed on neighborhood courts, basketball on the street is played with a passion.

The team dynamics are intriguing, but the really pertinent communication trait we will look at here is the one-on-one challenge, when two players take on each other. In some communities, the players will challenge each other up the court, with the defender shadowing the offensive player's every step. When the offensive player goes up for a shot, even with the defensive player's hand in the face, the ball goes in the basket and the scorer looks in the eye of the defender and might say, "In your face!" or merely "Face!" The interpersonal challenges that occur in sports may be bittersweet. Positive facework can occur through respectful coaching, strong teamwork, and physical exertion that do not threaten the dignity of others. Negative face situations can be created when the sport loses its focus on the skill and motivational factors and becomes personal affronts to individual players.

Face and Identity

What is accomplished when we do facework? Lim and Bowers (1991) have identified three types of face that emerge in most interaction situations. These are autonomy face, fellowship face, and competence face. *Autonomy* is a sense of self apart from others. It involves a feeling of freedom to act and an ability to control one's life, an idea of privacy, and a sense of boundary between self and other. Whenever you act in a way to distinguish yourself from others, you are showing autonomy face. Autonomy is more important in individualistic cultures, such as northern European, as the rights and responsibilities of individuals within these cultures are very important. Even in more collectivist cultures, such as many in Asia or Africa, however, there is always a delineation of self from other. Harré (1984) writes that in all cultures individuals have a consciousness that distinguishes between self and other, a sense of agency that provides an awareness of goals, and an autobiography that provides a sense of one's own life story.

Fellowship involves the need to be included and a sense of connection between self and other. While autonomy face emphasizes separateness, fellowship face centers on connection and commonality. Trust and cooperation are examples of fellowship face, as are shared values, relationships, and a sense of togetherness. Whenever you act in a way that builds a bridge between yourself and another person, you are constructing fellowship face. Notice, however, that autonomy and fellowship are somewhat at odds. There is a tension here that must be managed. How do you promote a sense of separateness while also building connection?

Competence, the third type, is the attribution of ability, respect for position, and contribution to society. Competence face is a feeling that you are able to do something positive and constructive for the community and that you are recognized for this. Competence face involves both autonomy and fellowship; it recognizes that you as an individual have special abilities that are valued within the larger community and that the community somehow benefits from who you are. Whenever you act in a way that brings honor to yourself for what you have accomplished, you are building competence face.

Although face always includes these three dimensions, they are not always equal or balanced. Different forms of face become more or less important as the situation, group, relationship, or culture shifts. At different moments, you may have greater concerns for one of these over the others. Within different relationships, they assume different values, and various cultures value certain forms of face more than other forms.

For us, these three dimensions point to something larger that is made through facework, corresponding to three levels of identity important to human beings. These are personal identities, relational identities, and community identities. The plural is important here, as you are constantly co-constructing a number of identities on each of these levels.

Personal Identities. We present ourselves and respond to others as persons. This we do in ways that build, maintain, or erode our personal identities. For example, we may come to feel validated, rejected, approved, respected, or confirmed (Ting-Toomey & Oetzel, 2001, pp. 42–43). We work to influence the face of ourselves and that of others in a way that affects both how we feel and how we think at the moment (Ting-Toomey, 1994, pp. 2–3).

Relational Identities. Part of what we seek in communication is social, or relational, identity (Cupach & Metts, 1994). Often called *mutual face,* this is an identity we want to build for the relationship itself, which entails "who we are" within this relationship (Ting-Toomey & Oetzel, 2001, p. 37). Thus, part of your own identity will help shape the nature of the relationship, just as relationship shapes your own identity. If you want a relationship of questioning, challenging, and arguing, then it behooves you to be seen as contentious. If you want to make a relationship of consensus and calmness, then within that relationship you must project an image of agreeability.

Community Identities. Community identities can be very large indeed. We are using the term *community* to mean a system of any type—family, neighborhood, organization, culture, nation, or any other human grouping that is important to us, important enough that our identity is both shaped by this community and contributes to it. Within a system, we perceive that we have a place, a role, and a set of connections with other members of the system. An important part of who we are within the system involves how well we believe we fulfill our place, our role, and our connections. This is really a question of competence. We want to know that we meet community expectations, live up to community values, fulfill our role, and contribute to community life. We also want to feel that the community itself has an identity of value to us as individuals and to our relationships within the community. In a business organization, for example, managers, employees, contractors, and others want to know that they fit in, that they are doing their jobs well, that others respect them, and that the organization itself is what they would like it to be.

An important part of competence is *general social competence,* which means communicating in ways that are consistent with cultural expectations within the community at hand (Metts & Grohskopf, 2003). Good facework—being polite, deferential, respectful, and appropriate—is important in building this identity of the socially competent person. In many parts of the world, this means asking people about their families, sharing tea, honoring people's position, and many other forms of basic social etiquette. It other parts of the world, it means being direct, not wasting time, getting to the point, and saying what you mean. One of the reasons that social violations are problematic is that they can harm one's image as a competent individual within a community of integrity, and they can threaten the identity of the community itself.

How Is Face Created?

We know that face is an accomplishment negotiated in communication. In other words, face results from a negotiated set of actions that build, maintain, or threaten our desired identities. But what does this process actually look like?

Presenting the Self and Responding to Others. There is always some image of self explicitly or implicitly embedded in what we say and how we say it (Goffman, 1959). Most of the time, we present ourselves in a favorable light or, more accurately, in the way we wish to be viewed within the situation. There are times when we threaten our own face because of some sense of shame or self-disappointment. Sometimes we put ourselves down in order to build others up. The point is that no matter what we do, an impression will be formed, and we usually act to influence that impression. Frequently, this is a major goal of the interaction.

SIDEBAR 1.4   Face Engagement

"A correctly staged and performed scene leads the audience to impute a self to a performed character, but this imputation—this self—is a product of a scene that comes off, and is not a cause of it. The self, then, as a performed character, is not an organic thing that has a specific location. . . . It is a dramatic effect arising diffusely from a scene that is presented."

Source: E. Goffman, *The Presentation of Self in Everyday Life,* 1959, p. 252.

While we are presenting ourselves, we also respond to others in ways that affect their own sense of identity. We may show politeness, deference, and goodwill. We may compliment, praise, or show approval. We may also criticize, demean, or attack others in ways designed to erode or reduce their image within the situation. An important aspect of every conversation, then, includes actions that affect the identity of self and other. These two are connected, of course, as we build our own identity by showing honor to others, and we can damage our own identity by attacking other people.

At base, we operate in communication with what has been called the *cooperative principle* (Grice, 1975). This means only that people understand the need to join together in some sort of coordinated way in order to negotiate or co-construct an outcome. When someone greets you, you greet him or her back. When someone asks a question, you answer it. When someone makes a request, you either grant it or not. Understanding the need to manage the face of both self and others is, indeed, an extension of the cooperative principle. We normally share a set of rules for building or even attacking face, and we expect others to follow those rules cooperatively. People do violate the cooperative principle by ignoring, opposing, or even changing expected rules of interaction, but they do not do so without the consequence of confusion and loss of face. You might intentionally or unintentionally respond "off the wall," but you will probably offer an account or explanation in order to regain the face you would otherwise lose.

Interacting Directly and Indirectly. Our actions are frequently quite direct, as would be the case of boasting and praise. Often, however, we act indirectly to accomplish the same goals. You could say, "I have done a lot of research on this topic . . ." or you could pepper your conversation with all kinds of facts that show that you have done the research. You could remark, "You have such good taste in clothes . . ." or you could touch your friend's jacket, look at it, and smile.

We often make judgments about how direct or indirect to be. In both building and threatening face, there are times when we feel the need to be very direct, and other times when directness itself would be threatening to one's perceived competence as a communicator. Directness is appreciated in cultures that value clarity and individuality, where indirectness can be viewed as "slippery" or "weak." On the other hand, indirectness is more appreciated in cultures that value relationships and context, where directness is seen as intrusive and impolite (Ting-Toomey & Oetzel, 2001, pp. 30–31). We may be more direct when we are uncertain about how the other person will interpret an indirect message, and we are probably going to be more indirect with people who know us well and can "read" our subtle cues.

Enhancing and Threatening. We can use a variety of actions ranging from those that build face to those designed to tear it down. Messages that enhance identities are more common in highly coherent situations that are consensual and relatively free of conflict. On the other hand, in power struggles or disagreements we often move to demean other people and their ideas as a way of gaining personal influence (Pearce & Littlejohn, 1997). This is especially true in individualistic cultures. Ironically, face threats used to help one prevail in a conflict situation may actually make such conflicts harder to resolve, as the struggle becomes increasingly personal and contentious. You may have encountered a rather common pattern of facework that involves pumping oneself up and demeaning the other person in what John Oetzel and his colleagues call *dominating facework* (Oetzel, Ting-Toomey, Yokochi, Masumoto, & Takai, 2000). This is an aggressive form of communication designed to defend one's own honor and competence, while demeaning that of the other. Whether face is enhanced or threatened, of course, depends not just on the intentions and meanings of the speaker but on the perceptions and meanings of the listener as well. What is intended may not be the actual effect. You may mean to compliment a new acquaintance only to discover that this person took your comment as a patronizing insult, or you may intend to reproach a co-worker, who merely thanks you for the constructive feedback! It always takes two to negotiate meaning, and the meaning for one person may or may not correspond with that of the other. Later in this book, we consider how facework is structured over time in the back-and-forth interaction of conversations and episodes.

Integrating. In contrast to dominating facework, Oetzel and his co-authors identify a broad category of cooperative behavior called *integration* (Oetzel et al., 2000). This is a complex form of interaction that honors self and other through good listening and exploration of a problem of mutual concern. Here two people of good faith attempt to work through differences constructively in a way that shows interpersonal respect and caring. This kind of facework does not depend so much on what people say about one another directly, but how they show respect through the manner in which they attend others' needs along with their own.

❖ CONSTRUCTING A FRAME

Barnett Pearce and Vernon Cronen (1980) created the theory of the coordinated management of meaning (CMM) to explain this relationship between meaning and action. This theory has evolved over the years through the contribution of a host of colleagues who have put it into practice and refined it through testing and application (e.g., Pearce, 2005; Pearce & Kearney, 2004). In CMM, parties coordinate communication to make sense of and mesh their respective actions into a coherent whole. Each communicator may understand what is happening very differently, but the parties feel successful to the extent that their actions are perceived as organized (Littlejohn & Domenici, 2001). The way people communicate is often much more important than the content of what they say. Instead of focusing on pieces of the conversation, we can focus on the interaction as a whole process. The meaning that is worked out socially through interaction develops over time. Facework is an integral part of the process through which we coordinate our actions and construct meaning through communication. Largely based on CMM, the facework theory presented in this book offers many points to enter an interaction from a variety of vantage points. Each "entry" has implications for the meaning that is jointly created and the resulting social world within which communicators will move forward.

The continual creation of meaning has implications not just for the individuals in the immediate situation but for larger networks and entire systems as well. Robyn Penman (1994) writes that facework is always understood within a conceptual context, or frame. The nature of facework depends upon the frame in which you view communication. The following framework explores the facework process and its impact, by expanding the breadth and depth of the concept. This framework is situated in a matrix, which applies a *focus of attention* and *scope of action*. The framework is outlined and illustrated in Tables 1.1 and 1.2.

❖ FOCUS OF ATTENTION

The focus of attention identifies the parts of the system most salient to the communicator at the moment. Although communicators can address virtually any level of concern, we call out three as important:

- *The person:* Communicators frequently engage in facework with the primary aim of affecting perceptions of self or other. In other words,

Table 1.1   Facework Focus and Scope

Focus of Attention	Scope of Action			
	Act	*Conversation*	*Episode*	*Lifescript*
Person	An act that aims to affect self or other face.	A conversation affecting face of self or other.	An episode of conversations affecting self or other face.	A long-term series of episodes creating an orientation to self and other.
Relationship	An act of facework aiming to help define the relationship.	A conversation of facework shaping the relationship.	An episode of conversations defining the relationship.	A long-term series of episodes defining relationships.
System	An act of facework aiming to help define the system.	A conversation of facework shaping the system.	An episode of conversations shaping the system.	A long-term series of episodes shaping larger systems.

they try directly to build or threaten a person's face as the primary goal of the interaction. A simple compliment or an apology is an example.

- *The relationship:* Although facework is directed at persons, its goal is not always just to affect the individual. Indeed, much of the time the aim of facework goes beyond personal feelings and may be designed to affect the relationship in some way. For example, we might compliment a colleague because we want to build a positive working relationship with this individual.

- *The system:* Facework may also be aimed at broader levels of the system, including, for example, the family, organization, community, nation, or world. For example, a manager may criticize a supervisor in the hope that improvement will bring about a higher feeling of achievement among all employees in the department. Alternatively, the manager may be trying to affect the whole company by positioning it as a company with high standards and a compelling vision.

Interaction, then, can impact face at several levels. When you respond to another person, you are not just targeting that other person

Table 1.2   Simple Examples of Facework

Focus of Attention	Scope of Action			
	Act	Conversation	Episode	Lifescript
Person	Praising a child for doing well in a sports game so that he will feel good about himself.	Having a positive conversation with a child about her sports game, resulting in the child's feeling confident.	Attending all of a child's sports games for an entire season to show that he is worthy and loved.	Showing a long-term attitude of interest and joy in children and their activities to help them become happy adults.
Relationship	Praising a child for doing well in a sports game to continue building a supportive relationship.	Having a positive conversation with a child about her sports game, contributing to a supportive relationship.	Attending all of a child's sports games for an entire season, which contributes to a strong bond between parent and child.	Showing a long-term attitude of interest and joy in children and their activities, which creates many positive relationships with children.
System	Praising a child for doing well in a sports game to help build the strength of the community sports league.	Having a positive conversation with the child about her sports game, contributing to a greater support for the community sports league.	Attending all of a child's sports games for an entire season, which contributes to increasing strength for the community sports league.	Showing a long-term attitude of interest and joy in children and their activities, which contributes to an increase in healthy activities for children in the community.

or even your relationship with him or her. Your actions may have profound implications for other people in a network of relationships well beyond the immediate situation, and often you will be aware of this fact and act accordingly.

In a basic sense, then, we can see these focus areas as "choices." When you enter a communication interaction, you will have choices as to where to focus your attention. If you are dedicated to managing face in the situation, you will engage in an interaction that may fall into one or more of the above. This choice could answer the following questions:

- *For the person:* What do I hope will happen for you? What do I hope will happen for me?
- *For the relationship:* What do I hope will happen for us?
- *For the system:* What do I hope will happen for us all?

Weighing or balancing the facework we do on one level with that on other levels is challenging and requires us to be aware of tradeoffs. Perhaps you have known a person who, no matter what is going on, will help others feel good about themselves and elicit a positive response for self. This may have positive face implications in the short run, but may come to be perceived over time in the group as placating and lead to a loss of trust. Or perhaps you have known a person who is generally face threatening in the interest of getting a "good group result," and in the process erodes the personal goodwill and positive relationships necessary to achieve those good results.

The most skilled communicators are able to integrate facework on all three of these levels. The focus of attention becomes intriguing when we consider that communicators work on multiple levels simultaneously. Facework is rarely isolated to one of the above levels. Indeed, the levels of person, relationship, and system cannot be separated in reality, as each provides a context for the other.

In street basketball, players challenge each other's face at the *personal* level. One player thinks, "I hope that I can prove myself in spite of the difficult situation my opponent offers me," while the other thinks, "I will try to stop my opponent, but I will have a chance to regain my face, even if my opponent scores." On the *relationship* level, one-on-one basketball emphasizes two players challenging each other to their physical limit. The "face" focus says to each other, "We know that together, we will push ourselves to a new level by challenging each other's face and skills, creating some kind of bond in the process." Of course, the choice could be one of damaging face, as one player may be attempting to demoralize the other player, knowing that many instances of "in your face!" create an uneven playing field, even though the rules of the game enable the player who just got scored on to take the ball in from out of bounds and get a chance to regain face. Of course, the entire game usually happens with and in front of others, who take turns challenging one another, and facework always extends to the larger *system* of players as well.

SIDEBAR 1.5   Move-In Day

Consider: It is "move-in day" at the dormitories. One roommate (out of four) is already at the two-bedroom dorm room, and has started unpacking. You are the second one to arrive, and see this situation. She has taken the choice spot, with the sunny window and ledge to sit on or use for storage. You can now begin to unpack and decide where you will stay.

You may want to demonstrate facework at these levels:

• *Person:* I want the next best choice, and want to make sure I can be comfortable. I do not want this new roommate to think I am selfish or assuming, so I will say to her, "Wow, what a nice bedroom this is. I am anxious to get unpacked and am willing to put my stuff in this side of the room. Would you mind if I shared with you?" With this focus on the person, you are creating a social world where you act quickly, but do inquire about the "other" and his or her preferences.

• *Relationship:* You know that this is a person you will be living with all year, and want to establish a respectful relationship with her and the other future roommates. You may say, "I wonder when the others will be arriving. I am thinking about waiting until they get here to discuss where we should all sleep. Would that be OK? Or do you have a preference for where I should put my stuff?" With this focus on the relationship level, you are trying to create a social world where you act and communicate deliberately with the "other" in mind.

• *System:* Maybe you are one of those rare creatures that think carefully about decision-making methods and setting precedent for future decisions. You may decide to sit and gab for a while with the first roommate, and then maybe talk to your Resident Advisor about the process this person suggests that roommates use to decide how to divide up space. If there is no precedent set, you may ask all your roommates, "Hey, it looks like we have an opportunity here to make our first important decision. Before we rush into putting all our stuff away, I wonder if we could talk for a moment about 'how' to make that decision, and maybe it will help us later on when we continue to face tough choices." You are focusing at the system level, and trying to create a social world where people make clear appropriate decisions using a method all agree on.

❖ CONTEXTS OF ACTION

Although facework is usually thought of as a single act, it rarely is limited to one message or behavior. Face is an accomplishment of inter-action as communicators work together over time to negotiate face issues. Four broad contexts are offered here to identify the scope of action within which facework happens (Pearce & Cronen, 1980).

- *The act:* Single messages and actions do have implications for face, and communicators frequently make a statement designed to threaten or build face. A parent might compliment his or her child on a good report card.

- *The conversation:* More often, facework is accomplished across a series of acts and becomes an important part of the conversation. For example, a couple may build one another's parenting confidence as they discuss their child's report card.

- *The episode:* More profound than simple acts of facework are the broader face implications that occur over time through a series of interac-tions. Rarely are conversations isolated. Instead, they are connected to other conversations in thematic and organized sets of conversations. An *episode* is an event or series of connected events with a common theme. For example, many times over the years the child picks up his or her report card and gives it to the parent. Parents study it, think about it, talk together about it, discuss it with the child, write a note back to the teacher or have a teacher conference—all connected conversations over time.

- *The lifescript:* As discussed earlier in this chapter, the lifescript is a guiding set of principles, an idea of who we are and how we live, that governs interaction over many episodes. Managers have a style, parents have a philosophy, and activists have a cause. Our identities as persons and communities affect and are shaped by communication patterns of facework. What you say to your child about his or her report card, the conversations and episodes about report cards, student progress, and childhood responsibility are guided by the larger lifescript.

As communicators who make choices about how to act in a situa-tion, we can look at these contexts for action and determine the point from which we want to act and communicate. We could consider the following questions.

- *The act:* What should I do or say?
- *The conversation:* What is happening here? How should we continue?

- *The episode:* Where are we going?
- *The lifescript:* Who am I?

Consider a manager trying to decide how to address an employee discipline problem. A first choice, and probably the most narrow-minded, is to communicate at the *act* level of facework. As the manager, you could place a letter in the employee's file and have a session to reprimand that person.

What would happen if you first considered communicating at the *lifescript* level to respond according to a set of commitments that you have made well beyond any single interaction or situation? For example, you may remember that you are committed to respectful communication that models the dignity with which you would like to be treated yourself. You hope that you can set a precedent with your communication, so that interactions throughout the organization may model this effectiveness and constructive interaction. This context may give you the place to act and you may create a training initiative called "ethics in the workplace."

You may also decide to put yourself into the *episode* context. From this viewpoint, you could ask yourself, "Where are we going, either as a department or an organization?" You could revisit the organization's rules of conduct and procedures for addressing violations. In a private meeting, you may share these rules and give your perspective on the matter at hand. These rules point to the organization's vision, and you can point out the connection between ethical behavior and the achievement of the vision.

Finally, you may enter the communication context at the *conversation* level. You look carefully at what is occurring in this person's life, consider the workplace and home life situation, and design a meeting to discuss the consequences for the behavior. Your message will be framed from the perspective of a manager whose duty it is to carry out discipline, while recognizing the personal and professional pressures and challenges in each employee's life.

Using a system's perspective, these four contexts for action are integrally connected, as depicted in Figures 1.2 and 1.3.

Human action is characterized by difference, and how we act in a situation will vary, depending on our life experience and cultures that form our lifescripts, the episodes that give meaning to our lives, the forms of conversation that comprise our social life, and the manners of speech and action we have learned in the many communities of which we have been a part. Differences can run deep, and the management of difference can involve the intricate coordination of meaning and action.

Figure 1.2   Focus of Attention

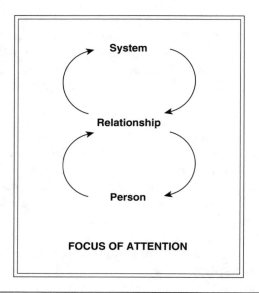

Figure 1.3   Scope of Action

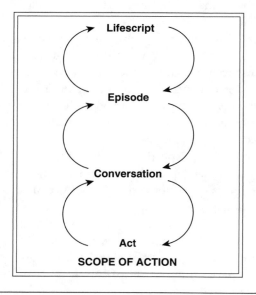

❖ PRINCIPLES FOR PRACTICE

We end Chapters 1 through 6 of this book with a small set of principles, or learnings, from the chapter that can be used as a guide for interpretation and action. As we use the term, a *principle* is a high-level guide that helps us understand complex and diverse situations and make decisions about how to act in the various settings of our lives. A principle is not a law; it does not state a universal causal relationship or dictate a particular outcome or way of behaving. Rather, we see principles as flexible benchmarks for moving forward in a coherent way. In this chapter we offer four principles:

The way you communicate will affect your identity and that of others close to you. Identity is socially constructed, and the manner in which individuals interact with one another affects their sense of self. You can think consciously about how to respond to others, always keeping in mind the kind of person you want to be, the kind of relationship you want to have, and the kind of community you want to make.

Show the most appropriate aspect of your complex identity to others in each situation, but also aim for a coherent lifescript. Your identity is multifaceted. It is dynamic and grows as you experience more of life. You do not need to worry about acting consistently, because the situations you face and the people with whom you communicate are not consistent. You can, however, find coherence in your lifescript at any given time in your life. Act in ways that reflect the kind of person you want to be.

Your relationships and communities are part of who you are. Nurture the connections that are most important to you. Even if your culture teaches you that you are independent and autonomous, you are not. Your sense of personhood and self are always socially constructed. Know your roots and branches and think actively about the relationships and communities that shape your life.

Treat others with the same dignity, honor, and respect you want for yourself. The golden rule lives. This does not mean that you act toward every person in an identical way, but that you use your best face judgment for that individual within the situation you are facing together.

2

Creating an Environment of Constructive Facework

A Practical Perspective

❖　❖　❖

W hen you arrive at a party, you probably stop to think, "How should I act in this situation?" Sometimes we ease into the party quietly and scope out the place before getting involved in a conversation. Other times, we decide to let everyone know, "Hey! Here I am, ready for an exciting evening!" We can affect the social interactions of the evening by the communication choices we bring to the situation.

The outcomes of our communication encounters are joint accomplishments, and when we communicate in complex systems, we achieve many things on a variety of levels. At the party, we can reconnect with a friend we have not seen for ages. We might organize a group of friends to leave the party and go catch a movie. By observing for a while, we may get a clearer picture of the type of people at the party. We may want to engage with the folks wholeheartedly or we may want to leave early, offering ourselves as "just stopping in." These *interactional accomplishments* are the *coordinated communication achievements that contribute to the creation of our social worlds.*

In the previous chapter, we explored facework as a central component in the social construction of identity, with implications both for self and other in the immediate situation and in larger systems and communities. Our efforts at facework can build a sense of personal identity by communicating in ways that preserve the social distinctiveness that each of us desires. This chapter takes a more practical turn and explores ways to create communication environments that permit constructive facework.

Action usually results in both intended and unintended consequences. The unintended consequences of interaction form a set of expectations that shape future possibilities (Giddens, 1977). So if you comment on a friend's dress, her response, your reaction to it, the comments or reactions from others in the room, along with other interactions, will create an environment that can impact ongoing interaction. Communication is never a simple cause-effect relationship. Our actions have both intended and unintended consequences that construct the very environment in which we act. When we act in ways that build, protect, or threaten face, larger systemic dynamics are created that, in turn, impact future encounters.

Intentional action, then, contributes to larger connections, patterns, and social worlds. From our perspective, facework affects this communication environment, and the communication environment affects facework. In this chapter, we invite consideration of patterns of communication designed to create a constructive environment of positive facework.

Constructive communication environments are highly cultural. We address culture later in this text, but for now it is important to keep in mind that the kinds of communication that build or threaten face depend upon the culture in which the communication takes place. In this chapter we present a set of concepts and skills that forms the basis for competent facework in many cultures, but certainly not in all. As you read this chapter, reflect on the cultural limitations of these ideas.

❖ FACEWORK AND THE COMMUNICATION ENVIRONMENT

Facework emerges from a reciprocal relationship between action and environment. What we say and do influences and is influenced by the larger conditions surrounding our interaction. The kind of facework we do shapes the environment in which we communicate, and that environment in turn shapes the kind of facework we can do.

Figure 2.1   Dimensions of the Facework Environment

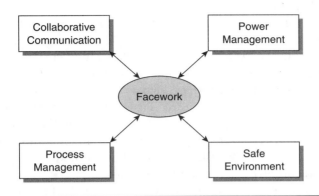

In this chapter, we outline four dimensions that result from this reciprocal relationship—the factors within the communication environment constructed through good facework that facilitate facework in the future (Littlejohn & Domenici, 2001). The dimensions are collaborative communication, safety, process management, and power management (Figure 2.1). Although we discuss each of the four dimensions separately, each involves the others in a cybernetic fashion.

Collaborative Communication

There seems to be a plethora of collaborative initiatives these days. For example, there is a whole field called "collaborative law" in which attorneys and their clients work together to develop a process to help all parties negotiate settlement proposals that are mutually beneficial. In a collaborative divorce, the couple together controls the process, the costs, and the outcome of their case. Collaborative practice in the medical field engages physicians, patients, and other practitioners working together to serve joint purposes. These medical practitioners understand and respect the abilities and knowledge of each other (Estes, 2004). Collaborative action in the business world sees organizations from one sector—particularly business—join together to form a partnership with a group or groups in another sector such as community groups or local government (*Our Community*, 2001). Other examples of collaboration are seen in education, where students and teachers become partners, and collaborative teams of teachers, librarians, and technology specialists work together to plan and offer curriculum.

Architecture, construction, real estate, and even the home are places in which collaborative teams work well.

These collaborative practices create synergy in which the whole is more than the sum of its parts. At one level, collaboration is common sense and practical. At a deeper level, collaboration creates an environment that is supported by all, and feels supportive to all, building an environment in which shared goals and processes are possible. Collaboration depends upon three basic practices (Donohue & Kolt, 1992; O'Hair & Friederich, 1992): (1) identify clearly the specific issues the group wants to address; (2) search for commonalities among the competing goals and priorities; and (3) develop new goals that incorporate and complement the competing ones.

Let's look at the example of a downtown neighborhood bustling with schools, businesses, restaurants, apartments, houses, and multiple services. The Downtown Neighborhood Association has been meeting for 10 years and is organized with officers and monthly meetings. The issue of rising violence on the streets dominated a recent meeting. The meeting led to a common set of goals and collaborative action, as neighbors came to see themselves as partners in a common endeavor:

1. *They identified the specific issues the group wanted to address.* Participants in the neighborhood meeting were able to clarify their own priorities and listen, observe, and ask questions of others. "What is it that has you most interested in this topic tonight?" "What are your hopes for outcomes of this meeting?"

2. *They searched for commonalities among the competing goals and priorities.* "I hear that many of us are very interested in working for a safer downtown area." "It sounds like we are all satisfied with the police efforts. Maybe we should move on to talk about the local high school security."

3. *They developed new goals that incorporated and complemented the competing ones.* "Ms. Mayor, it seems that most of the neighbors here feel very strongly that we get some attention to the local city park. Is that a topic of interest to you also?" "I hear a lot of energy around the violence problem, and see that we have some good ideas for moving forward. When do you think we should start discussing ways we can work with other neighborhood associations to accomplish these pressing goals?"

As this example illustrates, collaboration can change the communicators' orientation from one of competition and influence to mutual problem solving, from potentially face threatening to potentially face building. This shift marks a change from competing against others to prevail in a polarized situation to partnering with others to solve problems.

How would you know a collaborative environment if you experienced it? In short, a collaborative environment is one in which communicators (1) describe what they see and experience rather than attack, refute, or resist it; (2) talk openly with others to explore creative solutions rather than manipulate or control one another; (3) show flexibility and openness to new developments rather than demonstrate rigid conformity to a pre-established strategy; (4) show appropriate empathy and concern rather than distance and detachment; (5) work to empower everyone rather than stick to a power hierarchy; and (6) engage in open discussion of ideas rather than blind defensiveness (Gibb, 1961).

SIDEBAR 2.1   Recognizing Polarized Communication

"A good way to start creating alternatives to divisiveness is to recognize polarizing practices as they take place. Notice when participants in a discussion share only their certainties and none of their doubts; when they speak as members of a group rather than individuals with unique thoughts and experiences; when questions are rhetorical challenges or veiled statements rather than genuine invitations to share perspectives and gain understanding."

Source: Public Conversations Project, *Constructive Conversations About Challenging Times* (2003).

Process Management

Normally, we don't have trouble knowing *what we want to talk about*. The content of communication is usually glaringly obvious and begs for our attention, but in this book, we spend a lot of time inviting readers to consider the "how" of our communication. What people often forget in the pressure of the moment is that how you say something, even how you interact across time in a conversation, has consequences. Questions of process, then, are vital if we take a larger systemic view. Good facework means paying attention to *what* we say and *how* we say it. Process management is a way of ensuring that communicators consider carefully how they want to talk about the issue at hand. Process management is especially important when issues are complex, significant, and potentially face threatening.

SIDEBAR 2.2   A Process Management Checklist

Use the following checklist to address process considerations in communication interactions. When answering the questions, involve as many of the people who will be communicating as possible.

1. Where should we have the interaction?

2. When should we have the interaction?

3. Who will lead the discussion or facilitate the communication?

4. Who will set the agenda?

5. How long should the interaction be and what time constraints do we have?

6. What is the goal of our interaction?

7. What should we do if we veer off course and move away from our goal?

8. Who will take notes or record the progress of the communication?

9. What type of guidelines or ground rules do we need to make sure good facework is utilized?

10. What should we do with the issues we want to address but are not able to at this time?

11. What do we do with the final information or decisions regarding next steps?

Answering that "how" question is clearly important in group decision-making processes. Whether it is a small workgroup trying to move past a stuck spot or a large organization addressing internal strife, or even a large community of diverse people, look at process considerations early on. Addressing these "how" questions may seem like mere "agenda creation," but even meeting agendas can be individually and carefully designed with participants as co-communicators and designers. These are facework episodes that offer dignity and respect to all participants. Notice the connection between collaboration and process management. These two dimensions support one another. Good collaboration requires good process management, and good process management requires collaboration.

SIDEBAR 2.3   Guidelines for Time Management in Meetings

How can you keep people on track, help them share speaking time, make sure the group gets the job done, and finish on time?

- Generate an agenda and remind people of what they have covered and what is left to do.
- Give regular time reminders.
- Remind the group of the time limit and the need to keep comments brief.
- If participants seem to be getting off track, ask them if that is how they want to use their limited time.
- If you have to cut someone off, do it in a nice way. Acknowledge contributions before cutting someone off.

Comments like the following are gracious ways of controlling group discussion:

Thanks, Jim, I can see you are really concerned about the lack of a community center in your town. Let's hold that thought; we need to hear from some of the others now.

We're falling a little behind time now. Let's keep our comments just a bit briefer.

I appreciate your creativity, Sally. Let's get back to some of your ideas later, but for now, I want to hear the ideas of some of the rest of you.

These points are very helpful, and I want to make sure we incorporate them, but I think we need to get back to the agenda or we won't get through everything in time.

I notice that we have only an hour left and there's a lot of energy here for creative brainstorming. Is this how you want to use your time right now?

Thanks for your creativity, everyone. We have only thirty minutes left. What can we do now to make sure we get the job done by the end of this meeting?

Power Management

The third dimension that supports positive facework is the management of power dynamics in the communication interactions. We want to communicate in a way that enables everyone to say what needs to be said and hear what needs to be heard. Power is used, then, to express and explore, not to dominate and oppress. The empowerment question is: "What do we all need to do to be heard and taken seriously?" This is not a question of power "balancing"; balancing power assumes that you know what the bases of power are in every case and that equal power is the answer. Equal power is impossible. Different communicators will have different sources of power, and you can never equalize them all. The key, then, is empowerment, not power balancing. For purposes of attending to power dynamics, we must first begin to understand power in communication.

Personal and professional relationships are often hindered or helped by the management of power. Popular author Stephen Covey (1990) described three types of power (pp. 101–102) that correspond nicely to social science findings in this field (e.g., French & Raven, 1960)—coercive power, utility power, and principle-centered power.

Coercive power is the "big stick" approach. Controlling through fear is reactive and temporary, as it is gone when the controlling individual or system is gone. This type of power has people afraid of what will happen if they do not acquiesce to what the "other" wants to happen. The commitment is usually superficial and the energies can turn to sabotage and destruction (e.g., Asher, 1986; Windt, 1972). In attempting to "out-power" others through coercion, face needs are usually left in the dust.

Utility power is based on the useful exchange of goods and services. Each may have something that the other needs or wants (time, money, resources, talent, support, affection, etc.). Most organizations are held together by utility power, because it is based on a sense of equity and fairness. Relationships based on utility power can lead to individualism rather than team- or group-oriented behavior, as paying attention to their own perspectives and desires reinforces individuals. Social exchange theory concentrates on how people use utility power in making decisions about how to communicate with others (Roloff, 1981). Classic negotiation is normally a process of employing utility power. When communicators see ways to provide something others need— and get something back in return—they begin to recognize the quality of empowerment, especially when they define positive resources beyond the limits of material goods.

Principle-centered power is based on qualities that engender positive relationships, those things that lead others to believe in you and in what you are trying to accomplish. When you have principle-centered power, you are trusted, not because of what you can give or take away, but because of who you are. Principle-centered power is similar to invitational communication explored earlier, as the personal agendas of both "us" and "them" or of the leader and follower are encompassed by a larger purpose. A certain commitment is required of people who want to model this power. It is a sincere, long-term commitment to building trust and ethical values in the relationship.

Notice the relationship between principle-centered power and facework. Constructive facework builds principle-centered power. It builds confidence and commitment within the group for moving forward together.

How do we empower one another in this way? Ting-Toomey and Oetzel (2001, p. 189) suggest several strategies of power management:

- Know yourself and your power bases. Monitor your interactions to make sure you conduct exchanges evenly with diverse cultural and ethnic groups.

- Request and acknowledge comments and advice from individuals and groups that may have less power than you.

- Recognize that you are all integral pieces of the puzzle, and let the other "pieces" know how significant they are to the whole.

- Seek out and offer leadership opportunities for less powerful individuals. Give them challenges that they can accomplish, and recognize their best efforts and endeavors.

A judge we know, Anne Kass, once told us, "Sharing power is a different kind of power." When you undertake or encourage power relationships that build trust and respect, you are not losing anything, but are gaining a new kind of power. Whether called principle-centered or facilitative leadership, management of power in communication interactions can enhance a constructive facework environment.

SIDEBAR 2.4   Difficult Power Management Situations

The following strategies can assist in transforming negative behavior into a more positive pattern (Domenici & Littlejohn, 2005).

Interruptions: Acknowledge the person's need to talk: "I can see you have strong feelings on this, Bob, and we'll get to you in just a moment. In the meantime, I want to hear the rest of Jane's comment."

Non-participation: Acknowledge listening and invite comment: "Jim, I see you have been listening for a while, and I wonder what you are thinking about all of this."

(Continued)

Disruptive behavior: Address it as a group problem: "I notice we've been losing time by repeating things after people arrive. I wonder how we can make more efficient use of our time in this regard."

Side conversations: Talk to the offending individuals privately: "Betty, I've been distracted by your whispering in the back row. I'm sure it's nothing, but I just wanted to check with you to see if there is something I should know."

Offensive statements: Let the group handle them. (A group member makes a racial slur. Pause for a moment to let it sink in, see if anyone comments, then move on. If the problem persists, ask the group members if they would like a ground rule on respectful language.)

Hostility toward others: Reframe it and remind the group of the ground rules: [speaking to the whole group, upon hearing one participant call another a thief] "I want to remind you about the ground rule of maintaining respectful language. We have to work together, so let's make it as easy as possible."

Loud, emotional argument: Interrupt, acknowledge, summarize, and take a break: "Just a minute, just a minute. Excuse me. I can see that Tom is very upset about Elizabeth's new accounting system, and Elizabeth, you don't appreciate Tom's argument about it. I can see that both of you care about how records are kept, and I want to suggest that we look at that issue calmly. Let's take a break and come back to this situation when we return."

Griping and whining: Acknowledge the caring, state the positive vision behind the person's complaint, and ask for a solution: "I see you really care about making improvements here. I appreciate your vision for a really effective working environment, and I'm wondering what ideas you have for improving the situation."

Safe Environment

We maintain that collaborative communication, process management, and power management are three structural dimensions that affect the quality of facework. For many people, these are not customary modes of operation. They involve risk because they are different from what we normally experience. For this reason, we add a fourth dimension that undergirds the others: a safe environment. Effective facework builds a safe environment, which in turn makes good facework even more likely.

If we are to interact in a manner that accomplishes face goals, we need to feel safe. In addition to thinking of safety in the sense of "absence of danger," it is also essential to know we can talk freely and interact without fear of being attacked or sabotaged. Respectful communication is more than being polite—it is a conscious commitment to interactions that are safe. When we respect others, we generally trust them, and trust leads to the commitment to respond cooperatively and constructively.

Have you ever been approached by a friend or family member who asks, "Can I tell you something private and personal?" You could respond in a number of ways. You can directly address the need for a private conversation: "How can we discuss this in a way that is private and comfortable for you?" You can address the need for confidentiality: "It sounds like you have something to say that you would not like me to share with anyone else." Or you could address the personal side of the issue: "So, you would like to discuss something with me that might be difficult to talk about?" In each case, you are getting a bit more information about the type of conversation requested.

Look at the following example of creating a safe environment for communication. A non-profit organization was experiencing deep budget cuts. The unspoken assumption was that the organization, consisting of three paid administrators and 15 volunteers, would have to make the tough decision to close its doors. The presenting question was: *How could we create a safe environment that honored the efforts and achievements of the organization while at the same time being realistic about the choices for the future?* The three staff people needed to be engaged in the decision making and also needed to feel respected and safe enough to contribute to a conversation about the demise of their job. This is not a conversation to be eased into informally or without intentional thought to the communication environment. Here is the agenda they followed for 2 days:

1. Present a clear agenda review and discuss expectations of the participants.

2. Take a tour of the timeline (reviewing the milestones and accomplishments of the past 10 years, celebrating the achievements).

3. Acknowledge current strengths (identifying the strengths of the organization and the strategic priorities that are still most relevant).

4. Note current resource constraints (overview of all constraints, including money, time, agency support, and personnel).

5. Develop options for moving forward (brainstorming session, trying to get as many options out as possible).

6. Discuss option evaluation (discuss each option in light of the priorities in item 3 and the resource constraints in item 4).

7. Decide on the most appropriate option to move forward.

8. Do transition planning.

By the end of the two days, the staff and volunteers were sad and resigned to the fact that the organization would close, but they also had ownership of the decision. They felt safe enough to explore the decision at length, and they fully participated in all the dialogue that led to the decision. The first day could have begun with a clear announcement, "Due to budget constraints, we can no longer keep this organization afloat," but that announcement could have created feelings of defensiveness and resentment, as those who would soon have to find a new job would be caught unawares.

❖ CREATING A CONSTRUCTIVE ENVIRONMENT

Integrated decisions about creating an environment conducive to good facework involve attention to collaboration, process management, power management, and safety. To establish a safe environment, the following considerations provide the basis for constructive environments: appropriate self-disclosure, interactions that minimize anxiety, settings that are conducive to safety, and invitational communication.

Appropriate Self-Disclosure

Self-disclosure, or revealing information about yourself to others, has clear implications for safety (Chelune et al., 1979). You will normally think twice about whether to tell another person about private information, including some aspects of your past, your emotions, and your perceptions. Inappropriate levels of self-disclosure can make others feel unsafe; yet disclosure suitable to the level of the relationship may actually create safety through trust. Indeed, relationships are built on the kind of trust that honest self-disclosure provides. There seems to be a natural tension between the desire for privacy versus the need for openness (Altman, 1993; Baxter, 1993; Petronio, 2002). These two desires need to be managed, and they constantly present the question of whether or not to disclose information.

There seems to be a relationship between the amount that persons are willing to disclose and the depth of the relationship between them

(Altman & Taylor, 1973); but we know that there is not a simple linear relationship here. In fact, as people in a relationship struggle with the contradiction of privacy and openness, they go through cycles of disclosing and holding back. Petronio (2002) calls this *boundary management,* which involves decisions at any given moment about what should be private and what should be known. Individuals in relationships even negotiate what aspects of the relationship should be disclosed or not.

Self-disclosure is largely a question of what level feels safe to yourself and to others, what needs to be known in order to build and maintain the relationship, and the extent to which self-disclosure will contribute to collaboration, power management, and process management. The following guidelines are a good starting place for managing disclosure boundaries (adapted from Verderber & Verderber, 1992, pp. 179–180).

1. *Disclose to others what you would like shared with you.* The golden rule of self-disclosure is to convey to others the type of information that is easily generally shared. For example, in the meeting with the disbanding organization described above, participants were not asked to share with the whole group how they came to the conclusion that their respective budgets could no longer support the organization.

2. *Increase the depth of information you choose to share as the benefit exceeds the risk.* As trust is built in the relationship, the risk level may become more acceptable. By the end of the second day with the disbanding organization discussed above, they had increased levels of trust and could attempt higher levels of disclosure. The second afternoon ended with a question to each participant: "What will be the most difficult for you to give up as this organization closes its doors?"

3. *Gauge what you reveal in gradual increments.* We need to remember that receiving self-disclosure can be as threatening as giving it. Most people become uncomfortable when the level of disclosure exceeds their expectations. In the example of the disbanding organization, one of the opening statements was, "We will be experiencing a variety of communication methods and choices during the next two days. We will be discussing things in a divergent manner (brainstorming and option generation) and also converging on options (narrowing down choices and evaluating options). Some of you may prefer one type of communication over another, but we feel that both are necessary to move forward with the issues before us. If you feel uncomfortable at any time, please let us know."

4. *The most personal information should be revealed in the most intimate relationships.* People are often hostile or resentful of personal information shared early in a relationship, especially if it is embarrassing. If an ongoing relationship does not exist, there is usually no reason to get into deep secrets.

5. *Reciprocal sharing of personal information is safest.* When personal sharing is reciprocated, the most positive effects are realized for the relationship. If someone begins to share something personal and no one else in the conversation goes to that level, it may be time to steer the conversation another way. When someone in the organization began sharing how the loss of the job would affect his family and life plans, the group stopped in silence for a few seconds. No one responded to the comment. The conversation then can be skillfully reframed and the group respectfully reminded of the "transition" agenda item planned for later that day.

The construction of positive facework environments includes the establishment of a safe environment for communication that respects each person's comfort level and ability to share and receive information.

Anxiety Management

John Keltner (1994) believes that one way to minimize the potential for unproductive communication is to reduce anxiety. He tells the story of two roommates caught in escalating anxiety and struggle. Jerry was very anxious about getting his term paper completed on schedule and was working late one night when his roommate came in with a case of beer and a demand that Jerry join him in a little relaxation. Jerry cursed him, threw a book at him, and locked the door, thus feeling that he was getting some control of the situation. His roommate, in turn, became angry and started pounding on the door and yelling. Jerry at that point experienced another anxiety—the cost to him if his roommate destroyed his room. Thus, the original anxiety had been assuaged for a moment and now another arose, and the struggle between the two friends escalated and that raised still another concern for Jerry.

The presence of anxiety is often tied to the presence of stress. Anxiety does not decrease the tendency to continue in the undesirable behaviors because it clouds the thinking. In situations where differences occur, people can act out of anxiety and increase their struggles. In an effort to control his anxiety, Jerry only escalated the problem, causing more anxiety. This escalating cycle becomes more face damaging as the environment becomes less safe.

The following examples can be used in groups and relationships:

- *Allow thinking time.* In response to a question, give people a few minutes (or hours) of time to consider the question, so they do not have to compete for airtime. We recently led a discussion at a preschool class. Each time a question was asked, many of the kids threw their hands in the air. When we called on them, many were embarrassed and afraid, and could not formulate a reply. We then responded, "For this next question, no one will put his or her hand in the air. First, you will close your eyes and think carefully about the answer for one minute. When we tell you it is time, you can raise your hand." The responses after that thinking time were much more confident and thoughtful. Another way to offer this time is to give participants a worksheet or ask them to take out a piece of paper to address a question in writing before responding verbally.

- *Break into dyads.* Group conversations can begin with an option affording more safety: First break into groups of two to discuss the topic. Dyads can discuss the issue for a while, and then report out to the group. Or, a dyad could join another dyad and the foursome could continue to discuss, looking for common ideas or perceptions. Use of smaller groups can offer a feeling of safety and respect.

- *Frame issues productively.* Think carefully about how the question or invitation to communication is phrased. Negative or closed questions can invite brief and awkward answers. Open and positive framings can invite people to respond creatively and comfortably. We appreciate so many of the experiences of the Public Dialogue Consortium (PDC). Their work in the city of Cupertino, California, emphasized that how an issue is framed can affect the safety of the discussion. Two of the central issues addressed in their work were originally framed as *racial tension* and *crime prevention.* Speaking to those issues calls attention to the problem and not to the solution. People may be hesitant to contribute to those conversations because of negativity and fear. The PDC opened the discussion significantly when framing the issues as *cultural richness* and *community safety.* Participants were able to talk about the many dimensions of a safe community and to talk about actions that might be taken to achieve that vision. Conversations about *cultural richness* called attention to the many ways in which cultural diversity is a community asset, rather than the negative association of changing demographics (Littlejohn & Domenici, 2001).

- *Leave an out.* We often offer a "pass rule" in our conversations. If people are not immediately ready to contribute, they can pass this turn. They can request the conversation to come back to them if they feel more confident or prepared later. If they choose to bypass the opportunity to speak altogether, they are welcome to do so. At that point, we may do a bit of reality testing to make sure they know that this opportunity to give their input is significant and available.

Settings Conducive to Facework

When constructing a communication environment, a significant consideration is having a setting where people feel comfortable and respected. Note the safety dimensions of this example. A workplace mediation was about to occur, and one of the participants arrived about 30 minutes early. He limped into the room and asked if he could be seated before the other participants arrived. He did not want them to witness him limping into the room, calling attention to his disability. He was afraid that the others would see him as weak and wanted to be able to discuss the issues with confidence. He got comfortably seated in the mediation room, participated with ease throughout the mediation, and remained seated until after the session ended and everyone left. There are a variety of considerations when thinking about settings conducive to a safe environment. Two that we will discuss here are (1) arrangement of the meeting space and (2) including people in the conversation about the safe environment.

Spatial Issues

Communication interactions can be affected positively or negatively by the way people share space. The way people use and react to space between people and/or objects is called *proxemics* (Hall, 1966). An executive or person in power may deliberately sit away from the group, in front of the group, to retain control. In a large group meeting, participants often sit by those whose opinions and actions they most relate to. On the other hand, facilitative leaders and team members may choose to sit within the group, hoping to make everyone feel more equal and to balance power. When we consider the boundaries that people create to define the distances between themselves and others, the definitions can be as follows:

1. *Intimate distance* ranges from about zero to 18 inches. This distance is reserved for intimate relationships and other forced close

relationships such as contact sports. Usually, strangers do not enter this space.

2. *Personal distance* runs from about 18 inches to 4 feet. This distance is normal for team discussions and group work on common goals.

3. *Social distance* is from 4 feet to 12 feet. Strangers or business contacts often use this distance. Usually a desk or some other barrier gives the message that this distance is requested.

4. *Public distance,* from 12 to 25 feet, is a suitable distance for addressing groups. When a person or a panel is speaking to an audience, the distance between the speaker/moderator and the group makes it difficult to keep focus and build a comfortable environment for team dynamics. The audience members are probably feeling comfortable since they do not have to interact much with each other but usually will be focused on the speaker. In cases where the group needs to increase possibilities for collaboration, the speaker/moderator might want to decrease the distance. If there is a conference table between the speaker and the audience, that could be removed.

When we are trying to set up an environment for constructive communication, we look for ways to arrange the meeting room or the space that best meet the goals of the communication interaction. We are often faced with classroom seating with a podium at the front of the room, so we quickly move chairs into a semi-circle and push the podium aside. If we were setting up a speaker to address a group, we could leave the classroom style as is. People can communicate more freely when they see each other, but should not be forced into interactions with those they may be hesitant to share with on the topic at hand.

SIDEBAR 2.5   The Proxemics of a Classroom

Next time you are in a meeting room or a classroom, look carefully at how the chairs and tables are set up. Are there rows of chairs all facing the head table or the lectern? Are the chairs grouped in circles or one big circle, facing each other? Are there tables arranged throughout the room? Are these tables square or round? For each of the above questions, think about what type of environment is created and what type of communication would be most appropriate and comfortable in each.

Invitational Communication

Sonja Foss and her colleagues (Foss & Foss, 2003; Foss & Griffin, 1995) introduce a new notion about communication rooted in the idea of an invitation. Instead of working on the assumption that we cause, influence, or affect others to act in certain ways, *invitational rhetoric* looks at the ways in which we share a point of view and invite others to experience this. Invitational rhetoric both encourages and relies on a safe environment, and it does this by promoting three values—*equality*, a spirit of non-domination; *immanent value*, which acknowledges the worth of all participants; and *self-determination*, the right of everyone to make decisions on issues that affect their lives.

Moving away from conquest, conversion, benevolence, and advice, invitational rhetoric invites dialogue on issues of mutual concern. The object is to engage communicators in a joint process of mutual discovery. Following are a few statements one might hear in a communication event of this nature:

- I'm hoping to discuss this issue with you. How can we talk about it so we both contribute to the discussion and offer ideas for addressing the dilemma?

- There are a few things I'd like to discuss with all of you today. It is really important to me that we end this meeting with some shared understanding. Before I begin, could we go around the room, introduce ourselves, and share our perspective on the challenge we are here to discuss tonight?

- I can see that you feel very strongly about this problem. Let's move these chairs around so we are all sitting together. What would you most like to happen as a result of this conversation?

- What is it about this issue that makes you feel so strongly about it?

We also know that safety does not mean the same thing to everyone. Some people have communication competence that enables them to speak freely (and loudly) whenever they want. Others are uncomfortable communicating when they are with someone who does not share their viewpoint. You can model to others how to create the condition of safety by listening and speaking respectfully and appropriately. If you notice any verbal or non-verbal indication of discomfort, it is perfectly fine to say, "I see that not all of us are contributing to this conversation. Let's take a few minutes here for a process check. Is there anything we can do to make this environment more conducive to good communication?" Negotiate the structure that enables good facework.

SIDEBAR 2.6   Don't Open Birthday Presents in Front of Others

---

Our friend Carla Shibuya has this as a family rule. When anyone in her family has a birthday, they wait to open any gifts until later when all the guests have gone. Respecting the need for positive face, Carla sees that her family does not need to be confronted with a challenging communication situation where their responses to gifts may not be appropriate, truthful, or forthcoming. The family is very appreciative and caring, sending sincere thank-you cards afterward, messages that respectfully acknowledge and give thanks for the special gift. That note is written in a safe environment where the gift-receiver can deliberately form a response.

By communicating in a way that does not draw attention to those making difficult choices, does not create surprises, and does not force people into comments before they are ready, we give them a safe environment within which they can communicate. The point is to avoid putting individuals into an untenable situation in which any response could be a face threat.

A simple rule of thumb is to ask people what they need to feel comfortable. Whether you are in a private meeting or a public conversation, a good preface to the conversation might be, "What would be the best way to have this conversation so we both feel comfortable and able to communicate freely?" If you have a very large group, you might ask to meet with some of the participants in advance to discuss that question. If you do have the time to negotiate the collaborative creation of a safe environment, participants will build ownership in the process and utilize an appropriate communication structure to foster safety.

In the previous chapter, we identified three levels of focus in facework—the person, the relationship, and the system. Notice that this multi-level facework invokes all of the dimensions of a constructive communication environment. Looking back to the community meeting focused on rising violence, Table 2.1 offers three interactional accomplishments that may occur on the three levels:

1. The president of the Neighborhood Association is about to step down and is discussing this with another neighbor.

2. The entire Association is having a large group conversation about the leadership changes.

Table 2.1 Constructive Communication Environment

Focus of Attention	Collaborative Communication	Safe Environment	Process Management	Power Management
Person Two people discussing the imminent leadership changes in the Neighborhood Association, one of whom is the president of the association	I see that you are interested in preserving your good reputation. Let's discuss this in a way that helps you uphold your standing in the neighborhood.	Let's move past the "mistakes" that were made during your term as neighborhood association president. I am most interested in the accomplishments that you built during the last five years.	How should we talk about the leadership changes necessary in our neighborhood association? How long do you have for this conversation? Where should we talk? What would you like to accomplish by the end of the discussion?	What can I do to help you identify and discuss your interests and concerns in this conversation? Let's make sure we both speak freely and openly.
Relationship Neighborhood Association meeting with 25 people in attendance, discussing leadership changes	It seems that we all are concerned about the rising violence in our neighborhood. Let's keep that common interest illuminated as we move forward with this discussion.	How would you like to handle sensitive and controversial issues? Should we discuss some type of confidentiality commitment?	We have set aside two hours for this meeting, and we have 25 people here. Let's take a few minutes to discuss a process that meets our needs for this issue today. To begin, what would we like to achieve at the outset of the meeting?	I can see there is a lot of energy and experience here today. Each of you brings significant perspectives that need attention. Since we have only an hour, can we commit to allowing brief, uninterrupted speaking time for each of us?

Table 2.1 (Continued)

Focus of Attention	Collaborative Communication	Safe Environment	Process Management	Power Management
System Within the Neighborhood Association are representatives from local police, local government, and the school board	How wonderful to have all these interests represented in our neighborhood! We have the opportunity to build a successful neighborhood in a variety of ways, by tapping into the ideas and energy of all of us. Let's begin by looking at the larger system. What services are represented here and how do you relate to community development?	We all have a variety of challenges facing us in our community. Let's try to discuss our challenges as opportunities for improvement instead of failings of people or offices.	What other perspectives or interests are not here that would be interested or affected by our decision? How can we craft a process that includes all the necessary stakeholders?	Obviously, the police and local school board have been most involved in the violence issue. It also looks like the community members see this as an issue that requires strong leadership. How can we create a path forward in a way that allows each voice to be heard?

3. The Neighborhood Association has been joined by other community leaders and service providers to discuss possibilities for working together.

❖ SKILLS FOR POSITIVE FACEWORK

With a basis of collaborative communication—a safe environment, process management, and power management—a constructive facework environment can be built. Next we need to incorporate communication skills and methods that do justice to that environment. One way to package this scheme for quality interactions is known as LARC. The acronym stands for Listen, Acknowledge, Respond, and Commit (Littlejohn & Domenici, 2001).

Listening

Effective listening is more than just tuning in to hear the other. Good active listening is an ongoing process of actively focusing on the communication and attempting to understand. If we are to honor

Figure 2.2   LARC Model

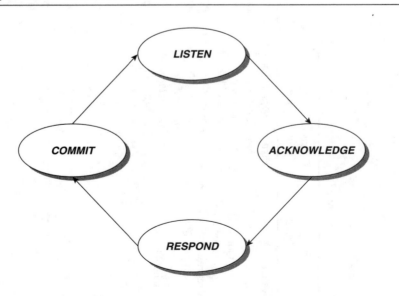

individuals and communities and systems by building effective relationships, we need to listen *first* before acknowledging, responding, or committing to next steps. According to an old saying, "There is always someone who knows what you mean by your message better than you do." The message we intend to get across is not always the one that is received. Listening requires vigilance, practice, and responsibility. The type of effective listening that honors facework does three things:

Delay Judgment. Wait until you have clarity on the intended message before you begin any further interaction. This clarification could come in the form of more questions, more patient listening, or more affirming non-verbal indicators.

    a. Open-ended questions allow you to gain more information than do one-word answers. Tell me more about . . . . How are you able to accomplish that? . . . What makes you so interested in that subject? . . .

    b. Non-verbal indicators include nodding your head, using focused and natural eye contact, offering an occasional "aha" affirmation, and leaning forward toward the person.

Attend to the Whole Meaning. A message has many parts, including feelings, experiences, opinions, facts, ideas, and questions. You can sort out what you are hearing and look for assumptions and information for which you would like clarification.

Ask Questions to Clarify. To further understand and organize what you are hearing, it is important to remember that questions are a significant form of listening. You can help develop a climate of shared understanding by asking, "Can you talk through that point again? I want to make sure I am clear what you are getting at." Stewart and Thomas (1990) offer skills for what they call "dialogic listening." This is a process of "sculpting meaning" from diverse ideas and interactions. Through communication, we are able to sculpt and chip away at the pieces until we have a shared meaning. Dialogic listening in our interactions might look like this:

    1. It focuses on *ours*. Rather than say that this idea or interest is yours, or mine, we can say *these are our interests, and this is our meaning*. When listening, you might say, "I think we are reaching shared understanding on the significance of this issue."

2. It is *open-ended and playful*. Encourage creativity with our questions and comments. Encourage the other person to expand on ideas, identify more possibilities, and think deeper about the issues at hand.

3. It centers on ideas and issues *in front of others*, not what is behind the responses. Try not to psychoanalyze the comments of others. Resolve ambiguity with clear questions and clear language so the idea becomes clearer to everyone, and does not contain hidden meanings.

4. It deals in the *present* rather than the past or future. Discussing the context of reference for comments can be used to explain the current statement. We want people to own their perceptions and opinions.

As you can imagine, listening to establish positive facework environments is active and interactive. The listener needs to be intensively involved in the interaction. As we continue to develop the trusting relationship that builds face, it is important to put off our instinct to jump in and give our own opinions and advice. We add an important step in the interaction. Listen first.

Acknowledging

We want people to know that they are being heard. We want to acknowledge that we are sculpting meaning, or creating some level of shared understanding. You do not need to agree with everyone, but showing that you heard what they said and are taking it seriously does much to build personal and relational face.

An acknowledgment is an act or statement that reflects in some way that you believe you understand what is important to the other person. You do not acknowledge everything you hear, of course, but when the issue is important or differences are encountered, acknowledgment is a powerful facework tool. People acknowledge differently in different relationships, depending upon expectations. Sometimes this means simply repeating what you heard. Sometimes it may involve saying what you see. Sometimes even a simple gesture, smile, nod, or touch will provide a sense of acknowledgment. Whatever its form, the acknowledgment simply says, "I hear you and understand that this is important."

Let's say, for example, that you are having a conversation with your friend about her wedding. She has just read you a long list of things she wants to make sure happen on that special day. Here are some of the responses you might have:

- Restate the content of what she said: *So, you want a church wedding, with four bridesmaids, a dance and reception afterward, and a huge cake. Is that right?*

- Reflect the feelings she displayed: *It sounds like you feel very strongly about making this day memorable for everyone.*

- Identify interests, goals, values, and needs: *I hear you saying that you need a party-like atmosphere so everyone will feel that the marriage is a really joyous thing.*

- Reframe comments in a constructive way: *You want only guests who love you and value your feelings, so you would rather not have any relatives you have not seen lately.*

- Acknowledge positive, respectful interaction: *You have just clearly and graciously talked through a difficult list of issues that need attention.*

- Respond non-verbally: *Gently take the list, look at it, smile, and give your friend a hug.*

The important thing to remember when making an acknowledgment statement is that you should always be tentative. You are telling the speaker what you heard him or her say, and want to make sure you have interpreted it correctly. Try to end your statements with something like, *Did I get that right? Am I hearing you correctly? Is that what you meant? Am I following what you are trying to tell me? OK?* If the speaker corrects you and says, "No, *what I really meant is this . . . ,*" then you will need to start the listening and acknowledging cycle again until you do reach some shared meaning on what the speaker is saying. After you have reached that shared understanding, you can allow yourself to respond.

Responding

This is the time for your statement, your own comments, your perspective or opinions, or your advice. In a high quality facework environment, here is another opportunity to communicate in a way that keeps people feeling comfortable and respected. We probably all know what it feels like to hear a comment that cuts deep, offends us, makes us uncomfortable, or makes us defensive. You want to respond in a way that keeps people engaged in the conversation. These suggestions for responses can keep the conversation going:

- State your own interests, goals, values, and needs. *I need to understand just what is expected of me for this wedding. I don't have much money for fancy clothes or celebrations.*

- Discover mutual or differing interests, goals, values, and needs. *I can see that we have a difference of opinion about these wedding plans. I think it is important to know each other a long time before making a marriage commitment and I gather that you are more interested in getting started in building the lifelong commitment as soon as possible.*

- Frame issues and options. *It looks to me like we need to get more information about a variety of things, including the price of the wedding that you would like and the interests of your fiancé in the wedding plans.*

- Discuss implications for relationship. *I am concerned that this wedding will take over all our time in the next six months, and our friendship will suffer.*

A response that is face-threatening can destroy a conversation or a relationship. Take a look at the difference between these two responses: (1) *Your plans are usually so inappropriate and impossible to achieve. When are you going to get real?* (2) *I am concerned that these wedding plans could be difficult to achieve.* We like to remind people to frame their responses as "I" statements rather than as questions or accusations. Here is a simple sequence to use when putting together a response that honors relationships and personal identity (Scholtes, Joiner, & Streibel, 2003):

1. *Describe what you are reacting to.* Describe the behavior or issue without judgment, exaggeration, labeling, or attribution.

2. *Tell how the suggestion or idea or behavior affects you.* Does it make you frustrated? Annoyed? Angry? Confused? Happy?

3. *Say why you are affected that way.* Describe the connection between what you heard and the feelings they provoke in you.

4. *Describe the change or idea you would like considered.* If you would like to see things change or would like someone to see your viewpoint, you can state it in a way that connects to the issue and its effect on you.

5. *Explain why you think the change will alleviate the problem.* Here is where you give the reasons for your suggestion.

6. *Listen to the other person's response.* Remember that you are sculpting meaning together and always be prepared to discuss options and come up with a mutual path forward.

Here is what an "I statement" might look like in the wedding conversation between two friends.

> I hear some very optimistic wedding planning going on. When I hear such confident planning about such an ambitious undertaking, I feel quite nervous because I would hate to see you let down again. It would be nice to bring in some other people who would be affected by these plans and include them in the discussion. They could give us some realistic insights into the logistics of a wedding such as this. What do you think of that suggestion?

People are more likely to remain open to the response if it is framed in a way that builds their face, while still bringing the issues into the open appropriately. When a communication interaction, whether at the level of acts, conversations, episodes, or lifescripts, has cycled through times of active listening, acknowledgments that signal a commitment to shared understanding, and responses that keep all communicators engaged, build in ample time to make commitments.

SIDEBAR 2.7   Affirmative Intervention

Inspired by such techniques as Cooperrider's appreciative inquiry, affirmative intervention involves a positive attitude or spirit with which you ask questions about a system—a search for the positive resources within a system that might be used as seeds for growth and change (Barge, 2001).

This approach can involve some rather sophisticated interviewing techniques that have good potential for helping groups get "unstuck" from negative, repetitive patterns of interaction. The approach is guided by several principles:

Maintain an attitude of curiosity: Be truly interested in the system and how it works. "It is remarkable that you all care enough about your situation to come today. How was everybody's participation made possible?"

Search for assets: Spend a minimum amount of time on the problem. Ask participants to identify their assets. "What resources can you rely on here?"

Inquire after the positive: Move as quickly as possible to questions designed to elicit positive stories and constructive resources. "I would like to hear about an event or situation here that worked very well, that was energizing or productive. What was it about this situation that made it work well for you?"

Reveal the positive shadow: Look for the positive vision that lies behind or under the negative story. "This constant arguing in the office seems pretty upsetting to you. How would things be different if you were not arguing all the time?"

Move forward: Invite the participants to imagine positive futures. "It is clear that you are all concerned about various disturbances in the neighborhood, like the barking dogs. I would like to know how neighborhoods come to manage and cope with these problems of living in close proximity."

Invite creativity: Instead of analyzing and advising, ask good questions that invite participants to be creative in generating their own solutions. "Jane, you have said that you are never consulted. What changes would you recommend that could lead to broader consultation in the workplace?"

Committing

It is a good rule of thumb to bring some closure to our interactions, so we can acknowledge the accomplishments and contributions that have occurred thus far. This step may just be a marker, a temporary commitment to continue the conversation, or it may be a firm commitment to next steps or to a collaborative decision. Whether it is two people in an informal conversation or a multitude of people having a system-wide conversation, set aside time to discuss what will happen next as a result of the interaction. We suggest the following types of commitments (Littlejohn & Domenici, 2001, pp. 113–117):

- *Decide on an appropriate course of action.* How frustrating it is to leave a meeting and see people shaking their heads saying, "We talked a lot but nothing was accomplished." For the issue in question, one commitment is that the communicators could make a decision or determine the appropriate next steps. This commitment could occur quickly—"It looks like we have agreed to invite the mayor to our next meeting"—or more deliberately—"We will now undertake an intensive assessment of our community, starting with an interview of the mayor and the police chief." When a decision is made, it is helpful to (1) reality test the solution by discussing how this solution will work, who will do it, when will it be done, and where the resources will come from; or (2) if the decision falls apart, be ready to revert to the LARC model: Listen, Acknowledge, Respond, Commit.

• *Create a constructive environment for discussion.* We call this a process commitment. Here is where the communicators decide to create a deliberate process for discussing the topic. Considerations would be given to the interactional accomplishments offered above: collaborative communication, safe environment, process management, and power management. "We will hold a separate meeting to discuss this one issue that divides us. We need to decide where, when, and how long to meet. Who will facilitate? Who will set the agenda? How will we make sure everyone's concerns are heard? Who will take notes? What will we do if we continue to disagree?"

• *Explore the issue further.* This commitment is feasible only if there are still time and resources to continue the conversation at hand. Sometimes a group may say, "It is almost lunchtime, how about if we keep on discussing this through lunch?" What is vital here is that people decide together if they are going to keep on talking together, even past their stated time limit. It is very frustrating when a conversation continues on and on with the assumption that everyone has the time and energy to stay engaged. We want people to *choose* the type of interaction they embark on and continue with. Take a process check (or "time out") and query the group members about their comfort level and dedication to the issue at hand before exploring it further at the current time.

• *Use collaborative problem solving.* This type of commitment says that all communicators will work together to address the issue at hand. We use this type of commitment step especially when we are addressing deep differences or face-threatened environments. We can use a process where all participants work together to create a mutually beneficial solution. Typical collaborative problem solving looks like this:

1. Define the problem as a shared problem. Make sure everyone sees the problem the same way.

2. Discuss goals. What do the different people want, and what should the group as a whole achieve?

3. Brainstorm possible solutions. List solutions that will meet as many goals as possible.

4. Try to achieve consensus on what will make a good solution. Keep in mind that you are going to try to meet as many of the participants' goals as possible.

5. Narrow the choices to a few realistic options.

6. Deliberate on the pros and cons of each option, and discuss the trade-offs you would be willing to make. Weigh each option against the goals and criteria.

7. Make a tentative decision.

8. Reality test the decision.

9. Discuss how to put the decision into action.

• *Bring in a third party to facilitate or mediate the issue or conflict.* The benefits of using an objective third party to help guide the communication are numerous. It is most helpful if this person has skills in communication facilitation, mediation, or group processes. Maybe this person is a member of a similar group that has dealt with an associated issue. In some cases, the outside person can be hired as a consultant to assist with process management. In either case, this commitment shows dedication to building an atmosphere of understanding and respect. A commitment to a respectful and face-building environment is seen clearly when outside resources are brought in to assure that high-quality communication occurs.

The LARC skills are a foundation that enables people to communicate with one another in ways that respect the dignity and contributions of everyone. We try to model these skills in an organic and dynamic manner. Even though they are presented in a linear way (listen first, then acknowledge, then respond, and finally commit), we know that our interactional accomplishments are a complex weave of communication. Keep these two assumptions in mind: intentionality—*what is **between** people is significant*—and cybernetics—*our social world and its structures are made by the communication patterns we establish.* These commitments to interactions that respect the other require patience and persistence. We cannot assume, take for granted, or demand respect for ourselves without a commitment to the other. We need to keep the other in our conversations (Arnett & Arneson, 1999). In the same way that housemates try to work through a distribution of household duties, facework can be addressed as an act, a conversation, an episode, or a lifescript (Table 2.2).

Table 2.2 LARC and Scope of Action

LARC Skill	Scope of Action			
	Act	Conversation	Episode	Lifescript
Listen	Tell me more about living with your past roommate and how you shared duties.	I am so curious about your experiences as a cook and cooking for others. These stories are fascinating!	I have heard so many good stories about your love of good food and experimenting with food. What is it about food that makes you so energized?	You are so consistent in your dedication to cooking and wholesome foods. I look forward to sharing meals with you in this relationship.
Acknowledge	I see, you always took care of cooking duties with your other roommates.	You have enjoyed cooking since you were a child, and still like to try new recipes.	Wow, you have impressed me with your experiences as a cook. Your stories and meals are a big part of my life now.	I see you as a person who illustrates "we are what we eat"!
Respond	It seems that we are at a crossroads here, and I would like to suggest that we create a new system for sharing the household duties.	Let me tell you a bit about my experiences in the kitchen with my family and with other roommates.	Even though we have discussed cooking and your love for food for weeks now, I am still concerned that I end up doing the dishes most of the time.	Please allow me to show you the lifestyle I think complements healthy and interesting eating principles.
Commit	OK, we will take turns cooking and doing dishes, except for weekends when neither of us will cook or clean!	Tonight at dinner, you will share your favorite meal, and I will do the same next week. We will continue to discuss kitchen duties.	So we have decided to take six months to try this new system for dividing up household duties. I will do the dishes on M, W, F, and you will do them on T, Th, Sat. We will cook whenever we have time, and evaluate the system in six months.	Since we are committing to this relationship and each other, we will explore the intersection of our love of food and the integration of exercise into our lifestyle.

SIDEBAR 2.8   Cultural Caveats

The practices described in this chapter are useful in many of the cultural situations in which we live and work. However, they are not universal and would seem odd, even inappropriate, in some cultural settings. Here are a few thought questions that you might consider in regard to culture and facework:

1. When might collaborative communication feel unsafe to communicators?

2. When might explicit discussion of process actually threaten the face of communicators?

3. Who might feel threatened by having their comments overtly acknowledged?

4. How do people in different cultures show that they are listening?

Culture is explored in greater detail in Chapter 6 of this book.

❖   PRINCIPLES FOR PRACTICE

In this chapter, we have built the idea that the communication environment affects the kind of facework you can do and that facework itself is part of that building process. We hope you find the four dimensions and four skill clusters to be helpful in managing face in the diversity of situations you will encounter. We think there are three general principles that can help translate this material into action.

Act with intent, but understand that you are always co-constructing something larger than the objective you are trying to achieve in the moment. Every action has consequences that can influence what you are able to do in the future. Notice what you are making in your ongoing social interactions and expand your goals as needed to create an atmosphere of positive facework. What is the larger system of expectations you want to create?

Remember the reciprocal relationship among facework, collaborative communication, power management, process management, and a safe environment. Building face means more than being nice. It means constructing an environment in which people can relate and work together in ways that enhance their respective lives. Every act of facework contributes to this environment, and the environment in turn contributes to facework.

When pondering how to respond in a difficult situation, ask, "What response will best help build collaboration, empowerment, constructive processes, and a safe environment?"

Communicate with others in a way that honors the complex identities of each person. You don't have to agree or comply with others in order to show that you are taking them seriously as fully formed, complex persons with a history of relationships and communities important to them. Show respect even when the experience of the other person is not consistent with your own. Walk the narrow ridge between self and other in a way that honors what is important to you as well as to others. Try to keep both in mind at the same time.

PART II

Realms of Practice

3

Facework in the
Personal Realm

Commercial portrait photographers have to be good with people.
Their livelihood depends on their ability to take pictures that
people actually want to buy. This is a bit challenging—as we have
discovered over the years in our amateur attempts to photograph
people—because most of us are pretty critical of our own image. We
have discovered that when we take digital pictures of people and show
them an immediate preview, they will more often than not reject two or
three shots before "accepting" one as the final product. Even then, they
often don't seem very happy about it. We have taken wonderful
candid shots of people, only to discover that our enthusiasm is not
matched by the subject's reaction.

People are conscious of their self-image—how others view them.
This is why so many of us spend considerable time in the bathroom
every morning primping with blow-dryers, makeup, tweezers, shavers,
and all manner of personal grooming aids. But our personal image
is not limited to how we look. We are concerned about how
we sound, others' judgments about what we say, our perceived
competence, and all forms of impressions that we make in interaction
with others. Most of the time, too, we want to reciprocate this desire by

complimenting people, being polite, and not hurting others' feelings. Effective facework, then, is a matter of presenting ourselves in ways that are consistent with how we want to be treated and honoring the identity needs of others as well.

Although we may be amused by how certain people dress, sound, or act, most of us know intuitively that deeper issues are involved— issues related to people's very sense of who they are as persons in the world. In this chapter we take a closer look at how we manage personal identity in communication. We concentrate here on the four levels of communication described in Chapter 1—the act, conversation, and lifescript.

❖ COMMUNICATION ACTS

A communication act is a "statement" that has meaning on several levels. In most cases there are both verbal and non-verbal dimensions of the act. For example, you might say, "What?" while your eyebrows show surprise. This act will be understood on at least three levels. The first is the *semantic* level, in which you look at the meaning of the words and gestures. Second, you look at the *syntactic* meaning or how the words and gestures are structured, the grammar of the act. Third, you look at the overall *intention* of the act—what communicators hope to accomplish when they perform the act (Cameron, 2001; Ellis, 1999; Searle, 1969). In the example above, the word *what* refers to "unspecified thing." When combined with a questioning tone in the voice, the meaning expands to be a question about what is being said or done, as in "What is happening here?" Now when you add the raised eyebrows, the overall meaning is something like, "I'm surprised at what is happening here." The statement could also mean, "I didn't get that; please say it again." The meaning results from semantic and syntactic interpretations—the word, tone of voice, and facial expression and the way in which these are structured or organized. This is sometimes called the *propositional meaning* of the act.

There is a third level of meaning as well, which is most important for our purposes here, and this is the intent of the act. Communication acts do not just convey a literal meaning, but they also accomplish something by getting across a larger intention of what the communicator wants to do with his or her words and actions. In the above example, the act might be taken as a question (What's happening?), a challenge (I don't like what you are doing), or the description of a state of affairs (I'm surprised at this). It could also be a request (Please repeat what you said).

Sometimes communication acts are quite direct, as they tell others just what the intention is. Other times they are rather indirect, gaining meaning more by implication. For example, "Pass the butter" is a *direct request* with no ambiguity about meaning. On the other hand, "Is there any butter in the refrigerator?" could be taken as an *indirect request* for butter at the table. You might say, "I promise to return the snowshoes tomorrow," which is a *direct promise*, or you might say, "I won't keep them long," which is an *indirect promise*. You might say to your child, "Give me that Coke!" which is a clear *direct command*, or you might say, "Who said you could have a Coke?" which could be an *indirect command*.

Notice that in each of these cases, the communication act does more than make a statement. It creates a certain intention to be fulfilled. Even a simple description or statement with no other motive is still doing something—communicating an idea or perspective. This is what is important about communication acts—they express an intention. In some cases, a single act may express more than one intention.

Facework consists in part of certain communications acts that build, protect, or threaten the face of self or other. If you tell someone, "You are an idiot!" the literal semantic and syntactic meaning, or propositional meaning (*You are unintelligent*), is inconsequential. What really matters here is the intent—*to insult*—and that is a direct threat to identity and face. On another occasion, you may want your friend to know that you think her dress is nice (propositional meaning), but the most important impact of the message is its intent—*to compliment*—which has important face implications.

In the process of commanding, directing, promising, vowing, stating, or questioning, face is almost always involved. For example, if I command or direct you to do something, this may reflect my perception of your competence. If I make a promise, it may be saying something about my reliability as a person, which is also a face concern. When you stop to think about it, almost anything you could say or do in an interaction has face implications, which is why we believe that facework is always central. It also reinforces our view that face awareness is important in all of our human relationships, and, in fact, why we are writing a book about this subject. With a full understanding that virtually anything you could say or do relates to face in some way, we want to take a closer look at communication acts for which facework is a primary intent.

Face Consciousness and Person Centeredness

We have known for many years from communication research that people vary in terms of how much they take other people into account in framing their messages. In public speaking, you would call this "audience analysis"—taking your listener into account when speaking. Communication scholars frequently call this *person centeredness* (Applegate, 1982; Delia, Kline, & Burleson, 1979; Hale, 1980).

Person centeredness means taking others into account and saying things in ways that the other person will understand and appreciate. We do adapt our messages to the audience, but we do so with varying degrees of effectiveness. People who are person centered are also face conscious. These people anticipate others' responses and show concern for face issues. Other people are less person centered and less face conscious.

Barbara O'Keefe (1988) claims that people construct messages on the basis of a certain set of assumptions that she calls the *message design logic*. How you frame a message is determined by the logic you employ, which in turn is affected by how person centered you are. People who are not very oriented to others make use of an *expressive logic,* which guides them to say what's on their mind without thinking about how others might receive this information. Just say it, get it off your chest, and express yourself honestly. Others are a little more person centered, but rely mostly on general rules of etiquette or social norms rather than thinking specifically about the person in front of them. These folks make use of a *conventional logic,* which is guided by social rules. A third group of people, highly person centered, follows a *rhetorical logic* that views rules as constantly changing, depending upon the context and persons involved. These individuals will think about how to integrate facework with other communication goals.

You may be more expressive on one occasion, conventional in others, and rhetorical in other situations. As a principle, we think that people can and should make an effort to become more person centered and face conscious to the extent possible in every important encounter.

Let's now look at the ways in which people use communication acts to accomplish facework. Here we will explore presenting the self, building the face of others, protecting the face of others, threatening the face of others, and responding to face threats (Ting-Toomey & Cocroft, 1994).

SIDEBAR 3.1   A Challenge

Imagine that you are a supervisor for the Postal Service, and one of your carriers is working too slowly, not getting the mail out on time, and making numerous mistakes. How might you handle this situation?

1. Think of what you might say to this individual if you were using an expressive logic. What would you say if you were using a conventional logic? A rhetorical logic?

2. What are the differences between these three messages?

3. How would your goals change as you move from an expressive to a conventional and finally to a rhetorical logic in your communication with this individual?

4. What are the differences in the kind of facework you would be doing in each of these three situations?

Presenting the Self

Imagine entering a conference room at the designated hour to meet a group of potential clients for an account you are managing. First, you will look your best. You will dress according to some sense of appropriateness to the occasion. You will pay attention to your posture, stance, and stride as you enter the room. Your introduction would be carefully considered to get across the most relevant and appropriate level of self-information for a first impression. Later you might have the opportunity to tell more about yourself, either directly in an introduction to the group or indirectly over time as you converse. Out of all of the aspects of your personal identity, in this situation—as in all situations—you select those aspects most needed to make the kind of impression you want to give (Jones & Pittman, 1982; Metts & Grohskopf, 2003).

This example illustrates a rather formal professional situation, but you are really doing this kind of thing all the time. You will present different aspects of yourself on the beach, in a bar, in class, and at a family Thanksgiving dinner (Goffman, 1959). Much of the time you do this indirectly by how you act and respond. You might, for example, tell stories that are interesting and entertaining, but that also communicate some important aspects of your own competence, your characteristics, or accomplishments that may be important for your image in the situation. Also, the manner of your interaction will also affect self-face. If you are friendly, responsive, and generally socially competent, you may make a positive impression.

Almost every time you communicate with others, you will have at least two goals. One is a content goal, accomplishing some objective, and the other is a self-presentation goal, managing the impressions others have of you. (As you will see in the following section, you probably also have a third goal, which is to manage the face of the other as well.) Actually, the presentation of self is an important part of the process of identity construction, which we discussed in some detail in Chapter 1. By presenting yourself in certain ways, for example, you may continue a process of establishing yourself as having autonomy, fellowship, and competence (Lim & Bowers, 1991). In other words, in this way you would, over time, establish yourself as a person who can run your own life and yet have relationships and connections with others and as someone who is proficient, knows what you are doing, and knows what you are talking about.

It is helpful to begin thinking about self-presentation using positive social examples like those above, but self-presentation may not always be "peachy" in this kind of way. Acts designed to present the self are aligned both with how you want to be perceived and your own self-image. Depending upon a host of personal, relational, and cultural factors, an individual may go either way here. You may actually present yourself in an unfavorable way because that is how you see yourself, or you may act in ways that build your own sense of self-worth. Psychotherapists and counselors often work with clients to help them build positive identities. Since personal identity is constructed through communication with others, finding some level of positive self-presentation contributes to building a sense of worth and dignity.

Sometimes, too, acts that are intended to present the self in a positive way work against that goal because they go against the relational or cultural grain. Talking extensively about yourself can be taken as boasting and quite rude in some cultures. In certain cultures, as well, people will deprecate themselves in order to build a positive image of the other person or group. Actually, people often anticipate that others will not always see them in a good light and will act to protect themselves or prevent loss of face, and, as we will see later in the chapter, people do respond by trying to mitigate or restore lost face when this has happened (Metts & Grohskopf, 2003).

SIDEBAR 3.2   A Golden Rule

"Society is organized on the principle that any individual who possess certain social characteristics has a moral right to expect that others will value and treat him in an appropriate way."

Source: E. Goffman, *The Presentation of Self in Everyday Life*, 1959, p. 13.

Building the Face of Others

All cultures promote face building as a value, though cultures accomplish this in different ways (Chapter 6). People learn from an early age the appropriate ways to do honor to others within their culture. Here we look at several ways in which people build the face of others.

Honoring. Honorifics are an important part of everyday communication (Penman, 1990; Shimanoff, 1988). We remain conscious of the social practice of placing others in a position of respect. Referring to someone as "Mr.," "Ms.," "Mrs.," or "Dr." is a perfect example. We know in our bones that it is better to call a stranger "sir" or "ma'am" than "hey you." In Japanese, the suffix "sensei" is often added to a name as a way of honoring as person. In court you refer to the judge as "Your Honor," and you may preface a religious leader's name with "Pastor," "Father," or "Rabbi."

We can honor people in many other ways as well. We may praise someone, introduce a person to friends or colleagues by mentioning something special about them, or share a positive impression of something they have said or done. We compliment other people for a variety of reasons, not least of which is just to make them feel honored and respected, to feel that they are worthy and appreciated.

Politeness. Honoring is a form of politeness, which means being appropriately deferential, acknowledging the contributions and needs of others, and showing appreciation. In most cultures, the local form of "thank you" always follows even the smallest offer. Rudeness is considered an affront because it is such a face threat. If you are too direct, fail to follow common courtesy, communicate in a socially inappropriate way, or are too openly critical at the wrong time or place, you would probably be judged as rude. Most people go out of their way to be friendly and polite precisely to avoid this attribution. It is interesting that in showing respect to others, we also engender respect for ourselves. A rude person is rarely enjoyed or respected in any social situation.

In their now classic theory of politeness, Penelope Brown and Stephen Levinson write that people want both autonomy, or independence, and acceptance (Brown & Levinson, 1987). Politeness really means acting in a way that enables others to have these, and we want these things for ourselves, too. If we say or do something that could erode another person's sense of autonomy or acceptance, then we are engaging in a "face-threatening act," or FTA. For Brown and Levinson, politeness means being careful about how we do this so as to minimize the impact of the FTA. When we act to protect someone's autonomy by trying to protect the person from intrusion or restriction, we are engaging in *negative politeness.* (In this case the term *negative* does not mean bad, but protective or mitigating.) For example, if you are about to make a request, you might acknowledge first that you know the other person is busy and that you don't want to intrude. When we are helping a person achieve acceptance, then we are engaging in *positive politeness,* which just means that we are showing that we accept, approve of, or respect them in some way. So, for example, you might preface a request with a compliment.

Generosity. The third way in which we build the face of other people is through giving (Lebra, 1976). Holiday and birthday presents are an obvious example. The offer of food or a nice dinner is another example. Spending the day cooking an excellent meal for a group of friends shows that you like them, care enough to give something of yourself, and directly acknowledge this through a personal sacrifice of time and money. Further, by showing your pleasure in giving, you are building your own sense of identity and face as well as that of the other.

Support. We show support in lots of ways. We can listen to another person's complaints, we can provide advice, we can show approval, and we can show that we support, even agree with, the other person's self-attributions. We can't be sure what counts as support, of course. In some relationships, being brutally honest may be taken as a greater sign of respect than giving equivocal feedback. Showing support in a professional setting is probably different from showing support with a friend. However delivered, support messages are taken as a sign that the other person is worthy of your attention, respect, and help.

Brant Burleson and his colleagues have conducted a mountain of research on the subject of communication and support (Albrecht, Burleson, & Goldsmith, 1994; Burleson, 2003). It is clear from this work that its effectiveness, or helpfulness, depends greatly upon the quality of the facework accomplished in messages of social support. Most helpful are statements that clearly express the desire to help, show affection and concern, and promise availability. Most people also find understanding and acknowledgment of one's feelings very helpful, as are signs of openness and a listening attitude. On the other hand, messages of support that threaten the face of the other person, such as minimizing the problem, denying or criticizing the person's feelings or behavior, accusing, or commanding the distressed person to "stop crying and calm down" are not very helpful. In fact, these kinds of statements would probably be taken as a face threat.

Protecting the Face of Others

We often act to protect the face of other people (Penman, 1990), and we do this in several ways.

Tact. We use tact when we deliver negative information in a thoughtful and gentle way. Tact means being diplomatic, discrete, careful, and often indirect. In many ways, tact is a matter of framing. If you don't like someone's new car, you may acknowledge that they are excited about it and share their excitement. When others' work performance is lacking, you might tell them that you would like to help them set some goals for the next year. The whole idea behind tact is to frame the negative in ways that will be helpful and constructive (Lim & Bowers, 1991).

Minimizing. We often work to minimize the negative impact of something we are doing (Kim, 1993). For example, if you make a request, you may do so in a way that minimizes the imposition. You may offer to help, make the request seem less daunting, give the person an out, and generally try to reduce the impact of what you are doing on his or her time and space or to make it worth his or her while. If you were to ask someone to help you move, you would probably say something like the following:

I'm moving next Saturday, as you know. I'm putting together a crew to help out, but I know you are pretty busy right now. I'm serving pizza, so come by for a little lunch if you want. That would be great. If you can't help, I'll totally understand.

Notice how this statement dances all around the request in order to minimize the possibility of intruding in some way. Here's another example:

> I'm sorry, sir, but we have to paint the wall here outside your office, and it'll be a little messy for a couple days. I'm really sorry, and we'll try to keep it quiet, because I know you do important work here. Please let us know if there is anything we can do to make this easier for you.

You can see that minimizing is really the same thing as negative politeness, as described above.

Avoidance. One of the most important reasons why some people avoid hard topics and criticism is that they don't want to hurt the other person's feelings (Brown & Levinson, 1987; Kim, 1993). They may also doubt their ability to maintain their own integrity and dignity at these difficult moments. If you passed an acquaintance whose spouse recently died, you would experience an awkward moment in deciding what to say. Usually, we are able to come up with some appropriate words, but some people might just avoid the topic or, worse, cross the street in hopes of not being seen, just because addressing the subject could itself feel hurtful. Conflict is often avoided for the same reason. We don't want to say something that would damage the face of the other, and, equally, we don't want to say something that could hurt our own credibility or level of respect. So we avoid the issue altogether.

Prevention. Sometimes we act to prevent face damage done by others: "Please don't tell your father"; "I know you don't agree with the boss, but you'll be sorry if you come on too strong in the meeting"; "No, you can't go over there because you are in no mental state for it right now. Calm down first." We may prevent face threats by deciding who should participate in a conversation, how we structure what people can and cannot say, and by invoking certain rules for how to discuss the topic. We also preface or structure our own comments in ways that mitigate a face threat we believe we are about to make (Gross & Stone, 1964; Metts & Grohskopf, 2003). For example, we might say something such as, "I'm really sorry, but . . . ," "It's not really your fault . . . ," or "Don't take what I'm about to say personally. . . ."

SIDEBAR 3.3   The Limits of Criticism

"In criticism, the language that we use often takes on a damaging, judgmental twist. We begin to use the word *you* instead of *I*. When we communicate from a place of discovery, we naturally use *I* or *we*. This involves more awareness of other people's needs and feelings, and of our own, and we become more specific as to our desired results. Consider the difference:

"You didn't fix this machine correctly, versus *I can't get this machine to do what I'd like. I'd like it to . . .*

"The first statement lays blame, and the second statement communicates specifically the outcome you want."

Source: T. F. Crum, *The Magic of Conflict,* 1987, p. 121.

Threatening the Face of Others

We use facework to honor personal dignity and show respect, but we also use it to do the opposite—threaten the face of the other (Lim & Bowers, 1991; Penman, 1990; Shimanoff, 1988). Criticism, rudeness, blame, attack, embarrassment, and deprecation are all face-threatening acts. Often these are done quite deliberately for personal gain, as an expression of anger, or as an attempt to prevail in a conflict situation. Too often people threaten the face of others in order to build their own, as if to say, "See how much better I am?" Ironically, this move, common as it is, will boomerang in most situations because it will actually hurt the speaker's image. Of course, the non-verbal manner in which we deliver a face-threatening act can have a major impact on how it is received. You can deliver criticism calmly and rationally or by yelling and being emotional. The latter is usually more threatening than the former. You can show caring in how you deliver a threatening message, or you can deliver it in a demeaning and damning way.

Sometimes we threaten the face of another person without meaning to do so, at moments when we are careless, unaware, distracted, or self-absorbed. Often unintended face-threatening acts are taken as purposeful, which can begin a negative spiral in the relationship, a topic we take up in Chapter 4.

Brown and Levinson show that politeness is a question of managing face threat (Brown & Levinson, 1987). The more polite we are, the less we are willing to threaten another person's face. Notice that there is a good dose of self-face in politeness as well. If we are polite and show sensitivity to others, we can gain respect for ourselves.

People are generally conscious of politeness and very deliberately speak in ways that prevent themselves and others from losing face. But there is so much potential for threatening face—often in unconscious ways—that we build little devices into our speech that provide a kind of ongoing politeness, as in, "I hate to bother you, but . . ." For this reason, politeness does require work, and we do make distinctions in the amount of work we are willing to put into being polite. You might be less polite with your brother than with your pastor, for example.

Brown and Levinson write that the amount of effort you put into being polite depends upon (1) the social distance between you and the other person, (2) the power the other person has over you, and (3) the risk of hurting the other person in some way. The situation also has a bearing on how polite you can be. In some situations, you need to be very efficient in making a request or demand or in intruding in some other way.

Brown and Levinson identify two forms of politeness: Positive politeness is designed to acknowledge a person's capability or competency in some way, while negative politeness is designed to mitigate or prevent a violation of one's autonomy or freedom. They created a politeness scale of the degree to which a potentially face-threatening act is delivered in terms of positive and negative politeness. There are five points in the continuum from most threat to least:

1. Deliver the face-threatening act baldly—this is a direct threat without any attempt to mitigate it. ("I need your car.")

2. Deliver the FTA along with some form of positive politeness— here, you try to mitigate the threat with a positive statement. ("You're always so generous. I wonder if I could borrow your car.")

3. Deliver the FTA along with some negative politeness—here you would qualify the threat in a way that would minimize its impact. ("I hate to bother you 'cause I know how busy you are, but could I borrow your car?")

4. Deliver the FTA indirectly, or off-the-record—here you would make an implication only. ("I wonder how I'm going to get to work today.")

5. Not deliver the FTA at all—this is complete avoidance.

Again, the greater the social distance, the more power the other person has over you, and the greater the risk of harm, the more you will move toward the polite end of the spectrum. This is why politeness looks very different in families and friendships than in professional settings.

SIDEBAR 3.4   Politeness Choices

Think of a situation where you need to communicate a harsh truth to someone. Use Brown and Levinson's five Face Threatening Act (FTA) delivery choices to compose your statement. Which would you feel most comfortable with? Why?

1. Direct threat

2. Mitigate the direct threat with a positive statement

3. Use negative politeness to minimize the impact

4. Make an indirect implication only

5. Avoidance

We feel that Brown and Levinson's ideas ring true for many of the situations in which we find ourselves; however, this theory has been criticized for leaving out many cultural and situational factors that could change things. This caveat provides an opportunity to say again that facework is never just a matter of the acts of one person vis-à-vis another. Rather, it is embedded deeply in relational expectations and cultural norms, as we will see in Chapters 4 and 5.

We must be cautious about judging a potentially face-threatening act based on what it sounds like in the moment. What may appear to be a face threat may turn out to be face building in the long run. Depending upon the relational and cultural contexts as well as the overall episode in which it is given, a piece of criticism—even sharply delivered—may turn out to be a turn in a longer series of acts that serve to build the face of the other. We recently heard a fascinating radio program in which several people talked about their favorite teachers, or teachers who had the most positive influence on their lives. Most of the teachers that these individuals identified were not always nice and polite. In fact, they were remembered because they challenged, criticized, and held high expectations and standards for their students. The speakers recalled instances when their favorite teachers responded with sharp rebuke, which must have felt insulting and uncomfortable in the moment but later proved actually to build face by helping students rise to a higher level of self-esteem and accomplishment.

The opposite is also true: A very nice face-saving act could turn out to be a manipulative move with the effect in the long run of degrading or demeaning the face of the other. This is why you can never judge the value of an act of facework without taking a larger, contextual view.

Responding to Face Threats

When our face is threatened, we may respond by moving to *redress* the threat in some way (Metts & Grohskopf, 2003; Schlenker, 1980; Schonbach, 1990). We do this with excuses, explanations, apologies, denials, agreement, regret, counter-complaining, and ignoring. You might not think of ignoring as a form of redress, but silence can sometimes be very loud. Silence can be taken to mean (1) I am taking this seriously and must think about it; (2) your comment is insignificant and not worth my time; or (3) I will not respond in kind to the disrespect that you have shown toward me.

How you respond—the behavior, framing, and language used—will contribute to the climate of facework as the conversation proceeds. When threatened by another person, you can be acknowledging, calm, solution oriented, and understanding, or you can be emotional, defensive, blaming, rude, or even violent in your response. Emotional and defensive responses return the face threat, which rarely accomplishes anything except a negative spiral of resentment.

❖   INTEGRATING FACEWORK INTO CONVERSATION

Face acts rarely stand in isolation. It is a mistake, then, to look at single communication acts apart from the conversations in which they occur. The pattern over time means more than the single instance. In this section, we broaden our lens to look at facework within conversations.

The question for any communication act is, "What does this act count as?" Is it an apology, an insult, a request, an offer to help? As we indicated above, you have a pretty good idea of the meaning of an act based on how it is stated and delivered, but its ultimate meaning always derives from a larger context of interaction (Tracy, 2002). The meaning of the act depends upon what kind of conversation we are having, what was said before and what we anticipate will be said in the future, and the place of this conversation within a larger sequence of episodes. The implications of what is being said and done in an interaction on the personal identities of the participants will depend on these larger structures.

The conversation we are having at the moment actually organizes specific turns of talk (Tracy, 2002). We must broaden our view of what counts as self-presentation, face building, face protecting, and face threatening by considering this conversational frame. Facework is rarely finished in a single comment or act but always builds over time on the back-and-forth exchange of an interaction.

In this section, we look at several facets of facework within the conversational frame, including face negotiation, supportive conversations, and facework in conflict situations.

SIDEBAR 3.5   Face Negotiation

Stella Ting-Toomey introduced the term *face negotiation* to refer to the process in which individuals establish one another's face needs and appropriate forms of response through interaction (Ting-Toomey & Kurogi, 1998). When you have a conversation with others, you establish a pattern of facework that functions for the group in some way. For example, an insult in one conversation may come to constitute a face threat leading to a series of defensive interactions. In another conversation, the insult may simply fix people in their pre-established identities, actually strengthening a sense of individual power among them. Debaters, for example, reinforce one another's feelings of self-worth by attacking and defending their respective arguments in what might look like a face threat in another kind of encounter. In certain conversations, an apparent series of attacks may be taken as fun or engaging, and participating in this repartee actually builds a feeling of camaraderie. In face negotiation, then, we establish the meaning of acts and the appropriate forms of response across time through a series of interactions.

Supportive Conversations

In their decades-long work on communicating social support, Brant Burleson and his colleagues have come to understand that genuine social support is developed over time through a series of conversations

(Burleson, 2003). It may feel temporarily comforting in a moment of distress to have a friend speak a few words of support, but what matters most is how you and your friend follow up in a longer series of interactions. Burleson and Goldsmith (1998) use appraisal theories of emotion to explain their position on this issue. According to this approach, your emotions are established by how you evaluate external events in light of your current goals.

Think about what a star athlete must go through after experiencing a serious injury. Any injury is distressing, but it is especially difficult when the player has to be benched during the recovery period. Athletes want to play, their team relies on their participation, and they are unable to meet important life goals at this time. Notice that this situation is a tremendous threat to personal identity. The injured athlete has been honored for his or her performance on the field, but is now vulnerable because of the injury. Providing emotional support at this time, if handled well, could become a great form of facework.

Burleson and Goldsmith show that providing support at a time such as this means using conversation to facilitate a cognitive restructuring of the meaning of the event (injury) or the person's goals (to play). In this example, the athlete's friends, other players, coaches, and even medical staff may provide this kind of support. Knowing just what to say and ask may not be immediately apparent but will have to be negotiated in a back-and-forth interaction between the athlete and those who are providing support.

Burleson and Goldsmith (1998) say that the support-givers will need to do three things. First, they should create a suitable helping environment in which it is safe to talk about the distressing situation. This means establishing trust, allowing the emotional issues to be explored, helping the player manage his or her emotional arousal, and keeping the setting comfortable and conducive to this kind of talk. Second, the support-giver will need to facilitate the discussion of the emotional issue. This means figuring out just when to introduce the topic, how to respond to the statements of the injured player, and how to organize or manage the conversation. Third, the support-giver will invite the player to explore alternative evaluations by using good questions, taking time, acknowledging the thoughts and feelings of the player, and avoiding advice. Through this process, the injured player may come to see his or her health as more important than playing the game, to understand that the injury is only temporary, to have confidence in the team to compensate for the loss, or to realize that the other players and coaching staff really care about the athlete as a person. All of these possible outcomes involve restructuring or re-appraising the situation in a way that can bring comfort and constitute a high level of facework.

SIDEBAR 3.6   Conversations That Restore

A thirteen-year-old girl came home from school one day and remarked to her mother, "Mom, we never talk any more." The mother was tempted to answer with an easy and almost defensive response, such as the following,

Mary, we talk all the time.

How can you say that? We talk at dinner, we talk before bed, and we talk in the car on the way to school.

If you want us to talk more, get your homework done on time, so you can have more free time in the evenings.

Maybe you could stay off of the Internet long enough to have more conversations with your family.

I tried talking to you last night and you seemed too absorbed in the television show.

Any of those responses may have closed off communication and further damaged a relationship about to enter the challenging teenage years. Instead, the mother paused for a few seconds, stopped her current preoccupation, looked at her daughter and offered this answer, "You seem concerned about our communication, Mary. Is there something you would like to talk to me about?" Mary seemed relieved and said, "I am being bullied at school." Now, the two of them could embark on a conversation aimed at reviving and strengthening a potential face-damaging situation. Mother and daughter then discussed the school environment and the intimidation Mary was experiencing.

If we dissect Mother's response, we see that she accomplished a variety of things. First, she acknowledged Mary's concern about the amount of communication that had been occurring between mother and daughter; *You seem concerned about our communication, Mary.* Next, Mother's response diffused any emotions that might exist within the statement or the ensuing conversation. Third, the response was invitational. It sought a continuation of the daughter's statement without making any value judgments. Lastly, Mother's response restructured a situation using constructive facework. It was much more comfortable to determine how to take care of the difficult school circumstances during this restorative conversation.

Facework in Conflict Situations

Face is almost always a central concern in conflict situations. Most conversations that involve open conflict are arguments in which the participants seem to be struggling to prevail, to gain something over the other person. Winning and losing have inherent implications for identity, and when you add the emotional component—anger, worry, remorse, blame, and guilt—identity needs are very much at stake. Sometimes the participants in mediation sessions say terrible things about each other to boost their own face and degrade that of the other person. Indeed, an important part of a mediator's job is to help the participants manage face.

So it is easy to see the face issues in a hot dispute, but many conversations involving conflict do not sound much like an argument and can have more subtle face implications. Years ago, Ralph Kilmann and Kenneth Thomas (1977) generated a useful model of five styles of conflict—(1) competing, (2) compromising, (3) avoiding, (4) accommodating, and (5) collaborating. These styles depend on the degree to which the parties wish to promote their own interests versus those of the other person. If you are mostly interested in gaining your own interests without allowing the other person to do so, you will be very competitive, which assumes a win-lose stance. If you are very interested in promoting the other person's interests over your own—a lose-win stance—then accommodation will be your style. If neither seems very important, you may avoid, and if both are important, you will tend to collaborate (win-win). Compromise means giving up (or gaining) a little of what each person wants.

Instead of using these "styles" to characterize individuals, we find it most useful to think of these five as response modes and to explore their implications for conversations in which conflict is present. Here we look at the face implications of common interaction patterns in conflict.

Compete-Accommodate. It often happens that one person moves to prevail in a conflict, while the other person gives in. This may happen after a period of argument, or no argument may occur at all. By winning, one person may experience at least a temporary face boost. Ironically, the "loser" may also experience a face gain, as one of the best reasons for accommodating is to avoid the threat that may come from a fight. The compete-accommodate pattern, especially if it comes quickly after little or no arguing, avoids face-threatening acts because there is no struggle and matters are settled quickly. It may also be the case that accommodators gain something important by preserving the relationship, maintaining the peace, or enjoying watching people they love get something they want. Giving up something important to honor another person can reinforce your identity as a person, which is a face gain.

At the same time, giving up something important can erode our sense of self-worth. The loss itself may hurt some aspect of your identity, and the act of losing, itself, regardless of what is lost, can be hurtful, depending upon your own personal values and characteristics. Either way, accommodating has negative face implications. So fighting for what is important to you, even when there is a potential face threat in the argument, may be an ultimate face gain in the sense that you stood up for yourself. There are always trade-offs in personal identity. If you have an argument, you may lose some face, but the struggle itself may actually help you gain face—a dilemma commonly faced in conflict situations.

Compete-Compete. This pattern is the one most frequently associated with an argument. This can be the most face threatening kind of conversation, as both people—especially if they are emotional—will say hurtful things. There is much potential in this pattern for face loss by both parties. However, this is not an inevitable outcome. One or both parties may find the argument exhilarating, it may reinforce an aspect of their own self-identity, or it may be part of a relational pattern of showing that you care.

A significant face issue in conversations involving conflict is the difficulty of backing down from a stated position. For many people, the move toward compromise is difficult because, after making very strong positional arguments, movement feels like giving in, which would be a loss of face. This is especially true for individuals who do not like to look inconsistent or to appear to be wishy-washy, a face issue important in negotiations. If negotiators take their positions too seriously, they risk an impasse. Mediators are all too aware of this possibility and provide many opportunities for disputants to reframe their statements and to explore the positive values of settlement or the negative consequences of not settling. Some mediators do not want to rush into settlement discussions too quickly in order to avoid parties' becoming stuck in positions from which they cannot retreat. It is far better to establish a basis of understanding and some trust in a safe environment before exploring options.

Collaborate. Collaboration, commonly known as the win-win approach, requires a sophisticated reframing of the conflict conversation. Instead of viewing the issue as a "conflict to be resolved," the communicators must come to see it as a "problem to be solved." Instead of saying, *You want this and I want that,* the individuals ask, *What can we do to make sure that all of our interests are met?* Instead of an argument, the conversation becomes a problem-solving session in which the parties create options for mutual gain.

In their landmark work on collaboration, Roger Fisher and William Ury (1991) say that collaboration is *principled negotiation,* meaning that it follows a set of principles that from our perspective are designed to maximize face gains and minimize face losses. The first principle is to *separate the people from the problem.* You avoid attacking the other person and instead concentrate on discovering interests, defining the problem, and exploring options. Notice how this principle immediately mitigates face threat. If you no longer see the issue as a personal fight, the potential for face gain is tremendous. Second, *focus on interests, not positions.* Positions lock us into a battle over who will win, but if we look instead at interests, we actually acknowledge what is important to people, which is a face gain. Third, *invent options for mutual gain.* The mere act of being creative in thinking of ways to meet everyone's interests is itself face boosting. When we see ourselves as collaborators, we can build a strong sense of ability and mutual concern. Reducing the chance of face threats in this kind of situation can open up possibilities for positive presentation of self and face building of the other. Fourth, *insist on using objective criteria.* This simply means that you negotiate what is important so that together you can evaluate options and ideas. Objective criteria help to remove the focus from the threat associated with personal attachment and open up the possibility of collaboration.

Although collaborative conversations have positive face implications much of the time, this is not always the case. For individuals who see themselves as highly competitive, collaboration may feel like giving in. Collaborative conversations also require a lot of energy and time, which can lead to a feeling of spinning wheels or wasting time, which in some situations can constitute a face threat.

SIDEBAR 3.7   Building Constructive Relationships

"The best time for handling people problems is before they become people problems. This means building a personal and organizational relationship with the other side that can cushion the people on each side against the knocks of negotiation."

Source: R. Fisher & W. Ury, *Getting to Yes,* 1991, pp. 36–37.

Compromise. Compromise is a common and useful solution to conflicts. Positional bargaining, as it is sometimes called, is just a back-and-forth negotiation in which the parties settle the issue by meeting somewhere in the middle. Compromise can be entirely free of face threat. Once the disputants show willingness to bargain, the focus will move to settlement, which can relieve potential face threats and even build face, as the parties seem empowered to reach an agreement. On many occasions, we have watched parties in disputes show satisfaction, occasionally even glee, at having settled a dispute.

But compromise can involve face threats as well, especially when parties watch something they really wanted melt away. Also, the process of compromise can involve face-threatening statements if the parties are unable to let go of their feelings of blame.

❖ EPISODES OF FACEWORK

You probably associate the word *episode* with television series. A large dramatic or comedic "situation" is divided into segments that are aired separately. Each episode has a stock set of characters and predictable narrative format. The term *episode* is also used in literature as an identifiable part of a larger story. The episode is like a little story that is part of a larger one. We also use the term *episode* to apply to segments of regular life.

An *episode* is defined as an identifiable series of actions with a beginning and an end (Pearce & Cronen, 1980; Penman, 1990). Having breakfast, holding a business meeting, playing a game of baseball, and having an e-mail conversation with your mother would all be recognizable episodes in American life. Episodes are recognizable and somewhat predictable. In this book we treat an episode as a larger frame within which to understand conversations. An episode may be small, even a single conversation, or large and filled with many conversations.

The annual strategic planning process in a corporation is an example of a lengthy episode that includes many conversations. Everyone would recognize the episode. It has a beginning—maybe a corporate e-mail from the CEO announcing the start of the process—and an ending, perhaps the presentation of the strategic plan to the Board of Directors. The many meetings, telephone conversations, e-mail exchanges, and other processes conducted as part of the planning effort are easily recognized by everyone as a stage in the process. Notice that each of these smaller conversations is understood and gains meaning in terms of the larger context of the episode. In many ways as well, the kind of talk that occurs in each of these smaller conversations is shaped in part by the episodic context, and the reverse is also true: The conversations themselves help to shape the meaning of the larger episode.

Now let's look at a smaller example—disciplining a child. If your son or daughter misbehaves, you probably have a regular routine for handling it, pretty much in one conversation. What is said and done in this conversation ("You misbehaved, so go sit in the corner.") is viewed as an episode of discipline, and the conversation gives meaning to the episode as well.

In this section we look at the way in which episodes of life involve facework.

The Gamelike Structure of Episodes

Games are a kind of episode. You would easily recognize a game of football, an evening of poker, or hide-and-seek as episodes. Using games as a metaphor, we can extend this analogy to all walks of life. Episodes provide a rule set for interpreting and acting within the conversation, just as the rules in an ordinary game structure what actions mean and what moves are possible. Tears mean something very different at a funeral, in an argument, or when receiving an exam grade because the rule structure of each of these episodes is entirely different.

Games provide two kinds of rules—rules of meaning and rules of action. *Rules of meaning* tell us what an act means, and *rules of action* tell us how to respond or act within the situation (Pearce, 1994; Pearce & Cronen, 1980). In highly structured episodes, rules are quite rigid, as in the case of landing on "Go to Jail" in the game of Monopoly. In less structured or less predictable episodes, there may be flexibility, even ambiguity, in how to interpret and act.

Think of an episode as a communication game. It is recognizable as an episode, different from other episodes, marked by a beginning and an end, and even given a name such as "business meeting," "college class," "talk with best friend," or "going to the chat room." You interpret and act on the basis of a rule set established within the episode.

Facework is very much influenced by the structure of the episode. What counts as face building or face threatening is established by the rule set. Responding to face acts within the conversation will also be determined to some extent by the rules of the episode. We need to look at the relationship between conversation and episode as a two-way influence. Not only does the episode affect interpretations and actions within the conversation, but the opposite is also true: Over time, inter-action constructs, re-constructs, and changes the rule structure of the episode. Let's look at an example of how this happens.

In North American families, parent-child interaction frequently involves direction and compliance. Many episodes of family life are structured around a pattern in which the parent assesses a situation, gives direction to the child, and checks to make sure that the child has complied. The rule structure within this episode defines parental direction as guidance necessary to teach their children. Within this episode, well-delivered directions are not seen as a face threat to the child, but as a face-building process that develops confidence, competence, and awareness on the part of kids. Most parents will tell you that they have the best interest of the child in mind and are working to help the child develop resources for high self-regard in the future. In middle childhood, we pretty much expect compliance on the part of the child, but things begin to change in late childhood and adolescence, as the rules of the game begin to change.

Ironically, as children develop the very confidence and capability their parents hoped for, they also begin to gain a sense of self in which directions from the parent start to take on the meaning of a face threat. Compliance may not be the automatic response, as the episode itself may change from one of (1) assessment, (2) direction, and (3) compliance to one of (1) judgment, (2) face-threat, and (3) resistance. This is an episode all too familiar to families with teenage children. You will also notice here that the adult and adolescent may not be operating in this episode with the same rule set. The pattern from the perspective of the parent looks like disobedience, correction, and resistance, which threaten the parent's face. The pattern from the perspective of the teenager may look more like bossiness, self-direction, and intrusion, which feel equally face threatening.

Episodes of parent-child interaction are very dynamic, but some episodes are quite fixed and even rigid in the expected pattern and rule set. These we call rituals.

SIDEBAR 3.8   Family Patterns

Consider family patterns that you have experienced. Think back to your family of origin or to your current family situation. Is there a typical interaction that has become a pattern? Can you name potential "rule structures"? These can be acts that have *rules of meaning* or *rules of action*. Are these rules rigid and structured or are they less structured and occasionally recognizable? What impact do these rules have on facework?

Rituals, Ceremonies, and Facework

Rituals are highly structured episodes that are repeated regularly and guided by a strong and often rigid set of meaning and action rules (Philipsen, 1987; Wolin & Bennett, 1984). A ritual may be particular to a relationship, group, organization, community, religion, or nation. Further, rituals are guided by a shared moral force that gives meaning to the entire episode. More than the individual acts and conversations that comprise the ritual, it has power in and of itself. As a result, the ritual as a whole can be an important kind of facework. Christmas morning in American Christian homes is an example of a face-building ritual. The Muslim Salaah, a prayer delivered five times every day and often done in groups, provides another illustration. Many rituals have face implications for an entire group or community, and we will return to this implication when we focus on these in upcoming chapters.

We normally think of rituals as face building, but they are not always so. A court hearing, which follows very strict process rules, is indeed a ritual that can have extremely negative face implications, depending upon your role. Lines of questioning often threaten witnesses, as their autonomy and competence are challenged. Disciplinary rituals in the military are inherently face threatening, as are getting a traffic ticket, losing a boxing match, and sitting through a damning sermon at church.

Once in a while, we encounter a pattern in conflict mediation that we have come to call a "degradation ritual." This happens when one party uses the mediation as an opportunity to belittle the other. We are not talking here about the occasional negative comment or face-threatening act, but a pattern of abuse deliberately designed to make one's opponent feel incompetent, unworthy, and ashamed, a "ritual" sometimes found in families and organizations. We use the word *ritual* somewhat loosely here because it does seem to have both the rigid rule structure and episodic force commonly seen in rituals, even though these particular individuals may not have participated in it before. We have learned that the face threat of the degradation ritual is so grave that mediators themselves may actually terminate the session rather than let it continue.

The face impact of this kind of episode is extremely negative. There may also be positive episodes that, like rituals, have strong face implications apart from any one act or segment of conversation within it. For example, many families put their children's artwork on the wall or refrigerator, almost in a ritualistic way, which makes a powerful face statement even when no words are spoken.

One kind of ritual that is designed to have positive face value is the ceremony. A ceremony is a formal ritual normally conceived to do honor to one or more individuals. Often public in nature (but not always), ceremonies involve individuals in formal roles, often decked out in regalia, to honor participants in various ways. Weddings, commencements, and retirement dinners are classic examples. The roast, one of the highest forms of compliment, is odd and interesting. Here participants use clear face-threatening statements to honor an individual. In a supreme note of irony, the rules of the episode define insults as compliments and jeering as admiration.

Funerals are especially interesting face ceremonies. They do honor to the deceased, but the real facework is aimed at the family, friends, and nearly everyone who attends. Funerals are an example of episodes that accomplish personal, relational, and community facework all at the same time, and like all rituals, the power of the funeral is not so much in any one thing that participants do or say, but in the whole funeral as an event.

SIDEBAR 3.9   A Toast at a Retirement Dinner

I will be sad to see Jack leave. He has been my mentor and guide for ten years. You know, I am not really a natural manager. Most of the time I don't even know what I am doing, but Jack was always there to help. When I couldn't figure out what to do, I could always count on him. I learned so much from watching Jack over the years, and that meant a lot because I didn't have a lot of experience myself. Now, whenever I need a helping hand, I'll just think about what Jack would do.

Our best to you, Jack. Have a great retirement. We will miss you.

❖ PERSONAL FACE AND THE LIFESCRIPT

You live your life as an open-ended journey along many conversational and episodic pathways. At any given moment, you have a sense of who you are, a kind of composite of possibilities that have built up over a lifetime of communication. This is your *lifescript* (Pearce & Cronen, 1980). It is a broad and inclusive context that gives meaning to the events of your life. Despite our tendency to tout free will as some kind of ontological potential, we are never really "free" to do whatever we want because of the many social constraints on our behavior, not least of which is the lifescript. Yes, standing in front of a shop window, you could break the glass, grab an item, and run. Are you really free to do this? Theoretically, maybe; but most of us would not consider such a thing because it is neither desirable nor permissible within our sense of self.

We are constantly amazed at what people will do or not do. When one of our mothers was dying, an old friend suddenly reappeared to help take care of her. This former friend was a constant companion and caregiver to our mother during her illness; yet, when the funeral was over, she disappeared, never to be seen again. We have often wondered what kind of "lone-ranger" lifescript guided her life's decisions. In contrast, a group of friends gathered around to provide care and support when a colleague was dying. Conspicuously absent through the illness and death was another close colleague who reappeared sometime after the funeral. We often wondered why he could not be part of the support group or even attend the funeral. Whatever the reason, a lifescript constrained what this erstwhile friend felt he could or could not do.

Across communication acts, conversations, and episodes, individuality shows through. People do orient differently to communication processes based on their own sense of what is important to them, what kind of "character" they are in the ongoing drama of life, and what part they should take in the narratives they encounter. Your unique lifescript sets values, establishes the bases of power, provides a repertoire of action possibilities, informs you of the meaning of events, and establishes a sense of personal identity. The lifescript is a powerful context for facework.

For some, the need to establish personal competence is so strong that they will nearly always work to present themselves in a favorable light. This might come from a strong sense of personal worth, or it might even stem from personal doubts. A different person might have a commitment to the face of others and work constantly to build the face of other people. Again, this could come from a strong sense of self, or a need to serve others. Some people take argument and attack to be personally threatening and even avoid these kinds of situations. Others find argument and attack stimulating and seek them out.

Some people are proud to think of themselves as flexible, adaptable, and growing. Others experience a more closed sense of who they are. The lifescript, then, may be more or less open. In some cases it can even feel "sealed off" from influence. The degree of openness in the lifescript will determine in part the range of episodes in which one is able to participate, how one will interpret the actions of others, and the range of alternative responses available in facework situations. An open lifescript is probably more amenable to redirection, as new life experiences may reconstruct aspects of it. A less open lifescript may be slower to change, such that interactions tend to reinforce rather than modify it. For some people, there is a strong force from the lifescript that influences interactions; for others, there is more force upward from interaction to lifescript.

A lifescript is always influenced by culture. This is understandable, since the conversations that create the lifescript over time always occur within a cultural context. In some cases, the lifescript is greatly influenced by a single culture; in other cases, it may be quite mixed. Cultures that are more collectivist in orientation will form lifescripts that guide facework toward building the identity of others, while individualistic cultures create lifescripts that guide facework toward individual gain and loss.

Barnett Pearce distinguishes between game players and game masters. A *game player* is someone who has all of the resources to participate effectively in a particular game, or episode of life. We would say that the game player's lifescript makes the person a competent participant in certain episodes. The *game master*, in contrast, understands the limits of a game, is able to re-invent the game, and can make decisions about when to play or not play. We can see that whether you are a game player or game master in some aspect of life reflects something about your lifescript.

We are all proficient game players of the episode called "surprise party." Most of us have participated in them many times, and we know that it is a ritual designed to honor the featured guest. A game master, however, understands that surprise parties have the potential for face building and also for face loss. A game master would probably think twice about who the party is for, what the person's face needs are, and how best to meet those. Will the reaction be embarrassment or delight (or maybe some combination of both)? In some cases the game master would be pleased to participate in or even plan the party, but on other occasions might refrain from doing so because he or she understands that its impact will vary from one situation to another. Better yet, the game master might even think of new rules for how to do a surprise party that are especially creative and adapted to the face needs of the honored guest. We once knew a man who planned an elaborate plot to walk into the restaurant in which his best friend was dining while on vacation in Paris. After dropping his friend off at the airport with good wishes for a great vacation, he secretly hopped on another plane for the same destination. Now, that's game mastery!

SIDEBAR 3.10   The Lifescript of a Mediator

Renowned mediator Peter Adler talks about his dedication to conflict management in whatever form it may take:

"For myself, I will keep tussling and fuddling and muddling my way toward the highest perfection I can, whether it be refreshments, door opening, data management, or the politics of face making and face saving. It's my life work and a quest."

❖ PRINCIPLES FOR PRACTICE

This chapter is dedicated to facework in the realm of the person. We have discussed a variety of ways in which we try to build, maintain, or threaten the face of ourselves and other people. As we review the content of this chapter, we find three generalizations helpful in raising our consciousness about this level of facework.

Every communication act can be understood on multiple levels. When you say something to another person, you express more than the semantic meaning of the words. You also express intent, a desire to do something with your words, and you want others to understand your intentions. Facework is the expression of the intent to address the identity goals of yourself and others. People understand (or misunderstand) one another not just in terms of the meaning of their words, but in their intentions as well. Most of our facework happens on this higher level.

Be face conscious and person centered. Because people are different, you need to talk to various persons in different ways. Think consciously about acting in ways that others will appreciate and understand. Your face intentions may not be understood, or they may be understood in ways you did not intend. The better you know your listener, the more effective your communication will be. The better you know your listener's face needs, the more effectively you can achieve face goals.

Larger units of communication are usually more important than single messages. What you say or do in the moment can affect people's feelings positively or negatively, but the most important identity work occurs across time in conversations, episodes, and the lifescript. Think actively about the larger communication processes in which you engage.

4

Facework in the
Relational Realm

H ere is a riddle: What is neither I nor you, but always you and I?
The obvious answer, of course, is a relationship. Our colleague
John Shotter (1989) suggests a deeper answer to this riddle by asking
how there can even be an *I* without a *you*, and his answer is that there
cannot be. Your identity as a person is always formed in relation to
others. Because identity is always constructed in communication, interaction establishes who we are at any given time.

In some cultures identity is somewhat restricted because relationships are narrower in the range of roles they ascribe to individuals. In
other cultures, identity is more flexible and expansive, because the range
of relationships that define identity is variable and vast. In individualistic cultures, your identity will shift as you encounter a variety of other
people in diverse relationships. Still, roles always involve certain rights
and responsibilities vis-à-vis others within the relationship. You cannot
have the identity of father without children; you cannot be a pastor without congregants; and you cannot be a teacher without students.

To help understand the complex ways in which identity is
established, we offered in Chapter 1 a model of embedded contexts
involving the person, the relationship, and the system (see Table 1.1).

Although we discussed these three levels separately, we must keep in mind that each of these contexts involves the other two. In this chapter, we look at facework at the level of relationships, but relationships cannot be separated from persons or from the larger community or system in which they occur.

SIDEBAR 4.1   "I" and "You"

Compare your relational identity in each of the following sets of situations. What are the differences in who you are as you relate to different people? Do you act, dress, speak, move, or feel different as you move through relational interactions?

1. Mother at the dinner table; friend at the dinner table.
2. Clerk in the grocery store; person in line at the grocery store.
3. Teammate on the sports field; person sitting next to you watching a sporting event.
4. High school friend with whom you have a long history; new friend with whom you are just establishing a relationship.

❖ THINKING ABOUT RELATIONSHIPS

We like to think of a relationship as a negotiated set of expectations for self and other (Duck, 1994; Jabusch & Littlejohn, 1995; Watzlawick, Beavin, & Jackson, 1967). Who am I in this relationship, and who are you? How should we respond to one another's actions, and what do these actions and responses mean? These answers are negotiated tacitly over time between two people. Sometimes expectations emerge more easily than other times. If the larger community (culture, organization, or group) dictates how you should act within a particular role, expectations will come easily, but when everything starts off fresh, that may prove to be more challenging.

Tacit relational negotiation happens as we interact: An action will have a meaning, and certain responses will come to be expected. That's what gives a relationship its unique color and flavor. Over time, new expectations emerge as relational partners experience new situations and interact in new ways. Some relationships are amazingly stable over time, while others are quite fluid, but all have moments of transition and change.

Think of a time when you were an employee in an organization. When you were a newcomer, you knew virtually nothing about other people in the organization and made decisions about how to act based on general social expectations such as politeness supplemented by a little knowledge about the company. You did have expectations, but they were quite general and not very relational at first. As you began to interact with others, you started to establish certain patterns based on an implicit understanding of what was going on. Over time in the organization, you developed various relationships with different co-workers, managers, and customers. As you developed relationships with others, your expectations became increasingly specific to those relationships. If you have worked in an organization for a long period of time, you can look back to see how your relationships have changed as new expectations emerged.

Relationships, then, are defined in terms of expectations. Often the expectations are so strong that violating them can create problems. Rule violation can also create solutions in cases in which the patterns are negative and need to be changed, as we will see later in this chapter.

SIDEBAR 4.2   Thinking About Work Relationships

Make a list of several work relationships you have had. What made each of these unique? How were you different in each of these relationships, and how was facework done in each? Try to identify a few relational rules that seemed to emerge in each of these work relationships.

If relationships consist of negotiated expectations, then they are made—they are accomplishments. The *metaphor of rules* is especially powerful in helping to explain how this is so. Rules are guidelines for meaning and action. How do you know the meaning of a touchdown in football? You know this by the rules of the game. How do you know what to do when you land on "Go to Jail" in Monopoly? Again, you know what to do because of the game rules.

In any social situation, your actions are guided by external or internal rules (Jabusch & Littlejohn, 1995). *External rules* are general guidelines for action within a larger culture, organization, or community. *Internal rules* come from the unique interaction within a relationship. A friend of ours has been going to the same barbershop for several years. At first, he acted in accordance with external rules for "being a customer," with some knowledge about barbershops in general. Over the years, however, he got to know the barbers and established a certain pattern of behavior guided by *internal rules* for meaning and action. For example, once he gets settled in the chair, the barber will always say, "Three-four-three?" You have no way of knowing from outside this relationship that this statement is shorthand for: *Let me check to make sure I remember. You want me to use a number three comb on the top, number four on the sides, and number three on the beard. Is that right?*

Relationships change as their internal rules change. Our friend would not expect his relationship with the barber to change very much, but the rules for his relationships with his spouse, children, and close friends do change as new rules of meaning and action emerge. Bourdieu (1991) refers to relationships in this sense as *generative structures* because they are reconfigured, not always in a major way, but certainly in momentary ways. Relationships, then, are much like a dance in which partners move back and forth, both generating new moves and responding to those of their partner.

❖ FACEWORK IN THE RELATIONSHIP

Personal identity is important in all kinds of relationships. Even as a customer, neighbor, or acquaintance, you want to be treated in certain ways. However, three types of relationship are especially important in the creation of personal identity, and it is here that facework is especially important. These are the relatively enduring and significant relationships that form our sense of identity and meet our most basic social needs—family, workplace, and friendship.

Mutual Face

Mutual facework is the process of constructing a shared sense of identity (Ting-Toomey & Kurogi, 1998). It involves establishing who we are together within this relationship, or what Tracy (2002) calls the *relational identity*. At any given time, relational identities tell us the character of our relationship and how we are doing. Working together to build, maintain, or threaten the status of the relationship constitutes the work of mutual face. Mutual face is not independent of personal face, as each feeds the other. If partners tend to enhance and protect one another's face, the relationship itself will benefit; if they work to build the face of the relationship, the partners themselves will benefit (Fincham, 2004).

Remember, however, that facework will depend upon the *internal* rules of the relationship. What may look like face-threatening behavior from outside the relationship may mean something entirely different to those involved. There is a difference, too, between the relational identities that partners enact with one another privately and those that they share publicly. We have all seen relationships that we very much admire as models, only to discover sometime later things weren't so sweet behind closed doors. Indeed, privacy is one of the things that relational partners negotiate as part of their internal expectations (Petronio, 2000, 2002). One of the most face-damaging acts is to reveal relational secrets to others, to violate expectations about privacy.

An important quality of many relationships is a sense of cohesion, or togetherness. Whenever you present a relationship verbally or non-verbally with pride as a solid marriage, an effective working relationship, or a meaningful friendship, you are building the face of the relationship and, indirectly, the partners as well. If a team accomplishes a difficult task by working effectively together, they may share some pride in their mutual accomplishment. Lim (1994) calls this *solidarity facework*. It is the kind of communication that minimizes differences and builds commonality. This is the kind of communication that shows cooperation and trust, and it helps to build *fellowship face*, which we learned in Chapter 1 is a basic face need (Lim & Bowers, 1991).

SIDEBAR 4.3   Wedding Vows

Consider the following vows written by an engaged couple for their wedding. How do these vows establish a context for mutual face?

Husband and wife to each other: I promise to sustain the love I now feel. I promise to seek and to renew the energy that will allow me to love you for who you are. I promise to respect you, to care for you, and to help you in your development as a growing person. I will always be honest with you, sharing both the good and the bad, the happy and the sad. In this spirit, I take you as my wife [husband].

Personal Face in the Relationship

The relationship, then, creates a context of mutual face, but it does more. It is also a powerful context for establishing personal face. Since identity is largely constructed within the relationship, the kind of facework we do depends upon the relational context. You will do a different kind of facework with your mother than with your daughter, a different kind with your employer than with your employee, and a different kind with your best friend than with a new acquaintance. *Altercasting*, literally "creating the other," is the work we do to maintain, support, or challenge the identity of others (Tracy, 2002).

William Schutz (1958) proposed that human beings have three social needs—inclusion, control, and affection. We find these three concepts useful, but we believe they vary from one relationship to another. In some relationships, you may have a strong need for inclusion, but less need for control. In others, you may have a strong need for control, but little for affection. We also think that facework often addresses these needs, depending upon the internal rules of the relationship. Within a certain relationship—employee-employer, for example—you will work out the level of inclusion, control, and affection that should be allowed and shown. You will also work out the way in which these should be shown. For example, there will be very strong rules about whether and how a manager should express affection toward an employee. Husbands and wives work out a diversity of ways in which affection, control, and inclusion are displayed, as do friends.

Of course, the partners may understand and orient differently to facework within the relationship. The success of a relationship depends in part on how well they are able to mesh their actions toward one another. Ting-Toomey and Cocroft (1994) suggest that relational partners organize their facework in various ways. First, they have a certain level of *co-orientation* toward facework, meaning that they have some level of knowledge about one another's face expectations and intentions. They may understand one another very well in this way, or not. An employer and employee may know exactly what they expect of one another in terms of identity management and how they show what they expect of self and other. Other bosses and workers may have little conjoint understanding of face needs, wants, and intentions.

Partners in a relationship also have some level of *coordination* in their facework behavior. Facework coordination refers to the extent to which partners are able to mesh their respective actions logically and comfortably. Again, some partners may have a high level of coordination, while others are a bit jerky and uncoordinated in meshing their respective facework activities. You would expect coordination to be challenging in new relationships and in times of change, while during stable periods relational partners are able to coordinate more effectively. If, as boss, you ask some workers to do a certain job, they do it effectively and efficiently, and you meet expectations for complimenting them, the facework would feel coordinated.

In addition, organizing a relationship involves *attunement*. Facework attunement arises from the other two. It is a kind of interpersonal and cultural sensitivity—knowing what, how, and when others need support and attention—as well as an understanding of the dynamics of the relationship, or what is appropriate at certain times and what is not. In short, attunement is "being in tune with" one another and with the rules of the relationship. A manager, for example, may know that some employees require a particular kind of facework, while other employees may require a completely different approach. If both partners in a relationship possess this mutual sensitivity, then attunement is achieved.

Facework and the Management of Contradiction

You might get the impression that good facework is simply knowing the rules and following them in a timely way. Research has shown, however, that this is rarely the case. Relational rules are often contradictory, and acts intended to build face may actually threaten it. For example, with the best of intentions, you might enter your 14-year-old son's room, ask what he is doing, and make a few suggestions about what he could do. That would certainly show engagement and interest, but it might also show intrusion and control. It could show availability and presence, but it could also be perceived as a violation of privacy. This is a balancing act: How do you show caring and guidance, and at the same time permit autonomy and grant control to the other person? This is a perfect example of the kinds of contradictions we must manage in everyday facework.

Consider the ways in which friends walk a tightrope of contradictions (Rawlins, 1992). Friends should help one another in times of need, right? But isn't it also true that they should not use one another? What is the difference between *being asked for help* and *being used*? Friends are supposed to accept us as we are, yet friends also should be honest in telling us what they think. How can we be both critical and accepting? You should be able to be honest with a friend, but, at the same time, you should protect his or her feelings. Again, a contradiction.

SIDEBAR 4.4   Making Friends

"Except for those maintained as memories, friendships persist only to the extent that individuals treat each other in mutually fulfilling ways, according to how they define their required contact, evaluative standards, and appropriate actions. Because of its voluntary basis, either friend can abruptly "walk away" or let the friendship gradually lapse if treated in a manner he or she deems improper. As a result, the interaction of friends is of particular interest for understanding inherently valued communicative practices as well as how and why people negotiate optional allegiances with others throughout their lives."

Source: W. K. Rawlins, *Friendship Matters*, 1992, p. 272.

Three clusters of contradiction seem common in relationships (Baxter, 1993; Montgomery & Baxter, 1998; Werner & Baxter, 1994). These are *integration and separation,* or the tension between wanting to be close and desiring more distance; *expression and non-expression,* feeling the tension between wanting to be open versus wanting to be private; and *stability and change,* or the contradiction between being predictable and being spontaneous. The important thing about contradictions is that within a single relationship, there may be a rule structure that sanctions, even encourages, both. What does this mean for facework? An act designed to build or maintain face may actually threaten it. An act designed to threaten face may actually have the opposite effect. The parties within a relationship must constantly negotiate what is right in the moment and sometimes even accomplish face in a variety of ways at the same time.

Let's return to the example of how to talk to your 14-year-old son. You want him to know that you are interested in what he is doing, which would be a sign of closeness (integration). At the same time, you want him to know that you value his independent decisions (separation). You want him to share with you (expression), but you understand his need for privacy (non-expression). You know that you want him to be able to rely on you consistently (stability), but you also want to honor his need for freedom (change). A common way of managing these inconsistencies is by alternating back and forth, sometimes doing one thing and sometimes doing the other. A more sophisticated strategy is to act in a way that accomplishes both goals at the same time. For example, you might make sure your son knows you are around, reinforce your availability without intruding on his space, and tell him what you are doing as a kind of invitation for him to share his life with you.

An even more sophisticated approach for managing contradiction is to redefine the situation so that the actions are no longer contradictory. This third approach can create a moment of change within a relationship. At some point, you redefine your relationship with your son so that you no longer (temporarily at least) experience the tension. You might reach a point where "distance" is jointly valued, so that integration is achieved via separation. You might define "non-expression" as a kind of "expression": "When he doesn't talk to me, he's telling me he wants to be left alone, and I can honor that." Or you might see that teenagers are predictably in a "state of change," so that change itself is a kind of "stability." You can reliably predict that change will occur.

A powerful way to manage contradictions—especially the tension between integration and separation, or connection and autonomy—is to provide an explanation for your response (Conlon & Ross, 1997; Robins & Wolf, 1988). Explanations build face through autonomy and connection at the same time in a single act. They also build face for both the speaker (self face) as well as the listener (other face). Explanations accomplish several things (Jameson, 2004): (1) they can show the speaker's experience and insight; (2) they can show how the response is intended to minimize imposition; (3) they can show connection through cooperation; (4) they can imply equality in the relationship; and (5) they can demonstrate that the relationship is valued. Which of the following manager responses feels more competent to you?

Jill, I'm getting irritated by these constant mistakes in the monthly account statement. Please be more careful! (direct order—no explanation)

Jill, I have to report our department financials to management every month, and these will be put together with the reports from all the departments, so it's really important that our reports are accurate. (context and explanation provided)

❖ COMMUNICATION ACTS IN THE RELATIONSHIP

Face Acts

Consider the following simple conversation:

Person 1:   I want some candy.

Person 2:   You can't have it. It will spoil your dinner.

Person 1:   You never let me eat candy.

Person 2:   Go wash for dinner.

It does not take a lot of imagination to figure out who Persons 1 and 2 are. They certainly are not manager and employee or pastor and parishioner. Employees do not ask their managers for permission to eat candy, and pastors don't tell congregational members to wash up for dinner. It is clear that these communicators are most likely parent and child. This simple example illustrates that persons in a relationship have particular roles, rights, responsibilities, and ranges of choice. The kinds of things you can, must, and may say will change, depending upon whether you are interacting with your best friend, your dentist, or your father.

Face acts are greatly influenced by the roles we negotiate within the relationship. What you can, may, and should say will vary depending upon the relationship in which these occur (Tracy, 2002, p. 65). When, for example, would the act of advising be permissible, required, or prohibited? When would advising be seen as face building or as face threatening? It would be permissible, even required, for a father to give advice to his 8-year-old son, but the same act 10 years later might be problematic. The implications of acts such as praising, criticizing, apologizing, and requesting will also depend upon the negotiated roles within the relationship. Also, the manner and timing of these kinds of acts will be determined by the relationship in which the parties are communicating.

Some Facework Dilemmas in Relationships

Although you can never know what a particular act means to the people involved, certain kinds of acts intended to save face can actually be face threatening within particular relationships. Here we discuss several kinds of acts that could have either negative or positive face implications (Tracy, 2002, pp. 72–84).

Advising. On the surface, advice is often a well-intentioned face-building act. You will take advice from doctors, attorneys, and tax consultants seriously. Often, however, giving advice creates particular constraints in the relationship that may not be wanted. Again, you have to look at the internal relational rules for advice. When is advice appropriate within the relationship, and when is it not? When someone asks for advice, what does the request really mean? How should one give advice, and when should one do so within the confines of the relationship? In most situations, honest advice is best delivered in a way that acknowledges the person's need for competence, inclusion, and autonomy—in whatever way this is done within the relationship (e.g., Agne & White, 2004).

If you take a friend's request for advice literally, you may risk failing to provide the support he or she wants. Often, a request for advice is really a request for confirmation and support, not advice. If you offer unsolicited advice, you may risk creating a hierarchy of authority in the relationship that will make the other person feel one-down. On the other hand, if you fail to give advice in a situation where you have the authority and expectation to do so, you may cause confusion, disconfirmation, and even anger. You also have to think about what advice looks like from the other person's perspective. Well-intentioned advice, depending upon the relationship, can be viewed as criticism, building one's own face at the expense of the other's, or unwarranted authority.

Reproaching. A reproach is a direct, negative criticism. It is a reprimand, accusation, or confrontation. In the moment, a reproach is almost always face threatening and frequently damages the relationship. Does this mean that we should never confront another person about a wrongdoing? There are times when we must. The manner in which the reproach is delivered can make a lot of difference. For example, criticism that uses insulting language, profanity, and loud anger will most certainly be face threatening in most relationships (though not necessarily in all). Criticism that is analytical, provides well-considered perspective, and includes the offer of help would probably be less threatening in most situations. Even profanity can serve different functions within a relationship and is not always face threatening.

Most parents want their kids to become competent, socially appropriate adults, and they realize that constraints will need to be enforced in order to achieve this long-term goal. For some children, direct, clear reproach seems to be effective as a way of shaping their behavior. A reproach can be face building in the long run, especially if it is delivered in a way that shows concern and caring in the larger context of family life. In many families, depending upon their cultural background, reproach judged as harsh from outside actually creates roles that provide meaning to the lives of all of the family members. In other families, however, the same kind of message might come to shake confidence and threaten self-esteem.

Accounting. In responding to a reproach, you may offer an account that excuses or explains the behavior in some way. However, you don't have to wait until someone criticizes you to give an account. People do it all the time in order to help others understand their actions and to avoid or prevent criticism. Many accounts are simple explanations, but some are actual justifications that attempt to make a potentially bad action acceptable, or at least better. Accounting is a perfect example of self-facework, but it can have implications for the face of the other as well, as it puts others in the position of having to respond to the account. It may also relieve them from the onerous responsibility of making a negative judgment. Accepting, rejecting, or ignoring the account will all have face implications, depending upon the rules of the relationship.

Again, rules for accounting are embedded in the relationship. Who has the right or responsibility to offer an account? Who should not be put in a position of offering an account? One of our fathers used to say, "Never argue with a child," meaning that acts of accounting will erode parental authority and pose a face threat to the parent. What counts as an adequate account? Who is permitted (or required) to make this judgment? Again, these issues will be negotiated within the relationship.

Disclaiming. Disclaimers are a particularly interesting form of facework. This is a communication act designed to separate yourself from your own statement so that you cannot later be accused of boasting, posturing, or taking an unwanted position on an issue. You have done this many times, as have we, by prefacing a comment with a qualification that lets you off the hook. So, for example, you might say, "I'm no expert, but I think that . . ." or "I don't have anything against her, but . . ."

Sometimes disclaimers are rather sophisticated: "I have never been very successful at fishing myself, but I have a lot of friends who are really good at it, and they tell me that fly fishing requires the most skill." When you use a disclaimer, you are trying to frame your comment in a way that will not create a problem for the other person so that person won't think badly of you. This protects your own face as well as that of the other person.

In some cases, disclaiming builds face. It can, however, create problems. You might be viewed as wishy-washy or even inappropriate. You might be perceived as trying to put your opinion off onto someone else, or your disclaimer may be taken as manipulative.

Ingratiating. Strictly speaking, *ingratiating* means acting in a way that incurs the favor of another individual, but it often has the negative connotation of acting in a manipulative way for personal gain. Fawning, suspicious compliments, and overpoliteness are examples of acts that can be perceived as ingratiating in certain cultures. We don't normally think of being ingratiating with one's spouse, best friend, or children; but in professional, hierarchical relationships, this attribution can be damaging. Even when people are not intending to incur a favor, others can perceive their actions in this way.

Each of the acts discussed in this section is interesting because of the questions it raises for the relationship. We have discussed these acts as threatening—and they often are; however, what appears to be face threatening at the moment may actually contribute to the building of face if we look at it from the perspectives of conversations, episodes, lifescripts, and the larger system. These are issues we will address in upcoming sections of this book.

SIDEBAR 4.5   Statements That Can Stop Movement

Beware of phrases such as the following that can evoke defensiveness, reduce trust, and hinder relationship building. Conversations can stop when we talk this way.

- You ought to/you need to . . . .
- Why didn't you do . . . ?
- That would be a bad choice for you. Here's what you need to do.
- How could you feel that way? You know better than that.
- Everyone has those feelings.
- Don't feel that way.
- Don't believe that.
- Let me give you my analysis of the situation.
- That is not very important. I suggest that instead, you talk about. . . .
- Why don't you do it this way?

Source: Adapted from Domenici & Littlejohn (2001, p. 144).

Emotion and Facework in Relationships

Feelings can run strong and deep within relationships. Emotion is especially important in close relationships such as family and is significant in friendships and work settings as well. How we manage feelings has serious face implications in relationships, which includes how we understand and respond to emotional expression as well as how we communicate our own emotions to others (Fitness & Duffield, 2004).

How we define, respond to, and express emotion has implications for self-face, other-face, and mutual-face. In the workplace, especially with superiors, we often keep our emotions somewhat guarded, maintaining professional respect and civility (Waldron, 1991). In families, however, holding feelings under wraps can do face damage (Feeney, 1999; Huston & Houts, 1998). Most of us would agree that we are more satisfied when positive emotional expressions outweigh the negative (Carstensen, Gottman, & Levenson, 1995) and that conciliatory and non-defensive reactions do more to maintain a relationship in the face of anger than do destructive outbursts (Noller & Roberts, 2002; Rusbult, Bissonnette, Arriaga, & Cox, 1998). Expressions of contempt are especially damaging because they may imply superiority, humiliation, and even shame (Tomkins, 1979). Sneering, sarcasm, mocking, and retaliatory anger or rage have obvious face implications.

Yet every relationship is different, and families socialize emotion in different ways. Think of the ways in which we teach children in the family how to orient to emotion. We teach emotional communication directly through a kind of coaching or indirectly by dismissing, punishing, or responding to certain kinds of emotional expression (Fitness & Duffield, 2004). Through these kinds of processes, we create a set of rules for emotion within the family, and, by extension, in other relationships as well. Emotional expression is also affected by culture, and the ways in which individuals in relationships come to understand and act on feelings may well be influenced by their cultural backgrounds. In some cultures, for example, strongly worded, angry outbursts are taken as a sign of caring, while in others they are taken as a sign of disrespect. This is why we can never say with certainty that certain kinds of expression are negative or that others are positive. It is always relevant to the rules of the relationship and embedded in cultural practice.

What, then, are the face implications of emotional expression? If you value clarity, passion, and directness and have learned that one should not mince words when the issue is important, your face will be threatened by someone who tells you to "calm down." At the same time, if you value tranquility, explanation, and tact, your face will be threatened by someone who jumps all over you. We think that one of the sources of tension in many relationships is that the partners have a different sense of what is appropriate and face saving in emotional communication. Over time partners will come to negotiate a shared set of rules for how and when to express emotion on the issues that matter most to them.

SIDEBAR 4.6   Are We Drifting Apart?

"Many of the social bonds that once unified us as a people now appear to be eroding. Average Americans, opinion polls show, suspect that our population is growing apart. Americans sense that civility and respect for one another are losing ground. People feel that their dignity and sense of self-worth are being assaulted in countless ways, small and large."

Source: D. Yankelovich, *The Magic of Dialogue,* 1999, p. 9.

Facework Challenges for Managers and Employees

The workplace offers a significant setting in which important life relationships are developed. Unlike romantic or family relationships, supervisor-subordinate relationships have special dimensions that can build or threaten face, and facework within organizations is a vital part of most of our lives. Here we consider two particularly challenging situations that managers and employees frequently encounter.

The Managerial Reproach. For most of us, what our superiors think of us matters, and, over time, does affect our sense of self-identity. When managers realize this, they will think seriously about *how* to talk with employees about concerns. Corrective conversations are especially challenging in this respect. Carson and Cupach (2000) found that the face threat associated with a manager's reproach depends on several variables. In general, employees feel less threatened if they believe the manager's perceptions are accurate and fair, the employee is given some freedom to handle the problem and feels competent to do so, and the manager is perceived as taking care and being sensitive in the communication. These authors advise that "managers who find it necessary to reproach an employee can improve the situation by making sure that they conduct the reproach privately, that the reproach is warranted and commensurate with the violation, and that they are courteous, positive, and informative" (p. 230).

Delivering Bad News. How do you deliver bad news to employees? Managers routinely do this in such areas as work performance, broken rules, denying requests, or explaining adverse circumstances. Such bad news can be face threatening to employees who want to feel that they are doing a good job, that their work is organized and integrated with others in the organization, that the organization will support their efforts and provide the tools necessary, and that their contributions are not hampered by situational factors. Wagoner and Waldron (1999) found that effective managers deliver news that may frustrate any of these face issues by combining some of Lim and Bowers's (1991) strategies, including *tact,* or the deliberate explanation of information in a way that will feel better to the recipient; *approbation,* which is the expression of approval; and *solidarity,* or a sign that "we are together in this." Again, the challenge is to think seriously about *how* to deliver a piece of bad news in a way that improves the possibility of a positive response, continued commitment to the organization, and a strengthened supervisor-subordinate relationship. Consider the following two versions of bad news. Which would you rather hear?

Version 1:   Sorry, Jane, I'm not going to get you a new computer this year.

Version 2:   Gosh, Jane, I wish I could find the money in the budget for a new computer for you, but the sales slowdown has really hurt us. I especially wanted to support you in this because you are one of the best workers here, but, sorry, I just can't do it this year.

The news is the same, but the second message is far more skillful and sensitive.

❖ CONVERSATIONS AND EPISODES OF RELATIONAL LIFE

We can all think of times when someone said or did something that had an immense impact on the relationship. These are *memorable messages* (Stohl, 1986) that stand out because of some importance they had for us. A single communication act can threaten, build, protect, or repair face. Yet because of the negotiated nature of the relationship, most facework happens over longer periods of time.

Relational Transgressions

The management of relational transgressions is an excellent example of the way in which facework is accomplished through conversation (Metts, 1994). In romantic relationships a variety of transgressions are possible, ranging from high threat to low. These include, for example, infidelity, lying, flirting, violating a confidence, forgetting a special occasion, violating privacy, not trusting, or breaking a promise. These kinds of actions can threaten self-face, other-face, and mutual-face, and if partners want to preserve the relationship, they will attempt to repair the damage in some way, which is rarely done in a single message.

Betrayals occur in close relationships when important relational rules are violated (Fitness, 2001; Jones, Moore, Schratter, & Negel, 2001; Metts, 1994; Roloff & Cloven, 1994). Violations such as lying, having affairs, and violating a confidence can be face damaging because they demonstrate greater concern for one's own interests than those of the other person or the relationship itself. Fitness (2001) wrote that "betrayal sends an ominous signal about how little the betrayer cares about, or values, his or her relationship" (p. 74).

When transgressions are severe enough, the relationship itself may fail; but partners are often able to repair the relationship in time (Emmers-Sommer, 2003). Studies have revealed several ways in which this happens (Roloff & Cloven, 1994; Roloff, Soule, & Carey, 2001). For example, one party may try to punish the other one to make the point that the betrayal will not be tolerated in the future. Other strategies are more sophisticated. For example, partners may clarify, or even change, the rules of the relationship, minimize the transgression, or focus on reasons why the relationship should be maintained. The latter strategy seems especially important because it helps the parties focus on the larger context of the relationship itself and the bigger question of whether and why the relationship should be continued, changed, or abandoned. The important thing about episodes of repair is that they afford the opportunity for partners to identify, clarify, and make explicit the rules of their relationship (Metts, 1994).

After a deception, for example, partners will often work to restore, revitalize, and/or reaffirm the relationship. Several strategies are common during the initial conversation (Metts, 1994): telling the truth, apologizing, making an excuse, justifying the action, denying, trying to build a positive image, referring to qualities of the relationship, and acting emotionally. In subsequent conversations, you are more likely to find avoidance or evasion, soothing, reaffirmation of the relationship, participation in rituals, and talking the issue through. It seems that the effort put into apologizing and trying to redeem oneself over a whole sequence of interactions is a kind of facework, as it shows good faith and wanting to do the right thing. It is probably this overall work that does more to restore face than any one thing the partners might say.

Gossip

Gossip is another conversational form with face implications (Tracy, 2002). Most of us have a conflicted view of gossip. On the one hand, we think of gossip as bad and even criticize people known as "gossips." On the other hand, almost everyone participates in gossip, and when we are gossiping, we often feel that it is a fairly harmless and downright fun thing to do. As a form of facework, gossiping shows that you trust the other person, which is a form of honor. It also puts the gossipers together in superior position over the person being gossiped about. At the same time, gossip does come with a moral cost; and "gossiping around" can erode trust and harm personal face, and when gossip gets back to the target person, the results can be devastating.

Social Support

Social support is another area that has particularly important implications for facework in relationships (Agne & White, 2004; Goldsmith, 1994; Goldsmith & MacGeorge, 2000; MacGeorge, Lichtman, & Pressey, 2002). In the previous chapter, we noted that supportive conversations involve creating a suitable helping environment, facilitating a discussion of the emotional issues, and inviting the individual seeking support to explore alternatives (Burleson & Goldsmith, 1998). Especially in giving advice, the face needs of competence and inclusion are also important, as is the desire for autonomy. If you are in need and seek the advice of others, you will probably most appreciate advice that is given with the acknowledgment of your own competence, in the spirit of affection, and with appreciation for your own sense of freedom to choose. Families provide perhaps the single most important source of social support (Gardner & Cutrona, 2004). Husbands and wives, for example, can make effective use of their relational knowledge in determining how and when to provide support to one another, and when they do this well, it is seamless and natural—the very best of facework.

Managing transgressions, gossiping, and providing support are just three kinds of facework in conversations. As friends, family members, and co-workers define the rules of their relationships, certain patterns of interaction emerge, and these patterns are a vital part of the structure of expectations within the relationship. You know what to expect, in part, because of the repetitive patterns that get established within a relationship. Indeed, one of the markers of relational change is a shift in the patterns of interaction. Patterns are repetitive and constitute markers within the episodes of a relationship. Routine patterns of interaction thus have episodic force: They determine how things get done within the relationship, and they influence the manner in which facework is accomplished. One of the surefire ways to change a relationship is to deliberately violate established patterns. This strategy is risky, but it can be a major step toward change in a relationship that is no longer working. In the following sections, we explore some of the episodic patterns that affect and are affected by facework within relationships.

Control in Relationships

Control is an aspect of interaction that shapes what "gets done" or "happens" in a relationship. Control is established by certain patterns of interaction in which one partner suggest, requests, or demands certain things, and the other partner responds by complying, denying, or diverting. Imagine that you are working as a teller in a bank and a co-worker asks if you would be willing to take a late lunch so that he can run an important errand. You could agree, disagree, ask a question, or maybe even make a different suggestion. Within a few minutes, the two of you would establish how you want to time your lunch that day.

We actually go through control interactions many times with a variety of people during the course of a day. It is helpful to think about these interactions as complementary or symmetrical (e.g., Jabusch & Littlejohn, 1995; Millar & Rogers, 1987). A *complementary interaction* is one in which both communicators respond in opposite ways: One person asserts control by making a suggestion, demand, or request, and the other person agrees. This type of interaction is most efficient and clear:

Teller 1:   Could you take your lunch at 1:00 today, so I can leave and run an errand?

Teller 2:   Sure.

A *symmetrical interaction* is one in which the parties respond in kind: Both assert control, or both relinquish control. Repeated attempts by both partners to assert control over what happens can turn into a power struggle:

Teller 1:   Could you take your lunch at 1:00 today, so I can leave and run an errand?

Teller 2:   No, I'm tired and wanna get out of here.

Teller 1:   But it would only be today.

Teller 2:   I don't care. I get my lunch now, and I expect to take it now.

Teller 1:   You are so rigid!

Teller 2:   [Walks away]

Another kind of symmetrical interaction is one in which neither party asserts control:

Teller 1:   I have an errand I need to run.

Teller 2:   Oh, should I take a later lunch so you can do it?

Teller 1:   Well, I wouldn't want to put you out.

Teller 2:   That's okay.

Teller 1:   Well, you shouldn't have to change.

Teller 2:   Whatever you want is fine with me.

Teller 1:   Well, why don't you decide.

These conversational exchanges have face implications in their own right. For example, complementary interactions can feel comfortable, coordinated, and competent, which builds face. On the other hand, if one party is giving up something important, it could actually threaten face. Symmetrical, one-up conversations can be face-threatening, especially if they escalate. Symmetrical one-down conversations can actually be a form of negative facework, as the parties try to minimize the imposition they are making on the other.

More interesting and important, however, are not these individual interactions, but the patterns of interaction that develop over time between two people. Let's discuss three possibilities.

Rigid Complementary Relationship. In this kind of relationship, the partners have worked out a pattern in which one person predominantly controls what happens. This individual usually asserts control, and her husband accepts this. This pattern of control involves a clear rule set about who makes decisions. This pattern does much to build the face of the controlling person, but its effect on the submissive member is less clear. It could be face-building in cases where it reinforces a desired ideal of being dutiful, as may be the case in some marriages, friendships, or professional relationships. It may also build mutual face when it reflects traditional cultural values shared by both partners. In the workplace, many supervisor-subordinate relationships quite comfortably follow this pattern, which is consistent with expectations about bosses and employees. In other kinds of relationships, however, this pattern could come to be a perpetual threat to the one-down partner. One of our fathers always believed that "the husband is the decision maker," and his mother and father enacted a rigid complementary relationship consistent with this belief. (Yes, this is the same father who said, "Never argue with a child.") Later in life, however, his mother decided that she would no longer remain in the subordinate position and began to stand up to her husband. This not only worked over time to build her own sense of worth, but it changed the pattern of interaction to a more flexible one that came to be quite acceptable to both in what turned out to be a remarkable relational change.

Flexible Complementary Relationship. Here we have a pattern in which control is rarely contested and flows smoothly, but in a more flexible way. The control may flow back and forth, sometimes taken by one person and sometimes by the other. Or, the partners may have certain topics or areas of life in which one takes control and other areas in which the other partner does so. One of the advantages of this kind of pattern is that both parties are honored as competent persons. In general, this pattern involves good facework across the board.

Rigid Symmetrical Relationship. This is a pattern in which the parties consistently fight for control or abrogate it. Long-term power struggles characterized by mutual dominance and reciprocated face threat are a signature of distress in a marital relationship (Fincham, 2004), and the pattern of facework in these kinds of relationships is typically destructive. In contrast, when neither party asserts control, stultification results. We suspect that close relationships are rarely characterized by submissive symmetry, but friendships often are. Friends sometimes come to use accommodation as a form of face saving. If you often defer to your friend, you are probably trying to show respect, but you also are guarding yourself from the criticism you might receive if you did make a decision. Deference, then, is a way of protecting the face of both self and other, but it does little to build mutual face. In the long run, then, rigid symmetrical relationships probably do not work very well, as neither partner helps to build the relationship.

SIDEBAR 4.7   A Wild and Crazy Teen

As a teenager, Chris was out of control. Despite his parents' best attempts to help him stay in school and off the streets, he spent most of his time running around, taking drugs, and failing to meet the most basic responsibilities of life. Every attempt his parents made to control his destructive behavior was met by obstinacy and refusal to comply.

Soon after he turned 17, the police once again brought him home, and while the officer was taking a report with his parents in the living room, Chris left through his bedroom window. He was gone before the officer had a chance to return to his patrol car. This event made his parents realize that they needed to initiate a new pattern of interaction and decided to make a risky move. At the earliest opportunity, they sat down with him and said, "Chris, we can see that you want full control of your life. We are not happy with the choices you are making, but there is nothing we can do about it. From now on you are free to come and go as you wish. We ask only one thing: Call us once a day to let us know that you are safe."

Chris could hardly believe his ears, but he accepted this contract gleefully as he turned on his heel and rushed out the door. About 24 hours later, the phone rang, and it was Chris dutifully reporting in. He would come home every two or three days to eat and sleep and then be gone again, but he always called in. Chris turned 18 in Juvenile Hall and continued for several years to struggle with his demons, but the pattern of the relationship—with its attendant roles, rights, and responsibilities—was forever changed. Eventually, Chris learned to take responsibility for his own actions. He came to see that his parents loved him and cared deeply about his welfare, and they learned that Chris could find the resources with which to make a life.

Unwanted Repetitive Patterns

People are usually quite aware of negative patterns of interaction in their relationships. An unwanted repetitive pattern (URP) is a pattern the parties neither want nor know how to change (Cronen, Pearce, & Snavely, 1979; Pearce, 1994). The partners hate it, but the rule set is so strong that they feel incapable of creating a new pattern. The behavior is guided by a logic that seems to have a life of its own. Constant fighting between a boyfriend and girlfriend is a case in point. Both are obligated by the belief that they are right and guided by the rule that when you are right, you must prevail. When you do not immediately prevail, then you get angry, and when you are angry, you can do only one thing: fight. The boyfriend and girlfriend don't want to fight—they want to get along—but the logic of this rule set is so strong that they cannot think of any other way to work through their differences.

One of the saddest examples of this state of affairs is domestic violence. Nobody except the most perverted would say that they want to hurt someone they love or that they would put up with being repeatedly battered, and yet spousal abuse is common. How does this happen? Sundarajan and Spano (2004) posit the following scenario based on interviews with both men and women involved in domestic violence. The relationship begins when the man privileges his need for self-importance and makes decisions based on this idea, while the woman subjugates her own interests to that of the relationship. Already, the partners have a formula in which the man wants to dominate his wife to protect his own interests, while the woman feels obligated to submit in order to protect the relationship. The man experiences increasing need for self-worth, while the woman experiences decreasing self-esteem. The male believes he has the right to show anger when his partner acts in a way that does not please him, and this trend intensifies to the point of verbal and physical aggression. Each time, the wife tries to placate his anger to repair the relationship. Because of his own strong face needs, he will typically deny or minimize the abuse.

Although patterns of abuse can continue for years, many couples are able to change the pattern eventually, often by terminating the relationship. This usually happens when the woman's fear for herself and her children finally escalates to the point that she must escape permanently in order to survive. This solution illustrates how couples can break a destructive pattern.

According to Pearce (1994), unwanted repetitive patterns can be changed if either or both parties (1) refuse to participate in the repetitive episode, (2) take action that prevents it, or (3) create new rules that change the pattern. Leaving home and finding refuge in a safe house accomplishes the first and second of these courses of action in many cases. Professional intervention can be helpful in accomplishing the third.

Creating new rules is possible through reframing the context of the relationship. Reframing makes it possible to understand what is going on in a different way, to reinterpret the actions within the pattern. For example, one woman stayed in an abusive marriage because she felt it was God's will for her to obey the marriage covenant. After a period of abuse, however, she came to see that her own disempowerment was not part of God's plan, and she was able then to shift the context of her understanding from preservation of relationship to personal health and well-being, which made it possible for her to file for divorce (Sundarajan & Spano, 2004). There are actually mediation programs dealing with child abuse and neglect issues (Milne, 2004). In these cases, mediation usually happens after the children have been removed from the home. In mediation, the parents are able to talk about how to restructure their patterns of communication with one another and with the children to build a positive bond and protect family members from harm, and they do this as a condition of getting the kids back.

Not all URPs are as serious or devastating as domestic violence, yet all constitute a threat to both personal and mutual face. The mere inability of a couple to change a pattern they hate has negative face implications. Finding the creativity and gumption to establish new patterns, on the other hand, can make major strides in rebuilding the honor and dignity that each partner would like to have.

SIDEBAR 4.8   Changing Patterns of Power

Stella Ting-Toomey and John Oetzel (2001, pp. 188–190) outline various ways in which participants in a conflict can realign their sources of power.
Less powerful individuals can:

1. Develop new sources of power.
2. Reframe their goals.
3. Make use of relationship commitments as a source of power.
4. Diversify their options.

More powerful individuals can:

1. Practice mindful self-restraint.
2. Solicit feedback and thereby empower the other person.
3. Acknowledge interdependence.
4. Expand options for less powerful parties.

Here are just a few examples:

A wife who has been emotionally abused by her husband for many years is able to rebuild her sense of self-worth by joining a women's group. **She has expanded her sources of power by forming new relationships.**

A professor who has been rejected for a promotion finds solace and strength in focusing on his excitement about classroom teaching. **He has reframed his goal.**

A manager accustomed to dominating others in meetings makes a conscious decision to stop talking and start listening. **He practices mindful self-restraint.**

A mother realizes that her child is becoming shy and withdrawn and works hard to find many avenues to stimulate the child's interest. **She expands the options for her child.**

Conflict Patterns

We discussed conflict patterns at some length in the previous chapter. Here we want to emphasize that patterns of conflict in relationships are most often worked out and are governed by the internal rules of the relationship. Van de Vliert and Euwema (1994) suggest a useful way of analyzing patterns of conflict in families. They divide conflict communications between those that are more active versus less active and more cooperative versus competitive. This yields four general patterns: (1) negotiation (active and cooperative), (2) non-confrontation (inactive and cooperative), (3) direct fighting (active and competitive), and (4) indirect fighting (inactive and competitive). We would expect family members to act in certain ways based on the pattern that emerges over time (Sillars, Canary, & Tafoya, 2004). *Negotiation*, for example, would include such actions as reaching agreements, being conciliatory, being descriptive and analytical, and solving problems collaboratively. *Direct fighting*, in stark contrast to negotiation, would look more like blaming, coercion, confrontation, and invalidation. *Non-confrontation* would include behaviors such as disengagement, irrelevant talk, non-commitment, and avoidance. *Indirect fighting* could include a host of strategies such as denial and equivocation, whininess, and withdrawal.

In surveying the literature on these patterns, Sillars and colleagues (2004) point out that the benefits of being direct or being indirect in managing conflict depend upon the relationship. Indirect communication is often fine, even salutary, if it is done in the context of an already happy marriage. At the same time, if "hit-and-run" tactics are used in an atmosphere of already hostile relations, they will probably be face threatening and reinforce the lack of satisfaction in the relationship. At the same time, direct conflict communication can also be appropriate, depending upon the internal rules for managing conflict in the relationship.

As for cooperation, many studies show that cooperative patterns of communication are more likely to be associated with marital satisfaction and adjustment. Unsatisfied partners are more likely to report competitive and negative interactions, while happy couples tend to report the opposite (Sillars et al., 2004). An interesting pattern that has been observed in dissatisfied couples is one in which the conversation starts out politely, but soon degrades into a shouting match.

You can see here how personal identity gets wrapped up in these patterns of conflict management within a relationship. How we respond to conflict not only resolves or perpetuates the conflict; it also can support or challenge the partners' identities as competitive, cooperative, clear, diplomatic, sensitive, or competent persons. Mutual face is also affected by these patterns. Who are we as partners in this relationship? Is this a relationship in which "things get settled," "we know our place," "we are tolerant," or "truth always wins out"?

It is clear from the rich tradition of theory and research in relational communication that patterns of interaction create opportunities and constraints for facework. Over time and across many relationships, you will achieve some level of coherence in how you see yourself as an actor in the world. Your orientation to identity and face will be shaped by larger moral images you carry within your ongoing and evolving lifescript.

❖ THE RELATIONAL LIFESCRIPT

When you think about your lifescript—ideas about who you are, where you have come from, where you are going, what you value, and how you treat yourself and others—you will find the power of relationships in your life. Our ideas about honor and dignity are not cut from whole cloth, but take shape over time based on an accumulation of understandings and a repertoire of actions that come to form the resources of our lives. Many kinds of relationship contribute to the lifescript. You might, for example, think back on certain childhood friendships, relationships you had in school, or even certain professional and mentoring relationships that are particularly memorable and important in your personal development. For most of us, however, family relationships are most important in forming who we are at any point in our lives. For better or worse, the voices that inform our way of being in the world are most often those of our fathers and mothers, siblings, and children. From the flux and flow of family life, we carry certain images that inform our sense of personhood and relationships, and we will come to characterize our family experiences in amazingly coherent ways that might resemble "a web, a flower, a tomb, a prison, or a castle" (Laing, 1971, p. 6).

From the time we are toddlers, we learn to create coherence in our understanding of family life, and over time the stories and rituals we perform in families constitute a kind of composition that is both artful and coherent (Bateson, 1990), though not always positive. Continuity becomes especially important as we are tossed around in the storms of family life. This is one way that we make sense of our life as a whole. Stories and rituals are the primary ways in which we achieve coherent memories that link our current views with the past (Jorgenson & Bochner, 2004).

Family stories are not mere descriptions or depictions of family life, but they actually provide a narrative that structures our sense of relationship. They tend to have a moral point that guides our commitments in terms of how to think, act, and live (Bochner, 2002). Certain kinds of stories are canonical, as they appear and reappear in many families and seem to have special power in structuring our moral orders (Jorgenson & Bochner, 2004). Stories of courtship, birth, and survival are commonly told in families, and within a culture they provide the basis for the standard cultural stories against which we measure our own experiences (Stone, 1988). From the courtship story, we learn about love, romance, and marriage. From the birth story, we learn about pregnancy, childbirth, and affection and inclusion of children. From survival stories, we learn about coping, friendship, enmity, and morality.

One's own life experiences, of course, rarely match canonical stories—even though we keep retelling them. In some cases, such stories may actually serve to marginalize the experience of certain groups that do not fit the culturally standard view. We may even find coherence in the contrast between our own life stories and those most frequently heard around us.

We are certain that the stories created over time in our most significant relationships affect what we need, are willing to provide, want to nurture, and wish to reject in daily facework with others. But stories evolve and change as we exit old relationships and enter new ones.

SIDEBAR 4.9   Family Stories

Think about your own family stories. Which ones do you remember as being especially important over the years? Think about the following:

1. Which of these stories relate to courtship, birth, and survival?

2. Which stories are canonical, reflecting general cultural values and norms?

3. To what extent do the stories you live match or depart from the stories your family tells?

4. How are your own values affected by these life stories?

5. What story do you tell about yourself? How is this coherent and how does it draw upon the relationships of your life?

❖ PRINCIPLES FOR PRACTICE

Facework is largely relational in nature. This is a clear thesis of this chapter and leads us to identify several principles to keep in mind as we navigate the relationships of our lives:

You negotiate the rules of facework. Facework practices are never universal, but always negotiated. Even public acts of facework, governed by external community rules, are learned through interaction with significant others. This means that you can think consciously about the kind of facework you want to create and use a repertoire of interaction resources in establishing what is right and good within particular friendships, workplace relationships, and in your family. You can never control this all by yourself, but you can think actively about how you want to participate with others in the tacit negotiation of face rules.

There is a tight relationship between mutual face and personal face. The honor and dignity you make for yourself and others is tied to the honor and dignity you make for the relationship itself. When you work to create a positive relationship, you are also working to create positive identities for everyone involved. When you work to treat individuals in honorable and respectful ways, you are also working to develop positive relationships.

Facework in relationships is complex, contradictory, and extended. Although single acts can make an impact, facework in relationships is constant and builds over time. Especially in close, long-term relationships, we must be constantly vigilant and creative in managing the face of self, others, and the relationship itself. Be flexible in how you frame and understand face needs within these kinds of relationships.

You can achieve positive facework practices by paying attention to patterns of interaction. Facework is accomplished through back-and-forth interaction. Patterns are inevitable and powerful. At the same time, patterns are made and can be re-made by the ways in which you act in the situations you face. You can abandon patterns that do not work and create new forms of interaction to improve personal and mutual face.

PART III

Facework and the System

5

Facework in the Community

❖ ❖ ❖

Human beings and chimpanzees share some 98% of their DNA. In her lectures and films, Dr. Jane Goodall (e.g., 1986) shows that the two species are strikingly similar. Chimps have community leaders, ritualized social activity, and family ties. They use tools; play together; fight; have wars; and, amazingly, even share something akin to culture. If you watch chimpanzees long enough, you get the impression that they do a kind of rudimentary facework.

Yet, clearly, there is a universe of difference in that last 2% of genetic material. Humans use language for advanced communication. They build high-tech tools, elaborate architectural structures, and amazing modes of transportation. They adapt to almost every niche and travel easily from one part of the world to another and into outer space. Humans attend conferences, do research, make records, negotiate complex agreements, mediate conflict, experience racism, and struggle with inter-cultural communication. Human society sets us unquestionably apart even from our closest evolutionary cousins.

We human beings often enjoy solitary activities, but even when we are acting alone, we are part of a community, and the community is part of us. We can never escape the social realities created within communities.

We are born into a community, we live our lives in communities, and we die there, too. We have a stake in our community, and often the stakes are high. As a member of the community, we have the opportunity to affect what happens there, but we can never do it alone. Like the chimpanzee, we are inextricably bound to social life, but for us, social life is the very essence of our being.

Most of us probably first associate the term *community* with a geographical territory. We think first of neighborhoods, towns, and cities. The community is the place where we live. Yet, a second thought will broaden the concept. Each of us is part of many communities, they are not always geographical, and we do not always live there. The community may be the place we work, worship, play, or go to school. It may be centralized in one location, dispersed among many places, or located in cyberspace.

A community is essentially a system of personal relationships drawn together by connected concerns, interests, and activities. Communities have what Joseph Pilotta and his colleagues (2001) call *thematics.* If you ask people to talk about the community, they will say many different things, but you will soon notice the same subjects coming up again and again, and these begin to paint a collective picture of "who we are." These themes hint at what Pilotta calls "the forest beyond the daily lived reality of the individual trees of life" (p. 70). Enough is shared for the community to identify itself as a community.

This does not mean, however, that everyone has the same interests, concerns, ideals, or even a vision of the future. But people do recognize that they are part of a system of connections that gives meaning to their lives. Indeed, within community, differences make a difference, and that is how we know what is and is not relevant. In other words, a defining characteristic of communities is a shared sense of relevance shaped by a common history, salient current events, and a sense that the community is marching together into a future. The communities of our lives are powerful in shaping who we are as persons—our values, our meanings, and our ways of acting in the world.

Returning to the theory outlined in Chapter 2, we explore facework here as a central organizing framework for communication in systems. As we unwind this complex ball of string, we see that the immediate action is usually embedded in a larger conversation, which itself has implications for facework. Systems such as organizations are built up through connected conversations, or episodes, and in this chapter, we look more closely at the episodes of community life. As with the other chapters in this book, we bring all of this back to the question of how our lifescripts as persons are infused with the moral values of community.

❖ COMMUNICATION ACTS IN THE COMMUNITY

Individuals are part of larger systems, as their actions contribute to the network of interactions that define the system. At the same time, the system places limits on what individuals can do. Defining what is possible, then, is a circular, systemic accomplishment. How we behave locally does impact the larger system, and the formation of the larger system does impact how we act locally. To refine the key question for action, we now ask: *Within my lifescript as a person, the communities of which I am a member, the episodes I am now enacting, and the conversation that presents itself to me at this moment, how shall I act?*

Sane adults know that their private fantasies are usually not options. We know what would happen if we pulled the fire alarm just to hear it go off. As individuals, we are never free to do anything we might want to do and are constrained by the context. Our choices are limited by rules established in the lifescript, episode, and conversation. At the same time, however, we always do have some latitude of choice. Sometimes we follow a tightly written script, and other times, we are free to improvise. If we are effective in communicating with others, our improvisations will be highly coordinated with those of others within some sort of conversational, episodic, or lifescripted narrative.

Several years ago, during a corrupt governmental period in Mexico, we had the opportunity to spend the morning with a group of Mexican high school exchange students in the United States. We were talking about dialogue, collaboration, and consensus building, and the students explained that the liberties we enjoy in the United States to change the rules of decision making were not possible in their country. This may have been true within the larger political context, but we asked them to think about where they did have freedom. "Do you have freedom to behave in different ways with your friends?" Yes. "Do you have freedom to try out new patterns in your families?" Yes. "Do you have freedom to act in different ways with neighbors?" Yes, they replied. "Then you do have the ability to establish new patterns of communication within certain boundaries, and that will make a difference."

Sometimes action is a simple question, but in difficult moments, especially in conflict or in making decisions where the stakes are high, the decision about how to act can be problematic. Facework in these kinds of situations is personal, but it is more than this. How we work with face impacts perceptions of self and other, of the ongoing relationships being built, and the larger systems that impact our lives. Usually, we are working with face on more than one level. Yes, we may be working to affect the feelings and image of self and others, but we probably also have the ongoing relationship in mind, and we may be working with larger systemic issues at the same time.

Consequently, we frequently encounter contradictions and paradoxes in facework: (1) How do I build the face of others when doing so might erode my own sense of confidence and esteem? (2) How do I manage immediate face issues when everyone will benefit by changing the nature of our relationship in the long run? (3) How do I manage face of self and other when changes are needed to achieve dignity and honor of the whole community? (4) How do I manage face when the larger system is threatening all of us? Often what looks like a face threat in the immediate situation turns out to be face saving in the long run, and conversely what looks like face saving can turn out in the end to threaten face.

Examples of these kinds of facework contradictions abound. Your child is doing poorly in school and must learn that her work habits are deficient so that she ultimately can succeed. A co-worker is driving you nuts and needs to become aware of this behavior so that peace can be restored to the workplace. A community leader acts in ways that create a threatening environment for everyone, and you must decide what to do.

SIDEBAR 5.1   It's a Beautiful Day in the Neighborhood

Surely, one of the icons of 20th-century popular culture was Fred Rogers. Every day for over 40 years, millions of children sat on the floor in front of their television sets to see Mr. Rogers arrive home, put on a sweater, and change his shoes. After he came in the door, Mr. Rogers had a predictable routine. He fed the fish, entertained a visitor, received a package, and took an imaginary trolley ride into the Kingdom of Make-Believe. Preschoolers loved Mr. Rogers because he liked them "just they way they are." The message was clear: No matter what else is going on in your life, you are a worthy person. This was, day after day, a supreme statement about the value of personhood.

Although Mr. Rogers enjoyed a good deal of teasing by talk-show hosts and impersonators about his mild-mannered style and childish voice, his message was not all joy and happiness. Indeed, *Mr. Roger's Neighborhood* was a place in which people died, got sick, experienced pain, felt ashamed, got so angry they were violent toward others, and experienced the anguish of divorcing parents. It was a place of dictatorial rulers, subservient citizens, aloof relatives, plotters, and planners. But it was also a place of creativity, art, music, storytelling, fantasy, and good fortune.

Mr. Rogers taught children to stay the course in the face of adversity. He taught them to value themselves and to be the best they could be. Mr. Rogers showed that social structure and rules are a necessary part of life, that different people know different things and should be valued for what they contribute. He always wore a tie and was always "Mister Rogers," not "Fred." And he showed that people could live in a world of reality, harsh though it sometimes can be. It may be true that, "You can never go down the drain," but it is also the case that, "Wishes don't make things come true."

We can learn a lot about facework from Mr. Rogers, and we see in his neighborhood that facework builds personal dignity, good relationships depend on this, and that the community at large both affects and is affected by how we treat others. No matter what harsh message he had to deliver, Mr. Rogers showed us the need to do the following:

1. Acknowledge

2. Show respect

3. Build constructive relationships

4. Honor contributions and appreciate assets

5. Value stories

6. Listen to all the voices

There is no magic formula for how to manage face in difficult situations. Good communicators are artisans who make decisions of judgment in order to mold a purposeful and salutary outcome. We have found it helpful to use certain principles as a guide:

1. Be cognizant of the larger contexts and work to change these as needed, including the pattern of conversation, the rules of the episode, and the moral guides of the lifescript.

2. Be as inclusive as possible and realize that the dignity and honor of many people, including yourself, may be at stake.

3. Speak respectfully, honoring your own and others' contributions.

4. Be explicit about broader systemic concerns, and bring others in as collaborators in making a better community.

❖ COMMUNITY CONVERSATIONS

How We Talk

The community is a network of inter-linked conversations. Perhaps the term *conversation* is a bit too polite and urbane to capture the sometimes-rough texture of talk, and we certainly do not use this term only to mean country club banter. For us, the term *conversation* is taken metaphorically to include community-wide "talk" of all types, including face-to-face interaction, broadcast and print media, visual images, and the Internet.

An important theme of this book is that we make our social worlds in these forms of conversation. The manner of our interactions literally creates the categories with which we understand the world of experience. Language is not a neutral medium, but forms and re-forms the arrangements of our communities. Communication, then, is the process in which we manage difference, and how we do so matters. The character of a conversation can be captured by questions such as the following:

• Who has the right to talk? Who has the obligation to do so?

• Who has the responsibility of listening? Who is permitted to ignore what is being said?

• Where does the conversation occur? Where is it not permitted to occur?

• When may the conversation happen? When can it not take place? When must it take place?

• How are communicators addressed? What do the participants have the right or even obligation to call other participants?

• What forms of language are permitted, prohibited, or required?

How would you answer these questions differently for, say, a court trial, an art opening, a street demonstration, a public hearing, a block party, an arrest, a high school basketball game, a political rally, or a department store purchase? Notice that the rights, responsibilities, and forms of communication used in a conversation create a little world in which some things are propelled to importance and others are relegated to insignificance. Notice also that in each of these examples, the manner of the conversation can threaten, build, or protect face. How you are honored or dishonored varies greatly depending upon your role in the conversation, the language used in the interaction, and the place of the conversation within larger episodes of community life.

Kerssen-Griep (2001) offers a clear example of how face is managed in the classroom in conversations designed to build a sense of student autonomy, competence, and relatedness. The teacher encourages conversations in which students feel that they can act skillfully and independently while building relationships with others. Such conversations encourage participants to "own" and "invest" in the class. They provide opportunities for decision making and honor individual student needs. Face building conversations also create a climate in which students can feel safe to take risks and to think independently and share their perspectives with one another. Such conversations also express respect and interest in everyone's contributions, and students are encouraged and given ample opportunity to share ideas, opinions, critiques, conclusions, experiences, and plans. Face building conversations in the classroom also encourage students to process and use course information in their own lives.

Talking to Honor and Explore Differences

Since the inception of the Public Conversations Project (2003) in the early 1990s, its founders realized that the form of a conversation is vital to the way in which participants work through their differences (Littlejohn & Domenici, 2001; Pearce & Littlejohn, 1997). The PCP has demonstrated many times over the years that conflict that had formerly torn a community apart can be handled with grace, dignity, and effectiveness if the form of the conversation is carefully considered.

The PCP is actually based on principles of family therapy. Laura Chasin and her colleagues at the Family Institute of Cambridge in Massachusetts knew that families face the same kind of struggles that communities experience. She wondered how family therapy methods might be used to restructure conversations on the important issues within a community. Although the PCP sponsors many forms of conversation, their methods share a common set of principles that include genuine listening, respectful address, mutual understanding, and self-reflection—all key facework goals. Indeed, we have learned so much about how to do facework from our colleagues at the Public Conversations Project.

It is fascinating to watch the PCP work. The power in shifting the conversation from persuasion and influence, even attack, to respectful listening is remarkable. We have used this style of dialogue many times over the years, and we are always amazed at how deeply participants are affected by a new kind of conversation. Regardless of the specifics of a particular public conversation, the PCP always follows certain guidelines:

- Participants relate to one another as persons, not advocates or representatives of a "side" on an issue.

- Participants speak from personal experience and tell personal stories.

- Participants reflect on core values, or what is most important to them as persons.

- Polarization is avoided. Public conversations are multi-valued, and participants are asked to reflect on shades of gray as well as pre-formed positions.

- Participants are asked to explore their own uncertainties.

- Conversations are carefully structured to build trust and to manage face. A facilitator keeps the conversation on track and helps to prevent destructive comments and interactions.

Talking to Inquire and Deliberate

The work of the Public Conversations Project shows us how inter-action is affected by the questions that people address. A church ser-vice, for example, calls our attention to questions such as these: For what should we thank God? How shall we provide one another spiri-tual support? Where do we need divine intervention? How shall we live as persons of faith? In the political realm, elections address the question of who should serve us, public hearings concern the question of what is our opinion, and polls attempt to answer the question of what the public wants.

In every way, the questions we address create the context for the episodes we conduct. Mary Alice Speke Ferdig (2001) found that episodes of public life can be understood as a kind of inquiry. She shows that the nature of dialogue can change drastically when the inquiry itself changes, and often a community needs to ask, "Are we even exploring the right question here?" Table 5.1 outlines a series of ques-tions that can structure the interaction in various community settings.

Albuquerque, the city in which we live and work, has a land-use facilitation program, in which affected neighborhoods have the opportunity to meet with developers in the early stages of a land-use

Table 5.1   Context-Setting Questions

Focus on identity	*Who am I? What is important to me? Who are we together? What do we both care about? What does each of us bring to this conversation based on our previous experiences around the topic that brings us together?*
Focus on principles	*What do I stand for? What do we jointly stand for? How do our choices and actions reflect our individual and collective values? How do we want to interact with one another in the context of this self-organizing process of change? What might that process look like?*
Focus on intentions	*Where am I going? What do I want to see happen here? What are we up to in this conversation? What can we create together that brings us to where we want to be?*
Focus on assumptions	*What aren't we thinking about here? What is our logic for these conclusions?*
Focus on exploration of possibilities	*What are the things you value most about yourself and the self-organizing experience of which you are a part? What are the core factors that give "life" and "energy" to the self-organizing process of which you are a part? What are the possibilities of that which we can create together based on the best of who we are?*

application process. Trained facilitators are assigned to cases, they consult with the adjacent neighborhoods, talk with the developer, and learn about the project from the city planner. If all parties are agreeable, a meeting is set up in a nearby school, community center, or other facility. At the meeting, citizens can share their concerns and ideas with the developer, and the facilitator submits a report of the input from the meeting to the commission as part of the approval package.

This program has been institutionalized in the city, neighborhood associations are well trained in its use, developers expect it, and the city in general benefits from early consultation. A few projects remain contentious, of course, but most turn out to be acceptable to the community because of this opportunity to work with the developer and help shape the project. With few exceptions, Albuquerque land-use meetings are constructive. They are cast in a positive light, and professional facilitators are able to provide a sense of safety and commitment. For the most part, participants feel confident that their concerns will be taken seriously.

Everything that goes into the land-use meeting involves positive facework. Everyone is consulted ahead of time so that they know what is happening and make a clear decision about the desirability of a meeting. The facilitator builds a strong set of communication guidelines assuring that everyone will have a chance to speak and to be heard. The notes and report give credence to issues, interests, and ideas. The developer has a chance to put his or her best face forward in a presentation, and the meeting is structured as a constructive experience that can lead to projects that work for the developer and neighborhood.

Talking to Build a Future

Washington State University, Tri-Cities, and nearby Columbia Basin College are Hispanic Serving Institutions. In a community summit, college personnel met with community members to explore ways in which the higher education institutions of the Columbia Basin area could meet the needs of Hispanic communities there. Entitled *Uniting Futures* (Uniendo Futuros), Hispanic leaders from the Tri-Cities area assembled to discuss issues facing their communities and ways in which the colleges could address these more effectively. This very purpose was itself an important stage in community facework, as the significance of Hispanic communities was placed at the center of attention.

The summit was really a kind of conversation, in which the members of the community could talk about their future in higher education, while officials from the institutions listened. Billed as "a way to explore where we've been, where we want to go, and how to work together to get there," the community summit provided a vehicle for creating a context of lifelong learning. College administrators attended, were introduced, and served as "keynote listeners." Their role was to sit in on sessions throughout the day without talking about their own interests, but to listen carefully to the concerns and ideas of others.

Flipping the focus from "keynote speakers" to "keynote listeners" can be an effective way to shift roles in a conversation. Normally, experts and influentials are granted the privilege of speaking, while citizens listen. Turning this around, the keynote listener concept asks high-level individuals instead to listen and learn from the wisdom of

Table 5.2   Guidelines for Keynote Listeners: Hispanic Community Summit

Listen deeply to the conversation of the day, at the following levels, and make notes:

- Listen to the content of what is being said.
- Listen to the sub-text (concerns, values, interests).
- Listen for differences, not only in opinion but also in concerns, values, interests, and style.
- Listen for shared values and concerns (even where there may be a difference of opinion).
- Listen for what can be learned about Hispanic communities by how people talk about their issues.
- Listen to prepare to make a commitment.

Postpone judgment, listening for the potential of ideas, and make notes about the following:

- What most surprises you?
- What challenges you and why is it challenging to you?
- What intrigues you?

Be prepared to share your comments and insights in an attitude of curiosity and interest.

the community. It does honor both to dignitaries and to the public. It acknowledges the importance of what ordinary citizens have to say, and it shows that their ideas will be taken seriously. It does honor to dignitaries as well, as it gives them the special role of listening. At the same time, keynote listeners can shift the conversation so that new things are learned, new directions can be taken, and new roles can be established. Table 5.2 outlines some of the things that keynote listeners pay attention to.

At the end of the day, these individuals participated in a fishbowl interview to reflect on what they had heard and to make a commitment about next steps. The interview can be remarkable. In the case of the Hispanic communities meeting, the college administrators showed that they had been listening, that they had learned from what they heard, and that they take leadership in a collaborative effort of implementation. This is the highest form of facework.

SIDEBAR 5.2   Protocols for Working With Tribes

- Meetings between tribal officials and staff should, if possible, be conducted between the same level of officials.
- Respect tribal council officials as officials of government.
- Tribal council officials expect to be treated in the highest professional manner when conducting business.
- Like all business relationships, honesty and integrity are highly valued. A sense of humor is appreciated, but generally, serious business-like behavior is appropriate.
- Personal interest in tribal political and cultural history is appreciated, but don't let your personal interest interfere with your mission or task. When possible, do your homework ahead of time to help you understand a situation or issue.
- During negotiations, prepare to discuss all aspects of an issue at hand simultaneously, rather than sequentially.
- Understand that there are different ways of communication. Seemingly extraneous data may be reviewed and re-reviewed.
- Always shake hands when introduced, meeting someone, and departing. It is customary to shake hands with everyone in the room.
- For business meetings, dress formally.
- Traditional authorities often do not relate well to written communication and may find face-to-face consultation more appropriate.
- Like most people, American Indians object to being "consulted" by people who have little intention of doing anything in response to their concerns. Be prepared to negotiate—to the extent that you have authority—to find ways to accommodate the group's concerns. And be prepared to respond with reasons why the advice may or may not be followed.
- Do not rely solely on letters or other written materials to notify tribal governments of proposed plans or actions or to seek consultation. Many groups lack the funding or administrative support to receive and respond efficiently to letters. Letters may not reach the people who are most concerned. Follow-up written communication with telephone calls or in-person contacts.
- Tribal governments usually are not wealthy. It may be difficult for tribal officials to come to meetings or exchange correspondence. In addition, traditional leaders are busy people with responsibilities in the social and cultural life of the community. Be careful how you use their time and avoid causing undue expense. In addition, tribal governments generally do not have large staffs to assign to meetings, follow-up, etc.

- Remember that American Indians may perceive themselves as having a long history of uneven relationships with the U.S. government. They may be suspicious of your proposals. Do not expect a sympathetic attitude to be automatic.
- Be flexible about deadlines, if possible. To be effective, try to follow the most natural schedule. If the mission requires that particular deadlines must be set, be sure to explain what they are and why they must exist. Expect to negotiate about them.
- Those you consult with might not be able to answer questions immediately. They may have to think about it and consult with others. As a result, it may be necessary to pose a question and then go away while they consider and debate the matter.
- Do not assume one American Indian speaks for all American Indians or tribal governments. Take advantage of organizations such as the Urban Indian Advisory Council for broad input.

Source: From the Minnesota Indian Affairs Commission (1999). Used with permission.

The Hydrogen Technology Partnership (HyTeP) is a confederation of agencies and businesses in New Mexico working to make an economic and technological future for the development of hydrogen fuel cells. The HyTeP group planned a national conference of businesses and industries, just to listen to industry needs and requirements. The group intelligently decided that the first kind of conversation that must occur in this future-building process is one in which stakeholders talk, as community leaders listen.

The HyTeP planners are acutely aware that this is the beginning of an ongoing conversation, they cannot predict where the conversation will take them, and they are determined to remain adaptive as new opportunities present themselves. The conference-planning effort was infused with facework, even if most of the members have never heard this term. The HyTeP conference planners carefully considered each of the participants in the upcoming meeting. They knew the players, were aware of the importance of each person, and openly discussed how to best honor each one. As a group and as individuals, the planners were engaged in positive facework at every stage.

Conversations are never isolated, but always connected to something larger. Each conversation is affected in part by conversations that came before, and each will affect both real and anticipated conversations of the future. When we look at the patterns of conversation in a community, we begin to see larger communication units called episodes.

❖ EPISODES IN BUILDING COMMUNITY

A community is marked by the regular activities and patterns of conversation that occur there. An organization has meetings, work schedules, shift hours, social activities, project cycles, and lots of other regularized patterns of activity. Towns have festivals, council meetings, school activities, neighborhood get-togethers, and elections. Communities of faith have congregational rituals, governance meetings, religious and social activities, and weekly schedules. These are the episodes of community life.

Communities come into being, are sustained, and are changed by their episodes. Some episodes such as festivals, graduations, and weddings do honor to the community and to individuals. Other episodes such as riots, criminal activity, political strife, and racial incidents threaten personal face and degrade the community. Such positive and negative episodes constitute the life of the common, and how episodes are structured, how they are accomplished, gives character and meaning to life.

In his book *By Popular Demand: Revitalizing Representative Democracy Through Deliberative Elections,* John Gastil (2000) describes typical episodes in the political life of the United States. In community after community, we see democracy enacted in predictable ways, including public opinion polls, face-to-face meetings with elected officials, talk radio, lobbying, and elections. Polls provide a way to "hear" public concerns and garner their ideas. Polls normally reveal norms, and public meetings provide an opportunity to state opinions in more elaborate form that can be heard directly by policymakers. Talk radio provides a forum for venting and sharing opinions. Lobbying affords an opportunity for interest groups to ply direct pressure on elected officials, and by listening to lobbyists, officials do get a strong sense of what is important to some constituents. In sum, all of these episodes make a community in which there is freedom to express ideas, officials are sensitive to public concerns, and people can participate in democracy.

Community episodes make some things possible, but also limit what can happen. The character of a community is established as much by the limits as by the powers of the episodes that define it. To continue Gastil's (2000) analysis, polls may tell us something about norms, but they do little to uncover the richness of the political fabric of a community, and they rarely afford an opportunity to talk about issues. Face-to-face meetings do provide such an opportunity, but if we look at the way public meetings are frequently run, there is little real dialogue or deliberation. In fact, in many communities, government agencies make a mockery of public consultation in the use of the DAD model (decide-announce-defend), in which public input is more or less irrelevant. If the issue is low-key, the public hearings may be what Gastil calls "empty meditation chambers"; if the issue is hot, "rousing political theatre" (p. 99). Public hearings also can provide a forum that encourages public face threat.

Talk radio can be even worse. Dominated by a single, often conservative voice, talk radio most frequently gives those who often feel otherwise trampled in the mass media a chance to vent. Although callers and listeners are more diverse than the conservative content suggests, hosts frequently pride themselves on the skills with which they threaten face of callers who do not share their opinions, not to mention those who do not dare to call.

Lobbying is a long political tradition and takes different forms in various communities. Unfortunately, lobbying rarely reflects a genuine public voice. Lobbyists are hired by interest groups to promote their own pre-established points of view.

As examples, these common political episodes provide ample opportunity to build one's own face, often in a competitive way, while tromping on the face of others. Despite its military overtones, the expression "rules of engagement" does capture an important aspect of community life, and that is how we engage others on matters of mutual concern.

We know of a small town torn apart over a highway improvement. The city had received a federal highway grant to improve a heavily traveled suburban boulevard that cut through the town. The idea was to get stakeholders together to make decisions about how to use this money for the improvement of the street and adjacent areas, but the matter was far from simple. The discussions had broken down, as business leaders and city residents, along with the council, quickly divided into two competing interest groups. The business interest wanted a narrower, two-lane option to slow the traffic down, which they believed would maintain business; and others, including the mayor and some other members of the council, favored widening the street to three or four lanes to improve traffic flow, safety, and access. This eventuality was both understandable and predictable, but the way in which the participants tried to work through their differences created a series of episodes that made it impossible to move forward constructively. The essential problem was poor facework, as key players spent years hurling vitriol at one another.

Over a number of years, this conflict played out badly. Previous consensus processes failed, a lawsuit was filed, and a court-ordered mediation was unsuccessful. Meanwhile, the city was unable to use, and indeed could have lost, some $8 million, and the badly needed renovations would not get done. Business owners and city leaders all knew that something different had to happen, but emotionally, they felt damaged, and it was very hard to muster the trust needed to engage in a new way. We struggled for weeks doing our best to encourage trust building, but after months of pre-negotiations, we were unsuccessful in bringing the parties to the table. Every time they were close to signing a process agreement, a key participant would take a unilateral action to subvert it. Although the parties knew intellectually that they should change their rules of engagement, they did not have the will to do so. In the end, however, the parties refused to come to the table.

After every effort to convene the stakeholders failed, the mediators realized that they had been co-opted into the struggle and set out strong conditions for continued involvement. These included the following:

1. The parties would need to communicate directly with one another and establish a committee to finalize the process agreement.

2. The parties would need to refrain from any public statements other than those permitted by the process agreement.

3. Side meetings and public events not approved by the process agreement would not be held.

4. Disrespectful language would end.

These conditions could not be met, and the attempt to convene a process failed. Here are the tacit facework rules that were followed:

- Look for, identify, and call out negative qualities in those who oppose you.

- Impugn the intelligence and motivation of the opposing group.

- Show your anger by using harsh, damning language in private and in public.

- Return accusations and blame in kind.

- Polarize the issue, and compete hard to get what you want.

Through many episodes, including community meetings, council meetings, court proceedings, mediations, and negotiations, these rules encouraged the parties as much as possible to build their own face while threatening that of the other. As a result, everyone felt attacked, and collaboration was impossible because, in the end, the parties could not speak directly to one another and could not imagine new rules by which they might have built honor and respect for the ultimate benefit of their working relationships and the quality of life in the community.

Changing the Rules of Engagement

In many ways, this book is about how to change our rules of engagement in a way that builds honor and respect; collaborative relationships; and adaptive, learning communities. When a community embarks on the task of addressing a difficult issue with which they are confronted, they can start right at this point: Design a process that can accomplish objectives such as those in the previous sentence. For us, process management is a crucial issue because it creates the conditions that can make constructive outcomes possible in the face of difference (Figure 5.1).

The rules of engagement in many communities empower people to speak out on their opinions, but often do not allow individuals to explore issues openly. Such rules frequently afford an opportunity to test ideas through polarized debate, but often fail to permit genuine dialogue that could explore the true complexity of the issue, including common ground and difference within a context of respect. When you have the opportunity to help communities design and manage processes for change, however, you can deliberately and clearly challenge groups to call their customary procedures into question in a way that can manage face and achieve mutually desirable outcomes.

Figure 5.1   The Face Management Triad

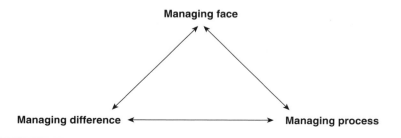

SIDEBAR 5.3   Tell Me a New Story

Those who care about communities and see a need for alternative processes for community collaboration owe a great debt to the Institute of Cultural Affairs International (ICAI; 2005). Long before the term *facilitation* was widely known, the Institute was a forerunner in designing creative processes for community change.

The ICAI began with the assumption that community change had to arise from community empowerment and that the community itself must enact new kinds of conversation in order to create new directions to rise above poverty, defeat drugs, and build social responsibility in the population. Using a Town Meeting format, the Institute went into some of the most problem-ridden communities in our country and abroad and brought community leaders together to talk in new ways about their futures.

The workshop was carefully designed. Beginning with a frank discussion of social issues, participants brainstormed their social issues such as education, crime, drugs, poverty, employment, social services, and the like. Using individual idea-writing, small-group work, and plenary sessions, participants list their concerns, cluster these into social action issue areas, and create an operating vision. The group then discerns underlying contradictions or factors that block resolution of these issues. Then a series of challenges is written, identifying the social issue, underlying contradiction, or block, and local illustrative stories. Responses to each challenge are then brainstormed and clustered into response categories. Formal proposals are then drafted.

The workshop ends as participants create a new image of the community in the form of new stories, new songs, new symbols, and a new drama. The Institute has refined and added to its methods over the years and is still going strong, having organizations throughout the United States and abroad. As a group they have shown us many things about facework:

- Communities and their members have the resources and power to change their lives.
- We are empowered when we acknowledge the limits of our present conversations and jointly create new, better ones.
- Conversations of creativity build feelings of honor and dignity, while conversations of despair threaten these.
- Collective imagination builds action-oriented relationships and healthy communities.

Breaking Old Patterns

In an attractive booklet published by the National Policy Consensus Center, Peter Adler and Juliana Birkhoff (2002) outline "Twenty things you can do to help environmental stakeholder groups talk more effectively about science, culture, professional knowledge, and community wisdom." This booklet presents a new set of rules for working through environmental conflict (Table 5.3). Together, these suggestions are just one example of how constructive facework can be the cornerstone of new episodes in the life of the community.

These twenty tools suggest tangible ways to break old patterns of interaction that may no longer serve a community. Notice that each of the twenty ideas suggests a new way of acting, and each helps to structure facework in some way on the level of the episode. Each is a guideline for how to conduct an episode of conflict resolution in a way that manages the face of all participants while building relationships and improving the quality of the community itself.

Reframing the Episode

Rules will change when the episode itself is reframed and understood in a new way. Steven Daniels and Gregg Walker (1996) point out, for example, that typical episodes of conflict resolution on environmental issues are complicated by a diversity of viewpoints, tension from differences in such factors as history and values, and strong emotional ties to the landscape. To help deal with these natural obstacles, Walker and Daniels have created a new kind of episode for complex policy issues. Borrowing from the field of education, they call their approach *collaborative learning,* or CL. Here is where reframing becomes important.

Daniels and Walker (2001) redefine the episode from problem solving to "improving the situation." The "situation" is not a specific problem or issue, but a system that must be managed. The question for participants, then, is, "How can we achieve desirable and feasible change through mutual, collaborative learning about science, the issues, and values?" Participants are teaching and learning together about their various views, cultures, and histories. Together, they learn too about the issues and gain necessary information for improvement. The method—a carefully organized episode of interaction—aims to create a safe environment and encourage dialogue and deliberation.

We are struck by the facework involved in this process. Instead of presenting the face-threatening frame of competition and conflict, they focus

Table 5.3   New Rules for Working Through Environmental Conflict

1. Begin with co-hosting.	*Have the major stakeholder groups co-host the negotiations.*
2. Create a game plan and group covenants.	*Include everyone in discussions about the process to be used and how to organize the event.*
3. Concentrate on relationships first.	*Share a meal. Have participants get to know one another as individuals rather than representatives.*
4. Be transparent about decision making.	*Establish ahead of time the rules by which decisions will be made.*
5. Pay attention to power.	*Think about how all participants can be empowered to use the resources available to them.*
6. Create rituals.	*Encourage participants to establish certain routines that have special meaning.*
7. Balance linear processes with iterative strategies.	*Create a process that allows forward movement, but also honors storytelling and repetition as needed.*
8. Talk about values.	*Encourage participants to explore their values explicitly.*
9. Acknowledge different kinds of knowledge.	*Acknowledge that different ways of knowing are legitimate.*
10. Generate multiple problem definitions.	*Permit participants to define the problem in various ways.*
11. Step out of the normal conversation mode.	*Think creatively about how to have meetings. Honor alternative forms.*
12. Create jointly owned knowledge.	*Encourage participants to collaborate in getting the information they need.*
13. Explore validity and accuracy with care.	*Encourage a climate of authenticity in which participants are free to ask for validation.*
14. Talk politics, but do it gracefully.	*Admit that important political pressures may be present, and allow frank discussion of these.*
15. Be patient teachers to others.	*Avoid mystery. Allow all participants to teach others what is important to them in ways that makes sense to the other.*
16. Organize sidebars.	*Make use of committees and special groups as necessary to explore certain issues.*
17. Create a public learning culture.	*Allow for difference and change. Admit new forms of information as they come available.*
18. Engage in storytelling.	*Stories are one of the best ways to tell others what is important to us.*
19. Explicitly articulate outcomes.	*Be clear about what is gained and what is lost by the outcome. Allow people to adjust to necessary changes.*
20. Create strong endings.	*Articulate the details of agreements and celebrate.*

on the face-building frame of learning and creative collaboration. Participants are first trained in the process. In a CL workshop format, participants—normally ordinary citizens and policymakers together— describe the situation they are facing, discuss interests and concerns, create transformative solutions, and deliberate on these. Later, ideas are sorted and processed for possible implementation. Throughout, the process is framed as a learning activity, and techniques are based on several assumptions about adult learning—that learning should be active rather than passive, that learning involves different modalities, that learning styles vary, and that learning is best when combined with systems thinking.

Facilitating communication and planning should always be based on the need for adult engagement and learning. Traditional ways of doing business within the community are not always structured in this way. Good planning requires a sense of purpose, clear vision, and commitment to a mission. Models for community change, such as the CL approach, honor previous experience, anticipate ongoing working relationships, and focus on visions rather than problems. They feature creativity, which in turn builds respect for self and other. And finally, they feature high-level thinking, which promotes feelings of value and honor for everyone involved and, in turn, honor face.

Examples of the power of reframing abound. The Public Dialogue Consortium approached Cupertino, California, to begin a quality-of-life project there, and discovered that the community was experiencing considerable racial tension because of immigration from Asia (Spano, 2001). Worrying that talks around racial issues could reproduce the very tensions they were designed to overcome, the discussions were reframed to an exploration of *cultural richness*. The result was remarkable. In Shawn Spano's (2001) book *Public Dialogue and Participatory Democracy: The Cupertino Community Project*, the city manager Don Brown wrote, "The 'light bulb' moment for me came when I realized that this project was not about changing people's minds, but that it was about giving people a way to talk about tough issues. I also realized that people's fears and concerns are real and legitimate and that they need a way of talking about them without the fear of being branded a racist" (pp. xi–xii). Can people overcome their fears of talking about hard issues, when we place facework at the center of the dialogue?

The character of the community is not a given, but is constructed and reproduced every day by the communication that happens there. The episodes, conversations, and acts of real people in daily situations constitute the social world of the community. The community is not the sum of the personalities of the people in it, but is a dynamic product of interaction. How we communicate impacts not only individuals but also the larger social world. A community, then, really is something that is *built*.

❖ LIFESCRIPTS AND THE COMMUNITY

The activity of the network of communications creates entire ways of thinking, ways of working, ways of understanding, and ways of acting. Shared history provides our most fundamental orientations to the world. That is why we always carry our communities around with us wherever we go. Our communities are part of us as persons. What we see, how we act, what we value, what things mean are all determined by ideas worked out through social interaction in communities.

If community interaction is so powerful, how do we account for individuality? We know that even within a single community, various interests clash, different values reign, and ideas compete. People do not necessarily see things the same way, and communities somehow hang together, if not always harmoniously.

If the community is a composite of persons, the person is also a composite of communities. Every person is different precisely because each is a unique combination of different social worlds. Our histories always differ, and our communities of association always vary. We may have some significant others in common, but each of us has particular relationships that influence who we are, how we understand our experience, and how we act in the world. This is precisely how the paradoxical human being can be both individual and social. We may be biologically unique, but, more important for human beings, we are individual because we are social.

And this aspect of the human condition—membership in many communities—is a crucial resource in human life. We can choose to honor other people because we ourselves have been dishonored. We can collaborate because we have experienced authoritarianism. We can remove barriers of prejudice because we have at some other time and in some other place come up against stereotyping. We can make new rules by breaking rules that did not work elsewhere. This is our power as social beings always living in community.

Our identities are shaped by our social worlds. Each of us possesses a dynamic and changing lifescript, a reflection of deep cultural ways of knowing. The lifescript gives a roadmap for how to live a life and how to respond to the constantly changing landscapes we traverse.

Lifescripts provide a sense of who we are as individuals, what it means to be a person, the nature of relationships, and even a way to understand the communities of which we have been, are, and will become members. The lifescript gives answers to questions such as, "What kind of person am I?" "What is important to me?" "How do I act?" "Where have I been, and where am I going?"

In Chapter 1, we introduced the term *moral order* to capture the assumptions that drive the lifescript. The moral order is a socially constructed set of understandings we carry with us from situation to situation. An important part of your lifescript involves face—how you want to be seen by others, how you want others to treat you, and how you treat others. Indeed, facework itself is the never-ending process of presenting self to others and acting toward others in the ongoing narrative of life. How we do this is very much part and parcel of the moral order, which is why different communities, especially cultural communities, do facework differently.

Indeed, the premise of this book is that facework lies at the heart of social action. How we build, maintain, protect, or threaten personal dignity, honor, and respect reproduces the very lifescript that guides decisions about how to do facework.

SIDEBAR 5.4   An Exercise on Stereotyping

Introduction

TIME: 1 minute

We've learned from our previous work that relationships of conflict are often fueled by distorted perceptions that people hold of one another—by assumptions people make about others who don't share their views or their culture or their experiences. Many people would like to feel less stereotyped by others. We'd like to lead you through an exercise that will allow you to communicate how you feel stereotyped and to indicate which of those stereotypes are most inaccurate or hurtful.

Generation of Lists

TIME: 15 minutes (in subgroup)

INSTRUCTIONS: We'd like the people who identify more with a pro-choice perspective to gather around this easel and the people who identify more with a prolife perspective to gather around that easel. Your task is to generate on the newsprint at least eight stereotypes that you think people on the other side of the issue hold of you. That is, when someone with a different view of abortion learns that you hold a PL or PC view, what negative attributions do you worry that he or she ascribes to you? What stereotypical beliefs, attitudes, and intentions do you imagine you are assumed to have? You will have 15 minutes to do this. You might want to start with a rapid brainstorming of many stereotypes, and then sort through and identify several that are somewhat discrete. One of us will facilitate this process in

---

(Continued)

each group. At the end of the 15 minutes we'll ask you to pick one of your group members to report on the list to the full group.

Marking the Lists

TIME: 5–8 minutes (in subgroup)

INSTRUCTIONS: Now we'd like to give you an opportunity to reflect on these stereotypes and think about which seem most inaccurate in your view. Which is most painful—which of these really hurts—to think that someone thinks this of you? We'd like each of you to put an "I" next to the 3 stereotypes you feel are most *inaccurate*. Then put a "P" next to the stereotype that is most *painful* or offensive. Finally, we'd like to invite you to put a "U" next to the stereotype or stereotypes that you think are most *understandable*—by doing this you're not saying it's true of you; you could be saying only that this is a stereotype your movement does too little to correct. This category is an option—we'd like to encourage you to give it some thought. Before any of you approach the easels, please take a minute to think. Then go up when you're ready. When you have finished marking the lists you'll pick a recorder to report to the other group on what the feared stereotypes are, what markings were made, and, if you'd like, you can say something about how the process went.

Group Reports

TIME: 8–10 minutes (in the full group)

INSTRUCTIONS: Now is the time for each group to report to the other. Each group has been invited to share not only the lists and the markings but also something about the process.

Sharing About the Most Hurtful Stereotypes

TIME: 20 minutes

INSTRUCTIONS: (This statement can be personalized or offered as it is here.) We'd like to have each person take the opportunity to say—again, you can pass if you'd like—something about the stereotype that you marked as most painful. And to say what it is about the way you understand yourself, the way you know yourself, what is it about your experience that makes the stereotype that you marked as the most painful, so painful. We'd like you to share just a couple of sentences. Again, what is it about how you understand yourself, know yourself, and understand your experience that makes one of these judgments or distorted perceptions so painful? This time, instead of doing a go-round, we'll do what we call the popcorn for- mat, which means, that you can speak when you feel ready. And then, when we get close to the end of our time, we'll check and make sure everybody who wants to speak has a chance.

❖ PRINCIPLES FOR PRACTICE

As we move through this book, we continually broaden the frame in which facework can be viewed. Our scholarship and experience leads us to see that face-related communication goes well beyond simple interpersonal exchanges. We learn two big lessons as we explore these larger frames.

Understand that every act is part of a larger set of interactions that, over time, connects people in relationships and communities. Think systemically and question the impact that your actions will have in the long run and the impact that the system will have on you, your relationships, and your communities.

We make positive communities through constructive communication. Communities and systems of all types are made in interaction, and if we want communities that honor human beings and their relationships, we must pay attention to the "how" of communication within those communities. Old patterns of interaction that do not work very well can be transformed.

6

Cultural and Global Issues

In a shift from common thinking, sociologist Anthony Giddens (2003, p. 16) identifies a kind of "reverse colonization" that happens when the developing world influences the West. We see this in cities in which immigrant groups bring a wealth of cultural products and when goods from around the world populate Western marketplaces. Globalization is an outward and inward phenomenon, influencing the world system of nations and markets as well as individuals' identities in local communities throughout the world.

We live in an increasingly globalized world in which intercultural contact is normal and necessary. If you call customer service for a computer problem from the United States, the chances are good that you will speak to a technician in India, but that isn't so odd because your next-door neighbor, even roommate, may come from India, Vietnam, or the Philippines. Or from Nigeria, Ethiopia, or Egypt. And your favorite restaurant may be managed by people from China, Korea, Thailand, Greece, or Lebanon. And you may be wearing shoes made in Vietnam, jeans made in India, or a sweater made in Ireland. In most large universities, class discussions are characterized by a range of world accents.

In Jakarta a few years ago, we visited a shopping mall where we could have bought products common in cookie-cutter malls throughout the world. We exited this mall into the teeming streets of the city filled with local food stands, bicycle cabs, and Javanese dress; and then we proceeded to the Asian market in the Chinese district, where we could have bought cobra blood, baskets, wild birds, hog heads, or live chickens. Jakarta, like so many world cities, is a mélange of cultural forms, including strong Western influence, but with an ironic resistance to westernization and strengthening of local cultures at the same time.

Personal identity is constructed locally. More than following simple rules of politeness, the social construction of identity consists of deep assumptions about what is right, good, and moral. We learn how to present ourselves and respond to others from the local cultures in which we live. For some—cosmopolitans, urbanites, and sojourners—the creation of personal identity is multicultural and diverse. For others, it may be restricted to a small cluster of cultural forms. Regardless, all peoples of the world face significant intercultural and international challenges in trade, travel, and tradition.

SIDEBAR 6.1   Consider Your Cultural Identity

Think about your own cultural identity. Where were you born? Where did you grow up? What are the cultural backgrounds of the most influential persons in your life? Where have you traveled and lived? What cultural artifacts are most important to you? What are the cultural traditions that give meaning to your life?

Intercultural contact is played out on a grand scale in international relations. We think of nations as individual actors that form alliances, trade, and even wage war, but in reality international contact always happens through the interaction of human beings—businesspeople, diplomats, national leaders, military personnel, and regular citizens. In an international negotiation, for example, individual human beings—usually representing governments, corporations, or international organizations—come together. They present themselves and respond to others in particular ways that have an immense effect on what happens as they communicate as well as on the outcome of the interaction. It is appropriate, even compelling, for us to extend our discussion of facework to the intercultural and international realm.

❖ THE CULTURE OF FACEWORK

Culture is hard to define. Johnson (2000) thinks of a culture as a complex system of three large sectors—a system of abstractions, a system of artifacts, and a system of language and communication. *Cultural abstractions* are the ideas that shape the values, morals, conceptions, and perceptions of a group of people. *Cultural artifacts* are products, including arts, music, dance, clothing, tools, and a host of other material objects created and used by the cultural group. *Cultural language and communication* consists of a symbol system with meanings commonly used and understood within a group. Language and other symbolic forms bind the overall cultural system together and give it meaning. The famous anthropologist Edward Hall (1959) wrote that "culture is communication and communication is culture" (p. 169).

Pearce (1994) feels that defining culture is a mistake because it is not a "thing," but a "difference" that can only be felt. Since culture is part of all human experience, it infuses human life and, according to Pearce, is like an eddy or current in a river. Cultures can be ethnic, national, regional, religious, gender-based, or based on any significant inter-group difference that affects meanings and practices. Culture is constantly made and remade in communication, and since we all live in a multicultural world, each person is a multicultural being. Today, Pearce asserts, persons are like a collage of cultures, and it is impossible to force fit any person or group into a mold. Although some stability and coherence is apparent within a cultural group, the forms of life enacted are always open ended, and we see constant change in cultural ideas as a result.

One of the ways in which we "see" culture is to encounter a difference that becomes problematic. Misunderstanding, lack of coordination, discrimination, and stereotyping bring us face to face with cultural difference. Carbaugh (1990) refers to such moments as *asynchrony*, or the failure of one cultural form to mesh with another. Asynchrony can result from differing notions of personal identity, appropriate forms of performance or behavior, or norms for structuring conversations and interactions.

Miscalculated facework is a good example of asynchrony. A northern European wants to compliment an East Asian business associate and ends up embarrassing him instead. An Israeli business representative traveling in South America wishes to be efficient and clear, but is perceived as abrupt and rude. A Japanese diplomat, trying to be polite, ends up "frustrating" a Canadian official because he nods, smiles, and says yes to everything. A British exchange student in the United States has heard that Native Americans don't like direct eye contact and offends a Navajo classmate because he won't look at her. Such examples are not limited to ethnic cultures. Consider, for example, a woman who tries to vent her frustrations with her husband, only to receive a quick piece of advice while he walks out of the room; a new employee who tells his boss a joke while putting his arm around the manager's shoulder; or a woman who tells her grandson that he will need to remove his tongue stud before meeting her friends.

SIDEBAR 6.2   Difficult Intercultural Moments

Think of encounters that have been challenging to you from an intercultural perspective. Re-read the paragraph about miscalculated facework and write a similar one based on experiences like this in your own life.

Cultural Forms of Facework

Clearly, facework is cultural. It arises from a strong sense of cultural identity, which is normally invisible until it becomes a problem (Pearce, 1994). How you would like to be treated and how you feel you should treat others depends upon cultural ideas related to (1) what it means to be a person; (2) what constitutes moral action; (3) what constitutes respect, honor, and dignity; and (4) how identity should be enacted in various communication forms.

Revisiting Directness. You will recall from previous chapters that facework is accomplished with varying degrees of directness. Sometimes we build or threaten face quite clearly and directly, and other times this work is more implicative. Hall (1976) observed an important difference among cultures, which he called *cultural context,* and it is clear that this variable very much influences the directness of facework (Ting-Toomey & Oetzel, 2001). Cultural context is a variable that ranges from high to low. At one end, the high-context cultures tend to assign most of their meaning to what is going on around the actual speech. Nonverbal action, personal history, and group and family affiliation are most important in determining what is happening. In low-context cultures, more meaning tends to be assigned to the actual words spoken. In low-context cultures, you often say what you mean and get right to the point. In high-context cultures, a great deal of time is taken to build a base of relationship, to feel others out, and to learn more about the context in which the communication is occurring. Consequently, people are more indirect in their expressions. In contrast, members of low-context cultures will tend to be more direct and detailed in what they say. A simple and direct compliment would be a clear form of face building among members of a low-context culture, while a compliment in a high-context setting could be felt as an embarrassment and a threat to face. On the other hand, complimenting one's family, which could seem almost irrelevant to a low-context communicator, would do much to build the face of communicators in a high-context culture.

Communicators in low-context cultures tend to value clarity and efficiency, while those in high-context settings prefer harmony. For many Asians, for example, expression of anger and conflict is to be avoided (Fine, 1995). The clarity and directness encountered by many Asian immigrants in Western countries is uncomfortable at best and more likely even embarrassing and offensive.

We once observed a mediation between a Korean tailor and an American college student. The student had taken her coat to the tailor to have the sleeves shortened and was unhappy with the results. The Korean man, speaking with a strong accent, found himself in a bind between his identity as a fine craftsperson and his desire to achieve harmony. The student just wanted him to pay for a new coat, but that clear request on her part was a direct face threat to the tailor. His answer was to offer a small amount of the money "to make a better world," which the student found confusing and irrelevant. He would not give the entire amount back because it would have been an admission of his failure as a tailor.

Individual Face and Community Face. How do we honor others? At times, we tend to focus on the other person as an individual. Other times, we honor a group or community of which the other person is a member. This is not an arbitrary choice, but emerges from a sense of connection that we make between the self and the group. *Individualist cultures* are known for emphasizing the individual over the group, while *collectivist cultures* give pre-eminence to the group or community over the individual (Hofstede, 1991; Triandis, 1995), and facework is directly related to these tendencies (Ting-Toomey, 1985, 1988; Ting-Toomey & Kurogi, 1998). Cultures, of course, are not either individualist or collectivist, but range along a continuum between these extremes. For those that are toward the individualist end of the spectrum, autonomy, individual responsibility, and achievement are important.

Individualist cultures create personal identities around individual traits and qualities. For individualists, good facework honors the individual as a person.

Cultures that are more collectivist in orientation develop personal identities around group affiliation. Consequently, facework centers more at the levels of relationship and community than the person. Spending time learning about a person's family and community are considered a high form of honor, but anything that would single a person out could be face threatening. Further, there is much more self-facework in individualist cultures, where putting your best foot forward is considered important. In collectivist cultures, by contrast, much more effort is put into other and mutual facework. Honor is achieved not by individual accomplishment, but by fulfilling one's role and expectations within the larger group.

Many African Americans display a unique pattern that integrates individualist and collectivist styles of facework (Collier, 1991; Fine, 1995; Ting-Toomey & Oetzel, 2001). As a result of a history of racial oppression, combined with a strong sense of cultural values, many African Americans can be very self-protective with outsiders, while maintaining a high level of mutual-face and solidarity within their own groups.

Power Distance. Cultures vary in the extent to which they think of social relations in terms of power (Hofstede, 1991). Status, authority, class, caste, sex, and even age can be the basis for *power distance* in which one person is considered to be higher in authority or status than another. The pattern of facework in cultures with high power distance is considerably different from that in lower power-distance cultures, in which equality is valued.

In low power-distance cultures, participation and inclusion tend to be strongly felt needs. To be left out is to have one's face threatened. In high power-distance cultures, inclusion is necessary only if one's own status or rank grants authority. Deference is an important kind of facework in high power-distance situations. In such situations, self-effacement is not thought of as face threatening, but as a form of deference to a higher authority.

Mexican culture is one example of a high power-distance culture. It is also rather collectivist in orientation. Dignity is very important to Mexicans, but dignity is an internal spiritual matter rather than a question of personal accomplishment, so there is no need for one to maneuver to get power within a situation. Power comes instead from roles arising from fate or circumstance, and powerful people are always to be respected (Fine, 1995).

Reciprocity. Reciprocity is a universal way of connecting, forming relationships, and creating community, but cultures vary tremendously in the manner and extent to which reciprocity is performed and what it means. In every case, reciprocity constitutes a kind of facework within the culture. Even in White, suburban United States, it is customary to bring a host a gift of wine, candy, or flowers, which simply acknowledges the desire to make a contribution. In collectivist cultures, however, gift-giving is more profound (Fine, 1995). Indeed, the Chinese concept of *quanxi* suggests that friends have a mutual obligation to one another. To fail to reciprocate is to fail to live up to a deep responsibility to the other person. *Quanxi* literally means "relationship, connection, obligation, dependency" (Wenzhong & Grove, 1991, p. 61), and it is manifest in an elaborate system of gift giving.

When we travel abroad these days, we normally bring a suitcase of gifts, usually small mementos from our region. We give these gifts as a form of honor, sharing our part of the world, and as a token of appreciation to our hosts. In Asia, we can always expect that the recipient will give a gift in return, and sometimes the gift-giving goes back and forth several times! This is more than being nice; it is building a sense of connection and community, common to high-context and collectivist societies.

SIDEBAR 6.3   What Makes You Feel Good About Yourself?

June Smith (Minneapolis surgeon): Saving lives. When I finish a hard operation, and I know the patient is going to recover . . . that's the best.

Maria Caccioppo (mother of six in Rome): A great family dinner! When my daughters, my mother, my aunts, and I get together every Sunday to cook, there is nothing better, and to see the smiles on everyone's faces when they sit down to dinner. That's the best.

Esau Kiplagat (Kenyan farmer): Drinking the beer with my friends. We get together at someone's house, and we men sit together with our straws drinking from the beer pot. The women sit around the outside and watch. It's a great feeling.

Sarah Winston (Utah housewife): There is nothing better than a quilting bee. All the women in our family bring our patches and then sew the quilting pattern. All we do is talk, talk, talk.

(The above are fictional.)

Special Issues of Culture

Emotional Expression and Conflict. Emotion, particularly anger and other negative emotions, presents a special challenge for facework, and cultural differences can truly influence the role of emotion in facework. Because conflict so often involves strong feelings, this too challenges our facework sensibilities, especially in light of cultural difference.

Marlene Fine (1995, p. 96) tells the story of a meeting among senior executives of a large organization. The group consisted of six White managers and one African American man, the affirmative action officer. At one point, the Black man accused the organization of not valuing affirmative action, and, in a manner typical of many African Americans, did so in a forceful and emotional way. The other members of the group remained silent, which seemed to inflame the affirmative action officer even more, which, in turn, made the White representatives even quieter. It was clearly a negative spiral that looked from the outside like attack-retreat. Fine gained insight into this situation later by talking separately to the African American executive and the others.

The affirmative action officer was irate because he took the others' silence as "not caring." In other words, he took the group's calmness as disconfirmation, which was a clear face threat to him. The Whites, in contrast, were angry that their Black colleague was so "unprofessional" and "inappropriate" in his outburst, finding this behavior very face threatening. The result was an escalating conflict caused by intercultural difference.

This example poignantly illustrates the importance of cultural forms in handling emotion and conflict. Fine (1995) writes that African Americans often feel that it is their right to express strong feelings, but to do so in a way that does not escalate to violence. Individuals with a northern European heritage, in contrast, often believe that strong expressions of feeling are inappropriate in professional settings, a norm that is firmly established in many organizational settings in the United States. The differences between Black and White expressions of feeling are obvious (Kochman, 1981, 1990; Ting-Toomey, 1986).

Asian cultures offer another example. The strong value of harmony, so common in many Asian cultures, makes the direct, explicit discussion of conflict difficult for many people from Asian countries. In meetings such as the one described above, people of Asian descent may remain silent and appear affirming in their demeanor. Others often take this as a sign of assent, when in fact the Asians may disagree (Fine, 1995).

Non-Verbal Aspects. It should come as no surprise that people from different cultures assign various meanings to non-verbal behaviors.

Behaviors taken as signs of closeness or liking—commonly called *immediacy* (Mehrabian, 1972)—are critical to facework, but they vary significantly from one culture to another (Burgoon & Bacue, 2003). Being highly expressive, standing close, directly facing the other person, maintaining eye contact, and even touching are valued in some cultures, but considered aggressive or invasive in other cultures. Patterns of eye contact provide an excellent illustration. Blacks typically maintain greater eye contact when they are speaking than when they are listening, but Whites tend to do just the opposite, at least in the United States (Hecht, Ribeau, & Alberts, 1989). You can see how this difference would create a problem (Fine, 1995). Blacks and Whites tend to stare at each other when the Black person is speaking, which could be interpreted as confrontational by both; but, then, when the White person is speaking, both may appear inattentive! Both speakers may feel disrespected by the other when, in fact, neither means to be disrespectful.

Eye contact is only one of many possible non-verbal factors in any communication situation. When the speakers share a culture, these may not be problematic; but they do emerge as significant in intercultural situations. It is not necessary to know every possible non-verbal difference, but to be aware of the potential for problems in this area and to be flexible and open in how you interpret the behaviors of others. More complete discussions of non-verbal communication and culture are readily available (e.g., Ting-Toomey, 1999).

Workplace Issues. The workplace is one setting in which facework assumes immense importance. When you consider that most of us spend as much as 25% to 30% of our time at work, organizational relationships become extremely important in forming personal identity. Beyond how we treat individuals and even form relationships, honor, dignity, and respect must extend to the whole system. How a manager treats one employee, for example, will have an impact in an entire department. It is also the case that organizations throughout the world—certainly in North America—are increasingly intercultural.

What do the changing demographics of organizations have to do with facework? Fine (1995) writes that a truly multicultural organization

> values, encourages, and affirms diverse cultural modes of being
> and interacting . . . creates an organizational dialogue in which no
> one cultural perspective is presumed to be more valid than other
> perspectives; and . . . empowers all cultural voices to participate
> fully in setting goals and making decisions. (p. 36)

All of this is systemic facework. Achieving this ideal on a system level requires a number of interventions, including (1) educating the workforce; (2) providing support groups as needed; and (3) creating policies that encourage constructive interaction, fair treatment, and interpersonal respect among workers.

Discrimination. We have written repeatedly in this book about the ways in which personal, relational, and systemic issues impact one another. We stand by our claim that facework happens at all three levels and that we cannot separate how we treat individual human beings from the qualities of our relationships and the nature of our larger communities. Because we live in a diverse world, issues of discrimination emerge as a significant factor in dialogues about the kind of society we want to create (e.g., McPhail, 2004). When a person behaves in a demeaning or disconfirming way toward another because of a personal stereotype, the face implications are significant; but when oppression becomes institutionalized, the interaction pattern is multiplied a million fold and thereby impacts the lifescript of untold numbers of individuals. This truism is especially important when we remember that face is not just a matter of "feeling good" about yourself, but goes to the very roots of personal identity. Thus our deepest conceptions about who we are as persons in the world can be shaped by entrenched patterns of discrimination across history within the institutions of society. Whether Jews, homosexuals, gypsies, and Seventh Day Adventists in the era of National Socialism in Europe; intellectuals during the Cultural Revolution in China; or Blacks in South Africa during Apartheid, members of oppressed groups form their sense of worth, aspirations, communication styles, commitments, and even pride based on these experiences. Featuring one example, Fine (1995) writes,

> Racism is the defining experience in the lives of most African Americans. It is a pervasive, historical fact of everyday life that has melded African and mainstream American beliefs, values, and behaviors into a unique set of cultural characteristics. Both the experience of racism itself and the internalization of the implicit and explicit attitudes in racist behavior and assumptions shape the African American world view. (p. 70)

The same could be said for the experience of Jews in the aftermath of the Holocaust, Native Americans living in the shadow of European expansionism, gays and lesbians now emerging from outdated social and psychiatric thinking, and many other groups. Global liberation movements aim to change long-standing and institutionalized forms of discrimination and oppression precisely to build honor, dignity, and respect among all populations. For this reason, activists in these movements find it essential to address and redress the wrongs of the past, and they become impatient with attempts to underplay or minimize history (e.g., McPhail, 2004).

SIDEBAR 6.4   Culture Matters

"It is precisely in times of international crisis when the political stakes are highest and emotions run hot, that culture is likely to matter the most. It especially matters when the crises have to do with core cultural understandings—those, for example, central to the culture of diplomacy."

Source: K. Avruch, *Culture and Conflict Resolution,* 2004, p. 47.

Intercultural Competency

Discussions of cultural differences can be paralyzing. Just knowing how many different cultural forms we will encounter makes us wonder how we could ever succeed in communication. Sometimes you get the impression that everyone must learn to adapt to everyone else's cultural values and practices, but that is impossible and could lead to stereotyping, confusion, and even apathy. The opposite approach of assuming cultural similarity also fails except in the most homogenous groups.

Several scholars have addressed the issue of intercultural competency (e.g., Hajek & Giles, 2003; Pearce, 1994; Ting-Toomey & Oetzel, 2001), and the answer in every case involves flexibility and awareness.

Knowledge. Although you cannot know everything about all cultures, a certain amount of cultural knowledge is an important ingredient in developing intercultural competency. More important than knowledge about particular cultural groups is knowledge about certain variables, principles, or factors that affect cultural styles of communication, as these help us know what to pay attention to in intercultural exchanges. Ting-Toomey and Oetzel (2001) write that individualism-collectivism and power distance are central concepts for helping us understand how cultures communicate differently in conflict situations. We think that these concepts are helpful not only in conflict, but in all intercultural communication situations. Some knowledge about each of the topics touched upon in this chapter will help you become more sensitive and flexible in communication.

Yet, Pearce (1994) reminds us that "knowing about" cultures is not the same as "knowing how" to communicate interculturally. "Knowing about" is never sufficient to improve competency. "Knowing how" involves the practical wisdom that helps us make good judgments in complex situations. It enables us to assess the situation, decide what we hope to accomplish, and act both appropriately and effectively to achieve our goals. Practical knowledge requires two things—mindfulness and inventiveness.

SIDEBAR 6.5   Culture as a Bridge

"Culture has too often been described as an obstacle and used as a convenient explanatory for failures. But besides its scapegoat function, it can in fact serve as a bridge between the two negotiating sides. One party can rely on certain elements of the other's culture to start building that bridge."

Source: G. Faure, "International Negotiation," 2002, p. 412.

Mindfulness. Mindfulness means being open to new information and being able to take multiple perspectives (Langer, 1989). In other words, we actively think through a situation rather than respond intuitively or out of habit (Hajek & Giles, 2003; Pearce, 1994). Mindfulness is a kind of reflexivity in which we pay attention to our own thoughts and feelings while assessing the situation and the needs and goals of others as well. Mindfulness is essentially creative learning based on "an insatiable curiosity, constant invention, and attentive critique" (Lederach, 2005, p. 122).

Ting-Toomey and Oetzel (2001) outline several skill sets that contribute to mindfulness. These include observation, listening, and reframing. Mindful observation involves observing and interpreting, while postponing judgment. Mindful listening means attending to what other people say and how they say it, but, more, it involves responding, repeating as appropriate, and looking at the conversational pattern that emerges. Artful perception checking can aid listening as a tool of intercultural competence. Reframing means shifting the context for understanding what is being said. It means looking at a person's statements and actions from a different perspective. For example, instead of taking a statement literally, as individualists are apt to do, you could look at it in the context of individualism-collectivism or power distance. If a literal statement is a problem for you, what would happen if you looked at the comments not as a direct act, but an indirect one? Instead of looking at how a statement affects your own sense of face, look at it from the perspective of how it relates to the speaker's face.

Mindfulness, of course, requires presence, or the feeling of being in the situation rather than distracted from it. When you are present, the situation seems real, vivid, and immediate, and you sense that you are fully participating (Fontaine, 1993; Hajek & Giles, 2003). When we are fully present, we have a certain situational awareness that enables us to see *who* is involved, *what* they are doing, and *other things* that matter in the environment. Presentness involves something like "peripheral vision" that reveals "a sense of the larger picture and myriads of small openings and opportunities" (Lederach, 2005, p. 120). Mindless intuition will mislead; mindful intuition will lead to creative solutions.

Inventiveness. Good intercultural communication requires a certain creativity, an ability to create new forms that bridge established cultural patterns. Rather than thinking about one culture adapting to another, inventive communicators will work on ways to transcend old patterns that may not work very well for those involved. Many dialogue methods are precisely this: They invite participants into a new kind of conversation that will appear fresh, if not a little uncomfortable, to all the participants. We can think of new forms as constituting a "third culture" that will integrate features similar to our "home" cultures and some that are different from these.

Perhaps C. P. Snow (1964) was the first to introduce the idea of the third culture in his famous lectures, "The Two Cultures" and "A Second Look." Snow was alarmed by the gulf between opposing cultural forms. As a case in point, he described the polarization between science and humanities, but he also noted that polarization divides in other ways as well, including, for example, the rich and poor. The third culture is a creative fusion in which scientists and non-scientists can communicate with one another. If we take this as an analogy, third cultures might be possible among other cultural forms as well.

There is now a worldwide movement called "Third Culture Kids" (sometimes known as "Trans-Cultural Kids"), or individuals who have grown up in so many different cultures that they embody many integrated cultural forms. They become "culture-blended" persons and have resources to take leadership as adults in creating transcendent processes (Pollock & Van Reken, 2001). Such individuals, due to the power of their life experiences, are capable of being inventive in intercultural contexts. They have a lifescript that enables culture bridging; others can learn to be inventive in these ways as well.

The field of linguistics offers an analogy (Pearce, 1994). When different language-speaking groups encounter one another, they need a way to communicate, a "third language." One simple method is to establish a pidgin, which is a rudimentary vocabulary that both groups can use, but the pidgin is the primary language of neither group. On a more advanced level, a creole is a fully developed language arising from interaction between groups over time. Containing elements of both languages, the creole will eventually become the primary language shared by a joined group. In intercultural communication, then, we need to be inventive in establishing something like pidgins and creoles that groups can share.

When communicators are inventive, they surpass the idea that they must accommodate to the style of one of the cultures involved. Instead, they work on establishing, often tacitly, new patterns that work well for both. Intercultural families establish their own unique rituals, and organizations develop ways in which all workers can coordinate their efforts. Often new forms are established on the relational level between businesspersons, teachers and students, and friends. As we learned in Chapter 4, relationships have their own internal rules that provide great flexibility in how facework can be done, and knowledgeable, mindful, and inventive intercultural partners will be able to establish relationships that work. They will be what Jean Paul Lederach (2005) calls "smart flexible" (p. 85).

Lederach (2005) writes that inventiveness in complex situations requires the convergence of four disciplines. First, one must acknowledge the *centrality of relationships.* We never act alone, and our identities are a result of the complex webs of relationship in which we exist. In other words, it is not just you against me, but there is something larger of which we are both a part. Second, one must practice *paradoxical curiosity.* This means being curious about possibilities beyond either-or categories. Should I communicate directly or indirectly, invoke power or not, speak as an individual or as a member of the community? We should be curious about how we can overcome such dualistic contradictions. Third, Lederach suggests that we must provide *space for creativity.* We must open our attitudes and perspectives in ways that make new possibilities apparent. The fourth discipline involved in inventiveness is the *willingness to risk.* We should be willing to try new things withour certainty about the outcome. Together, these disciplines form what Lederach calls *moral imagination*. We like this term because it suggests that people are able to imagine forms of action and communication that are morally guided to achieve dignity, honor, and respect for all.

Arguably, good intercultural facework impacts the largest number of people—the system at its broadest level—in the arena of international relations, a subject to which we now turn.

SIDEBAR 6.6   Exploring Intercultural Competence

Get together with an intercultural group of friends. Tell them about the principles of competence outlined in this chapter: (1) knowledge, (2) mindfulness, and (3) inventiveness. Have the group members share stories of times they were able to achieve excellent intercultural communication and how these three principles helped them. What other principles do the group members think helped them?

❖ PUTTING A FACE ON INTERNATIONAL RELATIONS

People and Nations

International relations as a field rarely focuses on human communication, especially interpersonal. The predominant theories in political science look at the global scene as a field of sovereign states working to protect themselves and meet their own national interests. To do this, nations pressure others, form alliances, and make war against one another (Ruggie, 1998; Wendt, 1999). In economics, the world is seen—for good or ill—as an active field of international trade and increasing globalization (Krugman, 1996; Stiglitz, 2003). Political scientists and economists typically think of nation states, corporations, and international organizations as if they were individual persons.

Although helpful, the metaphor of nation-as-individual belies the complexity of the social construction of reality in the international realm. Ultimately, nations and other entities enact policies, ideas, goals, and values that are worked out interpersonally among national, international, and corporate leaders and others. If you have not had the chance to listen to segments of the tape-recorded telephone conversations of U.S.

President Lyndon Johnson or President Richard Nixon's meetings in the Oval Office, we encourage you to do so because these put a human face on national and international issues and make us very much aware of the importance of human social interaction in the world scene. If you prefer a more contemporary illustration, you might read Bob Woodward's *Plan of Attack* (2004), which details the ways in which the war on Iraq was planned and executed as a result of real conversations in the George W. Bush administration.

When you look deeply into processes of international relations, you will find that what persons do and say in conversations lies at the heart of global action. This is not to assert that the structures and larger systems that are out of the immediate control of any small group are unimportant, but that these larger structures are created by interaction at the social level. These larger structures also return in circular fashion to constrain and direct the actions of individuals and groups (Giddens, 1977). One of the lessons learned by looking at these "global" conversations is the importance of facework.

Consider: It is the mid-1960s, and the United States and Vietnam are engaged in a devastating war. Both countries desire to get out of the conflict, but actions taken by each side fail to achieve this goal. In the end, the war does not end for another 10 years! Fifty thousand American military personnel and perhaps 10 times as many Vietnamese military and civilians die. An exchange between President Johnson and Ho Chi Minh illustrates the role of personal face in this conflict. In 1967, President Lyndon Johnson sent President Ho Chi Minh of North Vietnam the following message:

> We have tried over the past several years, in a variety of ways and through a number of channels, to convey to you and your colleagues our desire to achieve a peaceful settlement. For whatever reasons, these efforts have not achieved any results. It may be that our thoughts and yours, our attitudes and yours, have been distorted or misinterpreted as they pass through these various channels. . . . I am [now] prepared to order a cessation of bombing against your country . . . as soon as I am assured that infiltration into South Vietnam by land and by sea has stopped. These acts of restraint on both sides would, I believe, make it possible for us to conduct serious private discussions leading toward an early peace. (McNamara, Blight, & Brigham, 1999, p. 219)

One week later, Ho Chi Minh responded:

In your message you seem to deplore the suffering and the destruction of Vietnam. Allow me to ask you: Who is perpetrating these monstrous crimes? It is the American and satellite troops. The United States Government is entirely responsible for the extremely serious situation in Vietnam. . . . The Government of the United States must stop the bombing, definitively and uncondi- tionally, and all other acts of war against the Democratic Republic of Vietnam . . . and withdraw from South Vietnam all U.S. and satellite troops. . . . The Vietnamese people will never submit to force; they will never agree to talks under the threat of bombs. (McNamara et al., 1999, p. 219)

We do not mean to reduce this war to the facework of two men, but in a dialogue on the war 30 years later, former Vietnamese and American officials and scholars had an opportunity to reach some remarkable con- clusions about the importance of personal communication (McNamara et al., 1999). It is clear that the war could have ended much earlier if the leaders of the two countries had been willing to talk directly with one another in a constructive and open way—fully conscious of their cultural differences—but this did not happen for some very good reasons.

The two countries were "speaking" to one another in two ways— with words and with military action. The Americans ran a relentless bombing campaign against North Vietnam to bring North Vietnamese leaders to the negotiating table essentially by force. This was a con- certed communication effort: "You will face an overwhelming cost if you do not negotiate." On this point, Nguyen Khac Huynh, a chief Vietnamese negotiator, explained why this strategy could never work:

The bombing of the North was an extremely serious violation of our national sovereignty. It demeaned our humanity. It wounded our national pride and our international reputation. So long as the United States bombed the North, we could not seriously entertain the possibility of entering into negotiations, at the end of which would be a compromise. (McNamara et al., 1999, p. 259)

Although the bombing was an honest attempt to end the war, it had the opposite effect, as it most certainly united the people of North Vietnam in opposition to the enemy.

Bombing was not the only way in which the administration tried to communicate with North Vietnamese leaders. In its extreme frustra- tion over its inability to reach the North Vietnamese leaders, the administration sent out a spate of intermediaries to tell North Vietnam that the United States was serious about wanting to enter negotiations.

This communication campaign came to be called "fandangle diplomacy" (Kraslow & Loory, 1968, p. 137). It seems that President Johnson often entertained Washington colleagues and foreign visitors by putting on a huge barbeque with everything—shows, food, dances, cattle, fireworks, and music—at his Texas ranch. This type of entertainment in Texas was called a fandangle (Kraslow & Loory, 1968, p. 137), a cultural form that could not have been farther from the experience of the North Vietnamese leaders. Of this campaign, Tran Quang Co, a former Vietnamese diplomat, said,

> So what was our analysis of this bewildering use of intermediaries by the U.S.? . . . The U.S. tried to convince the international community to justify the fact that the U.S., a big and powerful country, was fighting a small, poor country, and was doing so with such violence. The U.S. hoped that the international community would conclude that the U.S. had no choice but to "punish" Vietnam with the bombing—especially with the bombing. (McNamara et al., 1999, pp. 242–243)

In his analysis of the failure to reach the negotiating table, the former U.S. Secretary of Defense Robert McNamara wrote,

> There seems to have been an almost total disconnect between Washington and Hanoi. Preferring quiet, even secret talks, the North Vietnamese found themselves dealing with Lyndon Johnson, the embodiment of the American tendency to publicize and dramatize. But one finding in particular stands out: When in doubt of U.S. motives, as Hanoi usually was, they turned to their immediate reality—the bombing of the North and the arrival of U.S. troops in the South—as their primary evidence. (McNamara et al., 1999, p. 303)

SIDEBAR 6.7   At the Negotiation Table

"Feuds fascinate me sometimes. It is difficult for me to understand why anyone would want to feed one. They are overly stultifying and lead to chronic fatigue and stagnation. While I can understand the fear beneath them, they seem very contrary to the richness of life and the fullness of potential. Thus, staying in our dialogues, all of them, promises more and delivers more to everyone. It takes energy to sustain a dialogue but it also takes energy to sustain a feud."

Source: P. B. Kritek, *Negotiating at an Uneven Table,* 1994, p. 299.

Three Orientations: Enemy, Rival, Friend

Think about the facework associated with different kinds of relationships. How do you act when you think of the other as an enemy? As a rival? As a friend? Alexander Wendt (1999) extended this analogy to the world of international relations, in which countries relate to one another in these ways. We think the metaphors of enemy, rival, and friend are useful in helping us understand the nature of international facework.

Treating the Other as Enemy. The relationship of enemy is normally characterized by the desire to eliminate, disable, or conquer. An enemy is someone who is out to get us, so enmity by definition is face threatening in the extreme. Communication necessarily aims to justify self and destroy the other. Most of us do not really experience relationships of enmity in everyday life. Except for soldiers in war, street gangs, politicians, and certain corporate executives, ordinary people do not usually have real enemies (instead, they have "rivals" as defined in the following section).

However, the model of other-as-enemy has been the most common logic of international politics throughout history. Power and violence have been the key to national security, and alliances are merely instrumental agreements designed for mutual protection. This view, commonly called *realpolitik* in international relations, imagines the world as a theater of nations in struggle in which international systemic forces can only hope to keep mutual destruction at bay. All action is essentially self-protective.

Realpolitik is a socially constructed idea with consequences in the actions of nations. When taken seriously, as it usually is, this idea affects the larger system of national relationships in a way that makes enmity real. In a circular way, the system of enmity returns to constrain the way that national leaders think about their environment and what they do about it. In other words, treating others as an enemy becomes a vicious circle, even spiral, that rigidifies the ways in which international players can and do respond to one another.

This explains why the national players in Vietnam and the United States were highly constrained in the kinds of communication they were able to have with one another and why virtually every attempt was taken as a face threat. McNamara said during the Vietnam dialogues that one of the greatest tragedies of the war was that a collaborative solution would have been possible, but that neither side was able to understand this because they were locked into thinking only in terms of other-as-enemy. His advice: "Communicate with your adversary at a high level" (McNamara et al., 1999, p. 393). The skillful interventions of former President Carter in North Korea and Haiti probably prevented war in both cases, high-level talks with Slobodan Milosevic in Belgrade at least defused a crisis at that moment in the Balkan conflict, and Clinton's direct dialogues for 77 hours with Israeli Prime Minister Benjamin Netanyahu and Palestinian leader Yasser Arafat led to a signing of a land-for-peace deal that at least forestalled armed conflict in that region.

Avoiding direct communication can exacerbate the face threat. Trying to work around direct communication can appear to be manipulation, as we learned from Johnson's diplomacy in Vietnam. When you take another person seriously, you honor the person and open the possibility that differences might be resolved. This kind of action has great potential for changing the structure of relationships of nations from enmity to rivalry or even friendship.

SIDEBAR 6.8   Conflict Like a River

"We can view conflict as a river that has its calm moments and its rapids; sometimes it even has treacherous waterfalls that require avoidance at all costs. We can enter and exit this river at many different points, and just because we have made it through one challenging rapids and reached a calm stretch does not mean that another set is not around the next bend."

Source: B. S. Mayer, *Beyond Neutrality*, 2004, pp. 187–188.

Treating the Other as Rival. There is a fundamental difference between thinking of others as enemies and thinking of them as rivals. In a rivalry, there is competition for resources, but rivals do not normally move to eliminate or conquer the other. Even though there may be passionate battles over limited resources, in a rivalry we affirm the other's right to exist. This belief leads to a level of restraint in our actions. Sports competition is a perfect analogy. Rivalry can be fierce, and players can ply their greatest strength and skill to win; but in so doing, they affirm the value of the competition itself and the right of the other team to play. This may look like face threat, but in the sports world, at least, it is a high form of face building for both self and other.

In international relations, competition can be severe, even violent, but force is at least somewhat restrained. War is accepted as part of the rules, but as a limited tool not for demolishing other states, but winning needed resources for self-interest. The analogy between a hard-fought sports game and a hard-fought war is probably valid. If diplomats and state leaders take a rivalry stance, they will be more apt to talk about "rules of engagement," the "limits of conflict," and "national rights and responsibilities."

Market economics is predicated on the rival model of relationships. At the current time, economic globalization is guided by a logic of rivalry. Although open international trade, at least in theory, is supposed to lead to win-win outcomes, in rhetoric and practice it is often conducted as a rivalry. This is why we hear so frequently that nations must become more competitive. They are still feeling and acting protective. In some cases, while espousing the virtues of open trade, nations implement trade barriers to protect their own industries and agricultures (Krugman, 1996). International organizations such as the International Monetary Fund (IMF), the World Bank, and the International Trade Organization (ITO) are supposed to build emerging economies and stabilize world markets, but they often serve the interests of their most powerful members instead. As a result, many critics believe that these organizations are too often unwilling to engage in open dialogue about meeting the needs of impoverished nations (Stiglitz, 2003).

As part of its "Article 4 consultations," the IMF meets annually with every country of the world, purportedly to ensure compliance with articles of agreement, but these have become IMF monologues in which the nation's economy is graded and the agency's agenda is pushed (Stiglitz, 2003). This doesn't matter much to industrialized nations that are already powerful and can afford to ignore the IMF report card, but in many cases developing nations must submit to these demands. Imagine how this process might be different if participants took a more collaborative approach and opened dialogue between the international community and the representatives from the nation involved.

In fact, many economists believe that the international trade situation is not a rivalry at all. Leading economist Paul Krugman (1996) claims that nations can never be like corporations in this regard. Corporations can and do compete, but the concept of market competition is irrelevant to what states are. Indeed, nations do influence markets, but they do not compete, at least economically.

Treating the Other as Friend. This new model of international relations began to emerge in the twentieth century. A friendship relationship—among nations as among persons—is one governed by the rules of non-violence and mutual aid. Friendships are characterized by reciprocity, as friends share a certain amount of interdependence and mutual identification. Friends do have disagreements and differences, but they agree to resolve these without violence. The friendship model is "prosocial," meaning that we treat others with respect and help them even when doing so does not necessarily serve our own narrow interests (Wendt, 1999).

Wendt (1999) presents four master variables that he believes can make the difference in whether or not nations move from rivalry to friendship. These are interdependence, common fate, homogeneity, and self-restraint. When you think about it, these are factors that would probably predict the likelihood of a friendly relationship between persons as well. When are people most likely to do good mutual face-work? When the have a relatively high level of interdependence, a strong sense of common destiny, some degree of similarity or common ground, and the willingness to act mindfully.

Taking international relations back to the personal level, then, what would change if state leaders, diplomats, international governmental and non-governmental organizations, and others began to shift their conversational patterns from the rhetoric of rivalry to that of friendship? If international dialogues explored areas of interdependence, common fate, and homogeneity, they might open up new possibilities.

In their book, McNamara and colleagues (1999, pp. 391–398) identify six lessons learned from the Vietnam dialogues. As a group, these lessons summarize well the qualities of good facework in international conflict situations. Without distorting the original intent, we have re-worded these points to help us understand qualities of good facework:

1. Learn how leaders of other nations think, how they understand the world from their perspective, and what is important to them.

2. Communicate directly at the highest levels. Meet with leaders of other nations, treat others in those meetings with respect, and take their ideas and perspectives seriously.

3. Follow democratic principles in diplomatic relations and consult widely among legislators and citizens within your own country as part of the process.

4. Bring larger numbers of stakeholder nations into the dialogue. Do not isolate yourself.

5. Acknowledge that solutions are not always possible and that it is sometimes just necessary to keep the conversation going.

6. Understand the damage that can result from protracted, slow-motion conflicts. Act quickly, intelligently, and decisively when needed to resolve situations that promise to harm many nations and people if allowed to continue.

SIDEBAR 6.9   Cases of International Relations

This chapter features the Vietnam War as a case. Select another high profile case of international relations. The case may have been very successful or not. Research this case and write a paper on the role of facework in the situation. Some possibilities include

- The Palestinian-Israeli situation

- The war in Iraq

- The terrorist attacks of September 11, 2001, and the aftermath

- The war on terrorism

- The current China-Japan conflict

❖ PRINCIPLES FOR PRACTICE

Much of the scholarship on facework is highly cultural and framed in terms of Western cultural norms. Yet, cultures do differ in the ways in which they accomplish facework, and this is important because of our increasingly global world. In thinking about culture and international communication, we find the following principles helpful.

In intercultural encounters, act mindfully. Be aware of the contexts of meaning that shape your understandings and actions and consider various other contexts in which the interaction might be framed. Think about the possible perspectives of others in the same way.

Understand that with culturally different communicators—even in an adversarial relationship—each has a coherent cultural perspective with integrity and history. Everyone's interpretation makes sense to each participant within his or her own contexts of meaning and action.

Intelligent inventiveness is the key to creating a common ground of communication among culturally different people. Third cultures can be and are created in order to bridge difference, but this requires openness, adaptation, and creativity.

In intercultural encounters, consider new ways to frame the relationship that will open up fresh possibilities for action. Relational definitions create a context of meaning that shapes how we act toward others, especially when cultural difference is present; but relational definitions can change, and a key to effective intercultural and international communication is to reconsider the kind of relationship we think we are in.

PART IV

Principled Practice

7

Toward a Practical
Theory of Facework

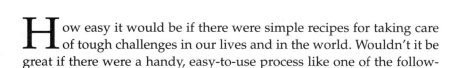

How easy it would be if there were simple recipes for taking care of tough challenges in our lives and in the world. Wouldn't it be great if there were a handy, easy-to-use process like one of the following (offered lightheartedly!)?

WAVE

Wonder

Actively pursue the problem

Verify that we see the problem

Expertly resolve the problem

GUTS

Go after the culprits

Uncover their motive

Tell them to stop that disruptive behavior

Shame them into being a better people

The truth is that working with human differences and the resulting problems requires more than cute acronyms. It requires us to work organically. Sometimes we have to decide how to act in the situation based on what is happening at that moment. If we are open to change, we can invite our relationships, organizations, and systems to adjust or even transform themselves as appropriate. If we hypothesize that it might be a suitable opportunity, we might pull out a reliable communication process or method. If we are feeling brave, we might try some strategy we have never tried before, all in the hopes of making an impact on a difficult situation.

In this book, the face dynamic is the common thread offered in the communication skills and methods, and is central to the practical theory we are calling *facework*. We all can put together a toolkit to bring to our communication interactions. Assembling the toolkit will require time, energy, commitment, and patience, but when ready to go, it can be helpful at all levels of communication: intrapersonal, interpersonal, group, workplace, family, and system contexts. The principles of good facework can provide a sturdy carrying case for the tools. This chapter will explore the practical nature of this assembly of tools and the corresponding theory that supports those principles.

SIDEBAR 7.1   The Toolkit Metaphor

Think of your own personal strategies and *ways of communicating* as an assortment of tools, and use the "toolkit" metaphor to explore the usefulness of your tools. List common tools on one side of the paper (hammer, tape measure, nail) and list a corresponding communication interaction you use that fits the metaphor. How useful is each type of communication? What gets built?

❖ PRACTICAL THEORY

How can we make complex judgments about how to act in the situations of life? The key for us is in practical theory (Barge & Craig, in press; Craig & Tracy, 1995; Cronen, 2001). Littlejohn and Foss (2005) summarize practical theory as follows:

A good practical theory enables you to (1) focus on a real situation you are facing; (2) explore what is unique about the situation;

(3) consider both the powers and limits of each action you could take; (4) take actions that enhance your life and achieve positive outcomes as well; and (5) learn from experience in the actual situations you face and prepares you to manage new ones. (pp. 28–29)

Littlejohn and Foss (2004) go on to say that practical theories enable us to act in coherent ways that lead to understanding, which in turn *might improve the situation.* We may bring about positive outcomes and develop new skills to manage the situation at hand as well as other situations in the future by our use of practical theories.

In this chapter we look back at the practical theory we have developed to see if it meets the test of four questions suggested by Cronen (2001):

1. Is the theory useful for identifying a system-in-view?

2. Does the theory construct judgments (systemic hypotheses) about the situation?

3. Does the theory implicate actions?

4. Does the theory implicate actions that lead to consequences that improve the situation?

❖ A THEORY OF FACEWORK

In Chapter 1, we introduced facework and the social construction of identity. We co-construct our identities through our interactions with others. We want to do it well, because we want to feel respected and to build the personal dignity and honor of the other. The interactions occur in the moment as a single speech act, or they may occur in the "expanded moment," as within larger contexts of action (conversations, episodes, lifescripts). Identity management is complex, indicating a need for healthy facework across the many different situations of our lives. Where and how do we select a starting place, or a hypothesis for acting in the situation? How do we know where and how to "join" others in the moment? Our Facework Matrix (Table 7.1) looks at the breadth and depth of the opportunities. We can work from a Focus of Attention, which identifies the parts of the system the communicator is trying to affect. Realizing that we do have the capacity to interact on multiple levels simultaneously, we can see that each provides the context for the other. We can also work from a Scope of Action—the broad contexts or ranges of action within which the facework opportunities exist.

Table 7.1   Facework Focus and Scope

Focus of Attention	Scope of Action			
	Act	Conversation	Episode	Lifescript
Person	An act that aims to affect self or other face	A conversation affecting face of self or other	An episode of conversations affecting self or other face	A long-term series of episodes creating an orientation to self and other
Relationship	An act of facework aiming to help define the relationship	A conversation of facework shaping the relationship	An episode of conversations defining the relationship	A long-term series of episodes defining relationships
System	An act of facework aiming to help define the system	A conversation of facework shaping the system	An episode of conversations shaping the system	A long-term series of episodes shaping larger systems

Usefulness in Bringing a System Into View

How does the practical theory of facework identify a current system-in-view? The social construction of identity challenges us to pay attention to the "how" of communication. If we attend to the manner of communication, we will be conscious of the system we are addressing. The following principles apply:

- *Create positive communities through constructive communication. Communities and systems of all types are made in interaction.*

- *Understand that every act is part of a larger set of interactions that, over time, connects people in relationships and communities.*

- *Communicate with others in a way that honors the complex identities of each person.*

Constructive facework requires that we think systemically, looking always for the situation at hand, the relationships present at the moment, and the system-in-view. People are complex, with a history of relationships and stories that are important to them.

Our colleague Wendell Jones is particularly interested in holding systems open to view, respecting the complexity of human systems and the nests of systems within systems. He looks carefully at groups and teams, positing that group disorder is *not* a natural state that must be thwarted in order to create processes that are productive. He sees that self-organization is inherent in human groups, and that leadership is challenged to maximize flexibility and creativity. This assumption asks leaders to provide open and natural environments for the teams.

Compared to traditional scenario planning (create a few possible futures and then determine which is most probable based on trends), Jones initiates what he calls *strategic conversations,* which make it possible to hold a multitude of possible futures open at once. Each future is kept in view, so that the people and work teams can compare their business idea, their organizational culture, and their emerging strategic plans to each scenario. He does not reduce the list to the most probable few, but adjusts and adapts the group processes based on the conversations that occur as the group considers the future scenarios. The plan is not the product, but the reflection about the institution and exploration of the nests of systems is the goal of the experience.

SIDEBAR 7.2   Shifts in Assumptions

"The next two decades will present challenges to Western thought unseen in almost four hundred years. Not since the seventeenth century, when such monumental figures as Newton and Descartes laid the foundations for the next four centuries of modern thinking, has a period of exploration and scientific discovery afforded more insight into what it is to be human and what it means to communicate and be in conflict."

Source: W. Jones & S. H. Hughes, "Complexity, Conflict Resolution, and How the Mind Works," 2003.

Constructing Judgments About Situations

Facework needs to be vigilant. It takes creativity and flexibility to understand the needs of the situation at hand and the system being addressed. Various principles for practice remind us that our facework accomplishments happen over time, through patterns of relationships that can be made and re-made. We can abandon patterns that do not work and create new forms of interaction (hypotheses) to improve personal and relational face:

- Facework in relationships is complex, contradictory, and extended.

- You can achieve positive facework practices by paying attention to patterns of interaction.

Tribal communities in the United States offer rich and complex stories of history and culture imbedded in nests of local, state, federal, and other tribal jurisdictions. A system of some 35 tribal colleges and universities has worked for at least three decades to make a difference in the quality of life on reservations throughout our land. For example, one tribal institution of higher education is interested in expanding from a technical institute to a 2-year community college. Who do you involve in the planning effort to move forward? Tribal leaders? Community College Association groups? Students and local families? Current faculty, staff, and administration? In this case, they decided to enter the system by beginning with the faculty of the institution. They explored the question of program expansion at a one-day retreat and discovered the priorities and visions of the faculty and administrators. After considering these results, they re-entered the system a month later and met for a day with the entire staff and representatives of the student body. They addressed concerns and also collaborated on visions and priorities. They now hypothesize that they can take these visions to the larger community and get its reaction and suggestions. These responses will guide a period of refinement and adjusting of priorities and vision. The tentative plan is to then have a larger community celebration in 6 months to introduce the more fully institutionalized community-based vision and priorities. Interviewing various parts of the system in the coming months to gauge the plan's suitability and appropriateness will test this plan. Interviews could take place at a student senate meeting, an athletics planning meeting, or could consist of individual queries to students, staff, faculty, or administration. The plan could change!

Early indications of interests, priorities, and challenges will guide the creation of the next steps. Engaging the larger system early on can help by scoping out before scoping in to the more timely decisions at hand. When you scope out to the larger system, the perspective broadens as questions are asked about relationships among entities (rather than individuals) and patterns of interaction (rather than examples of finite communication sequences).

Implicating Action

In Chapter 2 we offered the assumption that in choosing to privilege facework, we act with intention. We are conscious of the "other's" needs in the moment, and we hold a focus on the respect and dignity of the communication. Our ongoing social interactions *construct* a social world. This corresponding Principle for Practice proposes that we consciously choose our actions.

• Act with intent, but understand that you are always co-constructing something larger than the objective you are trying to achieve in the moment.

Honoring face does means more than just being nice. We are constructing an environment. We hope this is an environment where people can work and live together and feel respected. We once had a client at a major university who hired us to give a series of trainings to faculty. A horrible miscommunication occurred, culminating in a phone call to us from 700 miles away. We had planned on arriving the next day for the 2-day training, but, alas, the training had started that day! Some excellent facework occurred in this conversation, constructing an environment that was larger than the miscommunication at hand:

Tricia: Hello, Kathy. This is Tricia. How are you? *Where are you?*

Kathy: Hi Tricia, I am here in my office in Albuquerque. (pause) Why?

Tricia: Oh, no, I am here in the training room, with the participants for your workshop assembling as I speak!

Kathy: Oh, no, I thought I was arriving tomorrow morning!

Tricia: Well, this is unfortunate. Let's discuss a strategy to help us develop the best use of the time today. We can revise your training for them later.

What we loved about this conversation was that although it easily could have become blame centered (*Did my secretary give you the wrong dates? Didn't you read the e-mails correctly? Did you write it down wrong on your calendar?*), instead it looked for actions that would focus on the system-in-view. At that point, Tricia decided to focus on preserving our relationship, respecting our integrity, and helping the larger system function productively. It was so refreshing to bypass the blaming or fault-finding focus and instead look for ways to build the face of all of us.

Figure 7.1   Dimensions of Facework Environment

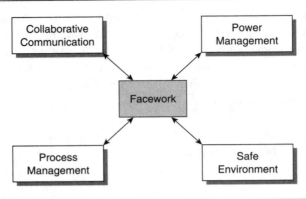

An important consideration in facework is to avoid focusing on "why things went wrong" and instead look for the positive resources for change. One tool to carry along in one's kit is *Characteristics of Constructive Communication*, which are exemplified in this facework principle:

- *Remember the reciprocal relationship among facework, collaborative communication, power management, process management, and a safe environment.*

In constructing this facework environment, our intent is focused on four dimensions of the communication environment (see Figure 7.1). In Chapter 2, we presented these four dimensions of facework, namely collaborative communication, safety, process management, and power management. Let's take one more look.

Collaborative communication privileges reliance on each other to accomplish shared goals. The implications for face entail a shared responsibility to treat each other in ways that honor *both* the personal and relational identity. A *safe environment* is constructed through facework when people are able to explore their differences safely. A commitment to honoring diversity and creativity is in place in a safe atmosphere. When individuals and systems make deliberate decisions about the processes and choices they will use to manage their interactions, they affect *process management.* By paying attention to the *how* of the communication interactions, facework actions prevent miscommunication and can clarify goals and conversation direction, so the participants are using their time in the most appropriate ways. *Power management* occurs when communicators are able to express their perspective and the good reasons behind their opinions. Facework asks us to listen with the intent to understand, while not necessarily agreeing. We often see that when communicators feel empowered, they say and hear what needs to be said and heard.

Consequences That Improve the Situation

The practical theory of facework proposes that situations within systems can be improved by thinking consciously about how to respond to others, keeping in mind the social construction of self and other in relationship and in community. Earlier we stated that *the Golden Rule lives!* Translated into facework principles, this means two things:

- *Treat others with the same dignity, honor, and respect you want for yourself.*

- *The way you communicate will affect your identity and that of others close to you.*

SIDEBAR 7.3   Embracing Respect and Responsibility

"Recent validation of students' insights comes from neuroscientists whose research has shown how the pain of social rejection affects the brain in much the same way as physical pain. Social pain is registered in the anterior cingulated cortex region of the brain, the same place where physical pain is registered. . . . Social pain may be more significant if it is revisited daily and remains unresolved."

Source: R. Heydenberk & W. Heydenberk, "Sticks and Stones May Break My Bones but Words Will Bruise My Brain," 2004, pp. 21–25.

If we are concerned with the manner in which individuals interact, we can think about the person we want to be, the kind of relationships we want to have, and the kind of community we want to make. These principles suggest that we can have a coherent lifescript. We can act in ways that reflect the kind of person we want to be.

- *Show the most appropriate aspect of your complex identity to others in each situation, but also aim for a coherent lifescript.*

We began this book discussing the lifescript of former President Jimmy Carter. By dedicating himself to a life philosophy and values, he is guided through life's choices. They may not always seem constant, but looking deeply, there seems to be consistency in the philosophy behind his choices. Consider the ghost of Ebenezer Scrooge's former business partner, Jacob Marley. In Charles Dickens's classic story, *A Christmas Carol* (Dickens, 2005), Marley offers this discovery from his post-death revelation:

> Mankind was my business. The common welfare was my business; charity, mercy, forbearance, and benevolence were, all, my business. The dealings of my trade were but a drop of water in the comprehensive ocean of my business!

Lifescripts are broader messages. They are our business. We acknowledge that some of the most important identity work occurs across time in conversations, episodes, and lifescripts.

With this intention to practice facework, we have the opportunity to communicate in a different, deeper realm. Margaret J. Wheatley (2002) speaks of her commitment to that type of conversation when she talks about the principles she has learned to emphasize before entering a conversation:

1. We acknowledge one another as equals.

2. We try to stay curious about each other.

3. We recognize that we need each other's help to become better listeners.

4. We slow down so we have time to think and reflect.

5. We remember that conversation is the natural way humans think together.

6. We expect it to be messy at times.

We live in a day when we are experiencing a strange and sad line between expressions of dissent and rude behavior in the name of dissent. Let us just look at the current 2-month period in which we are finishing the writing of this book, March and April of 2005 (see Walz, 2005): A conservative commentator was doused with salad dressing while speaking at a university public event. At another college address, a speaker got a pie in the face thrown by protesters. An audience member spit tobacco juice on an author signing her book at a public event. Looking at the broader context, we have a world with seemingly diminishing tolerance for opposing viewpoints. If we are to offer opportunities for constructive communication, intentionality about respecting and honoring difference could only improve our interactions.

❖ FACEWORK AS TRANSCENDENCE

Our communication challenges are not as simple or polarized as either "talking nice" or "throwing pies in the face of those with whom you disagree." The nuances and twists of our interaction choices confront us daily in so many ways. There is a regional collaborative project that has served multiple states for a number of years. It has accomplished its mission and made a significant impact on society. Some interest groups are eager to fight closure with attempts to raise money and stay open. Others want to be realistic, announce a job well done, and close the doors. Still others want to design a new format for the remaining energy and create a refined collaboration. They will enter this situation with a toolkit, with intentionality about honoring face, looking for the system-in-view, and crafting a hypothesis for how to begin interacting in the system. A first step might be to give honor to the history and accomplishments. *As we look at the past ten years, what are some of the stories of accomplishments and milestones that illustrate the mission of this organization?*

The organization might decide to be honest about the current situation and address it head-on: *As we make a decision about our future together, what are the constraints, trends, and realities that most affect our actions?* Another option it might examine is to address face needs up front, before entering into any decision making or planning: *Before we begin talking about our organization's challenging situation, let's create an environment in which we can speak and interact comfortably and respectfully. What needs to be in place for us to have the conversation we need and want to have? How can we make the best decisions as individuals and collectively as an organization?* The group members are still just discussing how to begin this conversation, but it is evident that they will enter tentatively and flexibly, ready to adapt or change as the system becomes clearer.

This tentativeness and openness is a form of transcendence. Carefully designed and developed processes can further generate new insights and new actions. Littlejohn (2004) sees this as *transcendent communication.* This type of communication does not eliminate difference. In this book, we have seen how facework engages difference and brings it to a place where it can be creatively tapped and explored to build the potential for paths forward previously unimagined. Not just for theorists or practitioners, the intention to transform the polarizations and differences means redefining what we are doing. We can redefine the questions that we ask and the forms of communication we utilize. The problem with our habit of relying on polarized views is that "one person's oppressive system is another person's revered tradition" (Littlejohn, 2004, p. 338). We probe the transcendent move that facework offers as a hope of escaping the damage that disrespect and incivility can lead to and illuminate the productive dialogue that can occur when people are afforded communication with dignity and civility.

SIDEBAR 7.4   Transcendent Communication

"We approach dialogue not only by experiencing difference but also by experiencing it in a new way. Namely, we hold what is important to us, while acknowledging the validity of the experience of others. I am convinced, however, that holding the tension by itself is not the whole of dialogue. We must transform this tension into a place where we can make meaning together, and this I believe is the heart of transcendence."

Source: S. W. Littlejohn, "The Transcendent Communication Project," 2004.

❖ PUTTING FACEWORK INTO PRACTICE IN UGANDA

Our conclusion to this chapter will offer noteworthy insight into the creative possibilities available to us when we are dedicated to face management in our communication. We bring to you a story from Africa, where a brutal guerrilla war has been raging for 18 years along the border between Uganda and Sudan. We are not suggesting that these fighters and communities have knowledge of the practical theory of facework, but we are encouraged by the capacity to transcend the war and violence with a respectful method of signaling a hope for peace.

The rebels speak earnestly of their faith in the Ten Commandments, at the same time that they kill and hack up civilians who get in their way. Their atrocities are numerous, from kidnapping children to indoctrinating youngsters as killers and commander's wives. In early 2005, the International Criminal Court at The Hague was investigating the war and was about to issue arrest warrants for rebel leaders. Some of the war victims were asking the International Court to back off. They recommended forgiveness, using an age-old ceremony with raw eggs. This capacity to forgive comes because the line between victim and killer is too blurred. It is remarkable to hear of the number of victims who have been hacked by rebels, who have seen their children carried off by the rebels, or who have endured years of suffering in the rebels' midst and can still say that their traditional justice and reconciliation ceremonies will have greater impact than arrests that would only make the rebels dig their heels in deeper.

What actions or interactions do have an impact on war, violence, or conflict that rages over human differences? If we enter the interactions at the place of polarization, we will create a more deeply polarized system. Promoting reconciliation is the ultimate facework action; it models a dignified move forward in tormented systems.

Recently, an assembly of Acholi chiefs put the notion of forgiveness into action. As they looked on, 28 young men and women who had recently defected from the rebels lined up according to rank on a hill-top overlooking this war-scarred regional capital, with a one-legged lieutenant in the lead and some adolescent privates bringing up the rear. They had killed and maimed together. They had raped and pillaged. One after the other, they stuck their bare right foot into a freshly cracked egg, with the lieutenant colonel, who had lost his right leg to a bomb, inserting his right crutch in the egg instead. The egg symbolizes innocent life, according to local custom, and by daubing themselves with it the killers are restoring themselves to the way they used to be. Next, the fighters brushed up against the branch of a pobo tree, which symbolically cleansed them. By stepping over a pole, they were welcomed back into the community. The victims and offenders can then sit down together to make amends. The wayward tribesman is required to pay the victim's kin compensation in the form of cows, goats, and sheep (Lacey, 2005).

These fighters used traditional cultural forms of facework to rebuild their relational community bridges. In the next and final chapter of this book, we look at other "artisans" and the kind of facework they demonstrate.

8

Guidelines From Artisans

Remember Jessica Fletcher, the murder mystery writer from the TV show *Murder, She Wrote*? In one episode, Jessica was teaching a class in criminology. One of her students confronted her the first day of class, saying, "How can you teach me? You are a writer, not a cop." After a pause came the response, "You're right. I don't know how much I can teach you. I do know I can tell you that you had ham and eggs for breakfast, you recently quit smoking, and you haven't been married very long." What did this response do from the standpoint of face management? It acknowledged the student's complaint (*You're right. I don't know how much I can teach you.*) and then the response framed the issue in a manner that did not cause a competitive conversation, did not offer a defensive reaction (*I do know I can tell you this . . .*). Jessica then told the student how she had come to those conclusions, which led him to finally remark that she probably *did* know something about being a detective. Jessica Fletcher *built something from the man's comment.* Her response was a bit creative, but was mostly practical. She built some credibility, created a base of knowledge about detective work, and modeled a way of communicating that was collaborative rather than competitive. At that moment, she was a facework artisan.

Whereas an artist creates for the sake of the art itself, the artisan builds something useful out of existing materials. The artisan assesses what is needed in the situation at hand, and determines the most useful contribution that can be fashioned. Artisans are often artful, and can be very creative, but they focus on utility and effectiveness. The artisans we introduce in this book manage face; they possess high skill and loads of patience.

Let's look at a simple example (Faber & Mazlish, 1999). Those of us who are parents are challenged daily with the task of using communication that *engages* rather than *closes down* further interactions. Look at the following example. The first interaction takes little patience or skill, and probably would flow easily from any of us.

Child: My turtle is dead. He was alive this morning.

Parent: Now don't get so upset, honey. Don't cry, I'll buy you another turtle.

Child: Wah! Wah! I loved my turtle.

Parent: Stop that crying! It was only a turtle.

Child: I don't want another turtle.

Parent: Now you are being unreasonable.

This second interaction engages the child with the intent to respect the child's feelings and experience while constructing a new conversation.

Child: My turtle is dead. He was alive this morning.

Parent: Oh, no, what a shock.

Child: He was my friend.

Parent: Losing a friend can hurt.

Child: I taught him to do tricks.

Parent: You two had fun together.

Child: I fed him every day.

Parent: You really cared about that turtle.

The second parent interacted as an artisan, accomplishing positive goals that ranged from the individual speech act (*I want to build my child's face by respect for his or her feelings*) to the lifescript (*as a parent, I want to show my child, as well as others with whom I communicate, that I honor them and our relationship*).

Throughout this book, we have introduced artisans in a variety of face management contexts. From our artisans, we learned four key lessons, which we have captured in things they said. These have become slogans for us, and in this final chapter we address these leanings in more depth.

❖ SLOGAN 1: I'M NOT HERE TO CALL YOU A THUG

In this book's introduction, we told the story of President Jimmy Carter and his encounter with military dictator Raoul Cedras. Carter's interactional accomplishment can be seen as impacting the *scope of action* at the level of the act, conversation, episode, and lifescript. His speech act, *I'm not here to call you a thug*, implied to Cedras a respect for personal identity and the desire to continue the conversation in a dignified manner. Carter's conversation built trust through a series of statements, created a context of safety and comfort. The entire episode offered an invitation to reconstruct democracy, with Cedras's choices being a key component. Finally, Carter's lifescript is one we see in the Carter Center's work and in Carter's books. Carter's principled life reveals his desire to secure worldwide safety, health, and freedom. How can we, as communicators, determine to interact in ways that "do not call people thugs"?

When one says, then, "I am not here to call you a thug," one is essentially saying, *I intend to be more flexible and open in how I conceive of you, my relationship with you, and what we might, if given a chance, do together.*

Honor Alternative Perspectives

Consider the example of a medical services office that had about 20 employees and was experiencing deep conflict about management style and leadership decisions. There was a chasm that had been strengthened by years of avoiding the issue. The agency decided to convene a process to explore the differences and create options for resolution. One of the exercises used that day was called "news of difference" (Pearce, 1995). The group members embarked on a discussion about the management of the conflict that was plaguing them. They had one rule for the discussion: *Each person must share a perspective or opinion that was different from the comments preceding it.* What a powerful discussion this was. The group members were able to feel and hear a vast array of good reasons for the perspectives people held. As each individual struggled to think of *another* perspective, each saw that the issue at hand was complex and full of opportunity for creative solutions. The group moved from a position of effectively calling one another thugs to exploring creatively a variety of perspectives that made solution possible.

SIDEBAR 8.1   Summarization Exercise

Choose a difficult conversation for your group to discuss. This issue should be something that each participant knows something about or can share some perspective on. A group size of 10 to 15 would be most efficient. Conduct the discussion in the following manner:

1. Each person will give his or her opinion or perspective on the issue, taking a couple of minutes to speak. Turn taking will occur popcorn-style: *Whoever is ready to speak next can jump in.*

2. Before the next person speaks, he or she needs to adequately summarize what the person who just spoke said. This summary needs to be objective, and should not hint at the speaker's own perspective. It should begin with a statement such as, *Let me see if I heard you correctly. You said that . . .*

3. At the end of the summarization, the speaker must ask for acknowledgment that the summarization was adequate: *Did I hear you right? Did I get the gist of what you meant?*

4. If the speaker indicates that the summarization did not exactly capture the perspective, the summarizer will give it another try until the summary is satisfactory.

5. Now, the second speaker can give his or her opinion on the issue.

6. When all members of the group have spoken, debrief the exercise.

   - How did it feel to summarize the person's comments before you could speak?
   - What was difficult?
   - Did you learn anything new about the issue?
   - Did you learn anything new about yourself or others?

Take a Risk

Carmen Lowry is an artisan who has provided valuable contributions to the world of constructive communication. Carmen works for the International Catholic Migration Commission and endeavors to bring community healing and transformation to struggling groups throughout the world. Her work in Maluku, Indonesia, aims to support sustainable relationships between communities that have experienced conflict resulting in displaced villages. In order to do this type of work, she concentrates on (1) building relationships between the communities; (2) ensuring that government entities responsible for the resettlement of displaced communities receive information about the situation in the areas in which they are working; (3) working with individual communities to help strengthen the leadership within each community; and (4) providing opportunities for communities to discover respectful, nonviolent ways to interact with government (in particular) and advocate for their needs. Carmen has helped us to explore the risks inherent in facework. She told us,

> I am struck by realizing that the risk of engaging in what I would see as respectful communication increases as the acts become less personal and more system-related. By this, I am referring to speaking with an individual, where being flexible in thought is seen to be highly desirable. However, systems often tend to reward those who are more direct and inflexible, so as to show strength of commitment, character, or such. (Personal communication, October 16, 2004)

Moving away from character attack does involve risk, but in many cases, it is worth it.

What are the risks that accompany good facework? We have already looked at Carter's work and the risks he takes by showing respect, even to seemingly unsavory characters. Even if our communication is respectful and invites safety, others may not engage in similar communication. People often feel that they have too much to lose. They know how to respond defensively or avoid the tough conversations. Not too many of us have training in good listening and constructive communication. The following risks are a part of high-quality face communication (Littlejohn & Domenici, 2001).

- *People risk change.* In constructive facework communication, people may change their opinion, they may question the way they used to do things, they may become sympathetic to someone they formerly despised, they may learn uncomfortable new things, they may find out that others agree with them less than they thought, they may experience new feelings, and they may go away stewing about something that never bothered them before.

- *People risk discovery.* They may find out things about themselves they had not been conscious of before. They may have to face facts formerly glossed over. They may have to make uncomfortable acknowledgments. They may be moved to tears.

- *People risk disclosure.* People can "say and hear what needs to be said and heard." Participants engaged in group processes could be asked, "What is at the heart of the matter for you?" and they need to figure this out for themselves.

We have offered methods and skills for constructive facework in this book that can help to manage those risks in face communication. Lederach (2005) reframed risk as *mystery.* When we embrace the risks that accompany our healthy interactions, we know we are stepping into the unknown, where the mystery awaits us. Often, our steps are worth the risk.

Hypothesize Freely

Assuming someone a thug is one possible hypothesis, but through reflection we move beyond this attribution to other possible ways of thinking about people. A sophisticated and powerful method of helping people preserve and strengthen their identity is through *reflecting.* We know that a system or a relationship can be understood in a variety of ways and offer reflection as a method to reach that understanding. Reflecting is a type of shared hypothesizing in which an interviewer reflects possible connections, contexts, and futures based on answers to systemic and appreciative questions (Pearce & Littlejohn, 1997). These reflections can give participants time to pause to consider relationships within the system that they might not have thought of. Reflecting teams have three or four people bouncing ideas off one another as the participants listen in. The reflectors must never be wedded to their reflections, but must shift and change reflections creatively and frequently. Sometimes these reflections will spark recognition in the participants, and sometimes they will not.

As part of a large collaborative planning initiative, a group of electronics associations addressed the issue of globalization and its impact on their companies and the industry, especially for U.S. innovation and education. The 60 leaders met for 2 days and alternated between sessions of planning and reality testing their plans. At the end of the first day, they experienced a "Reflecting Team" made up of the event sponsors and those most familiar with the system of stakeholders at the event. For about an hour, this small group sat in front of the room and "reflected" on the system in action that they had been observing for a day. They were guided by these words. Reflecting is a process by which a "system is shown to itself." It is a way for individuals and groups working within a system to get a *perspective* on "what is happening."

Reflecting is a way to help participants consider what their system looks like from various angles. There are many ways to look at a system-in-action. The reflecting team keeps shifting perspectives so that the participants can see the system from many points of view. The purpose of reflection is to stimulate thinking, broaden perspectives, and encourage creativity, not to control or influence the direction of the event.

SIDEBAR 8.2   Reflective Questions

1. What most intrigued you yesterday?
2. What surprised you?
3. What really stood out for you?
4. What interactions and connections especially sparked your curiosity?
5. How did [this development] most affect the system as you saw it?
6. What do you think you will be watching for today?
7. What do you hope the players learned yesterday?

Create a Container

Lucy Moore, a mediator and facilitator in Santa Fe, New Mexico, works mostly in the field of natural resources. Many of the cases she addresses have to do with dilemmas concerning the land in the Southwest. She often sits at the table with environmentalists and people from the traditional communities. The question on the table usually is, "How do we meet the community's needs and the environmentalist's goals?" In these cases, as well as many others that deal with diverse and complex interests, people concerned with facework aim to create a container large enough for all the stakeholder interests—at least at the beginning of the process. As meetings and discussions continue, options and ideas may be created that encompass many common and differing interests. Consider this scenario from Lucy's work (Moore, 2001).

"Just where is your land?" the polite, but confused Hispana from a Northern New Mexico village asked the environmentalist across from her. "I know where my land is, my community's land. What I don't understand is why you care so much about our land.

Where's your land?" The dispute was over a beautiful area in the mountains of Northern New Mexico. The community considered it a common area for grazing sheep and hunting; the environmentalists saw its potential as wilderness and wildlife refuge. (p. 26)

How can we create a container large enough to hold these needs and goals and their expression? Lucy believes that the first focus must be a long session of mutual understanding, where all stakeholders have a chance to explain themselves to each other. This is a common exchange in parts of the West where traditional communities are struggling to live off the land, and where activists are working to protect those resources, sometimes from local users. The "container" for this conversation is an agenda that provides opportunity to hear and say the good reasons for each side's perspective.

In Lucy's example, the local folks were Hispanic, but they were also rural, family-centered, and land-based in their economy and culture. The Anglo environmentalists were mostly urban, professional, uprooted, and relatively disconnected from extended family. The profound differences in values and worldview should not be ignored, but allowed to be explored and understood. Attributions of blame, retribution, and malice cut off any possibility of doing this.

❖ SLOGAN 2: DON'T OPEN
    PRESENTS IN FRONT OF OTHERS

We introduced the artisan Carla Shibuya in Chapter 2. Members of her family do not open their birthday presents in front of the guests, but wait until everyone has gone. Then the family can enjoy the gifts without the pressure of responding in certain ways. This is an example of a *delayed response technique*. One type of delayed response technique is to allow people to think about their response comfortably before offering it to the other(s). This "pondering time" can allow creativity, new options, and more depth in reasoning. One of our favorite delayed response techniques is the *Guided Tour*.

When a group of people is addressing a challenging issue, it is often difficult to present ideas for resolution without getting backlash or criticism from someone. Whether stated as a critique or as a constructive comment, these comments can stifle the conversation. We like to offer a new way to explore suggestions and options for forward movement, in a manner that allows everyone to ponder the ideas, without attacking the presenters. Here is the *Guided Tour* format:

1. *Brainstorming and prioritizing.* Small groups meet and address a question. They brainstorm possible solutions or ideas. Cluster these and prioritize the ideas down to the few that the group thinks will best address the issue. Display the few best ideas on a flip chart on the wall.

2. *Guided tour.* The entire group walks from station to station, where spokespersons (guides) offer the best ideas from their groups. The listeners offer curious questions designed to spur on further reality testing and development of the ideas. The guides do not respond, but simply write down the comments and questions.

3. *Refinement.* Based on the comments and questions from the entire group, the small groups refine and adapt or change their ideas or plans.

4. *Final presentation.* Each group again gives a tour of its priorities. This time, a discussion can occur. Steps 1–4 can be repeated.

Just the short amount of time groups spend in *listening without the pressure to respond* provides safety and comfort that empowers them to build on their ideas until they reach the most appropriate few. Another method to invite people to delay their responses is by using metaphor.

Consider this meeting where a complicated discussion about protecting an endangered species was made easier by using metaphor. Someone in the group stated that the decision at hand was like the comparison of *"Do I want to buy you a drink?"*(take care of the one species that is becoming endangered) or *"Do I want to buy the whole bar drinks?"* (get involved protecting the various species in the Southwest). By using the "buying drinks" metaphor, they were able to discuss the matter without feeling the weight of the difficult issue at hand. Others in the group then felt secure enough to enter the conversation, and added their own considerations. *"Maybe what I need is to buy only my own drink"* (I will act within the best interests of my own agency), *"I think we need to get involved with the whole liquor industry and change some policy"* (we should all work together to address the Endangered Species Act). When it was appropriate to address the endangered species issue directly, group members felt comfortable enough to speak freely because they had used a metaphor to discuss the difficult issue.

Our slogan, *Don't open presents in front of others,* is in itself a useful metaphor. It has allowed us to examine a wide range of research on gift giving and face management. This topic has implications for all sorts of communication interactions. Sunwolf (2004) looked at the relational strategies inherent in the giving and receiving of gifts. Though this issue has primarily been researched by marketing scholars (if we know why and how people give gifts, we can more effectively get them to purchase our product), we see vast implications for face research when looking at the relational dimension of *receiving* gifts. Sunwolf sees that, as a form of exchange, gifts both create and re-create relationships. A gift, which we also offer as a metaphor for a communication interaction, can match or diverge from our relational goals. When we receive a gift, we usually show delight and appreciation. These responses may be *deceptive* messages that mask disappointment or confusion, wanting to protect the giver's feelings. Just as in a communication situation, when surprised with a request for a comment, or a situation that requires communication competence, we might be surprised and be unable to contribute. This response to Sunwolf's survey, from a 10-year-old female, illustrates the face dimension of gifting (Sunwolf, 2004, p. 12):

> Christmas. I have to open each gift from extended family members in front of them. The entire situation is flawed. I will undoubtedly like one gift better than the other and will appreciate one the most. But because every giver is watching, I must equally show interest in all of the gifts. As a result, the people who gave the best gift won't ever know how much I appreciate it, because to them their gift is no different than any of the others.

Thelma Domenici, a corporate coach, specializes in contemporary social skills development. She sees that consideration of the giver is the most important factor. She admonishes us to respect the giver, "If you can remember that the gift is given with love, thought, and joy, you can receive it in that spirit. Then, what you do with it afterward may not be so troublesome." But what to do with an unwanted gift (along with the pressure to speak or contribute publicly) is still a matter of heated opinion. The popular television sitcom *Seinfeld* popularized the term "re-gifting." You can give a gift you received to someone else. When Thelma was asked what to do if the giver remarks on the absence of the gift they gave you, she paused and answered, "It would be wonderful if the giver did not put you in that spot" (Seldman, 2004). In the hopes of creating a face managing interaction, we invite consideration of our slogan, "Don't open presents in front of others." Surprises, confrontations, and pressure to perform usually threaten a person's desired identity.

❖ SLOGAN 3: THE BALL IS OVER THE FENCE

We are happy to relate a story about one of our daughters who is particularly adept as a face manager. At age 14 she was able to frame an issue as a problem to be solved, rather than as a blame-oriented statement. Instead of assigning the blame, in the case of Trevor who kicked the ball over the fence, she was able to report on the incident merely as "the ball is over the fence." We are committed to communicating in a way that does not search for right or wrong, or even who is responsible. In our communication, we want to model a quest to "manage difference" rather than "fix blame." Think of the implications in a variety of other situations.

1. The employer reports to the staff about an employee who is consistently late to meetings. The employer wants to invite the staff to address the problem:

He could say, James is consistently late to meetings and we need to figure out how to get him to be on time.

He did say, Our meetings are so important that we want to make sure all of you are included in the discussion. If someone is late, it stalls us. What should we do to ensure consistency in timely attendance?

2. The presidents of two neighboring countries are addressing border issues for which they share a common concern:

The president could say, You are ruining the environment on your side of the border. You have got to be more diligent!

The president did say, We share a common concern for upholding the environmental richness of our border lands. How can we work together to address the problem of ecological soundness on both sides of the border?

3. Two roommates are discussing the loud parties that one roommate has every weekend:

One roommate could say, You are so disrespectful of my apartment and my privacy! You have got to stop having parties.

The roommate did say, We have a difficult problem here that we need to discuss. We have some differences of opinion about roommate privacy and social events at our apartment. Can we discuss how to make sure that each of us has our needs for privacy met?

4. A large group of corporate executives is in a lengthy discussion about the need to downsize its central office:

The CEO could say, Because of the poor performance of this division, we are either going to have to reassign the division or fire a bunch of you.

The CEO did say, We are in a difficult position and need to make some tough adjustments. Due to budget reductions and corresponding performance issues, we are facing some downsizing decisions. I would like to include you all in a discussion about the situation and the process of making the decisions.

The important consideration to think about when we say, "The ball is over the fence," in whatever situation, is to frame issues in a way that enables collaboration.

Another of our wonderful artisan colleagues is a psychologist and consultant for the Mennonite Church. Carolyn Heggen assists struggling groups all over the world with training community trauma healers. She will meet with the therapists, counselors, medical personnel, and organizers of international relief initiatives to train them and counsel them in trauma management and mental health assistance. At the time of this writing, Carolyn is in India and the Andaman Islands, working with the disaster relief crews from the terrible tsunami of December 2004. One of the issues she faces is the internal conflict among the mental health workers. Working under very stressful conditions, these workers need their own communication and coping skills to deal with interpersonal challenges from within their group. Before the tsunami hit, she was working with a group of missionaries who were experiencing particularly tough conflict dynamics within their own group. Instead of inviting them to address their conflicts directly, Carolyn invited them into a conversation that transcended the conflict, enabling them to participate without fear of blame, guilt, or defensiveness. Her agenda with them went something like this:

1. Discuss as a group the vision for their work together. *Keep the discussion on the vision level. If your work here were very successful, what would it look like five years from now?*

2. Share positive resources, in small groups. *As you move toward this vision, what has been particularly successful? What has worked?*

3. Prioritize the characteristics that enable success. *In these successful stories, what was in place that made that success happen? What characteristics did people possess that made them able to act and communicate constructively?*

4. Compare the results. In the large group, list the characteristics of positive behavior and communication (both personal and for the group). *Cluster and discuss these.*

5. As individuals, determine where improvement is needed. *Look at the list and identify two areas where you need to improve.*

6. Build accountability. *Meet in dyads, with someone with whom you feel safe and comfortable. Discuss these areas that need improvement and steps you could take to build improvement. Ask each other how you could support the other's plan for improvement.*

7. Commitments. *On a slip of paper, write out your private commitment to improve and share it with one other person. Bring it to the altar, where all commitments will be offered to God and burned.*

8. As a large group, share any insights or commitments that people feel comfortable offering.

We remember the 1993 movie *Rising Sun,* where Sean Connery is an expert on Japanese culture and is teamed up with a Los Angeles detective to investigate a murder. Connery offers a memorable line: *In Japan, when something goes wrong, we fix the problem. In America, when something goes wrong, you fix the blame.* As communicators create their interactions, deliberately and with a systems view in mind, they can offer respect for personal and group identities by interacting in a way that separates the people from the problem. A regional director in the U.S. Fish and Wildlife Service, Dale Hall, is fond of commenting on this issue in a similar way. He says, "You'd be surprised how much you can get accomplished when you don't care who gets the credit." When we don't have to worry about who gets the blame, or who gets the credit, we can put a more significant effort behind the issue or challenge at hand.

SIDEBAR 8.3   Building Accountability

When we reframe problems as issues to be addressed collaboratively, how do we build personal accountability so people can learn from their mistakes and move forward productively? Isn't it important for people who are consistently late for meetings to see how their behavior affects others? Shouldn't the "partying roommate" know how disrespectful it is to keep everyone awake with loud music? Shouldn't the military dictator of Haiti be forced to realize how the rest of the world sees his horrible human rights violations?

❖ SLOGAN 4: IT'S A BEAUTIFUL
DAY IN THE NEIGHBORHOOD

Fred Rogers, fondly known as "Mr. Rogers," died on February 27, 2003, at the age of 74. CNN says of him, "He is always gentle, always courteous, and always a role model" (CNN.com Entertainment). With his cardigan sweater and comfortable shoes, Mr. Rogers liked all of us just the way we are. He invites us to aspire to be friends with others who are interested in us for who we really are . . . someone who makes us feel really accepted for the essence of our being. In his writings, *Thoughts for All Ages*, Rogers reminds us:

- The older I get, the more convinced I am that the space between communicating human beings can be hallowed ground.

- Young children sometimes look sheepish when they confide in us, as though they already suspect there's something amiss in their interpretation of the world; and have you noticed how often older children, even teenagers, will start a confidence with a question like "Promise you won't laugh if I tell you?"

- People have said "Don't cry" to other people for years and years, and all it has ever meant is "I'm too uncomfortable when you show your feelings: Don't cry." I'd rather have them say, "Go ahead and cry. I'm here to be with you."

- When you combine your own intuition with sensitivity to other people's feelings and moods, you may be close to the origins of valuable human attributes such as generosity, altruism, compassion, sympathy, and empathy. (*Mr. Rogers' Neighborhood*, 2005)

How can we model Mr. Rogers's face communication in our lives and work? We offer a variety of methods and models in this book. In this final chapter, we offer ways we can communicate honestly about difficult subjects, helping us to build trusting and confident interactional accomplishments. We can privilege storytelling. One of our colleagues, Kevin Barge, a communications professor at the University of Georgia, created a method of storytelling questioning that allows people to hear one another in new, more personal ways. It is a powerful method for helping a group explore its experiences and hopes. This tool helps us ask good questions and produce effective listening. We want to understand, respect, and appreciate the life experiences and stories of others. It is within these stories that important connections and relationships are taken seriously (Littlejohn & Domenici, 2001, p. 39).

Table 8.1   Story Questions

Situations

Explore what the situation means to the person.
Let's discuss this situation and what it means to you. How do you make sense of these circumstances?

Ask about the relationships among people.
How would you describe your relationship with Bob?

Ask about the relationship among groups of people.
You've said that the families must work very closely with the directors of the youth outreach program. How would you describe their relationship?

Time

Ask about the history of the situation.
What has brought you to this point?

Explore why this issue has become important at this time.
You said that this issue has become important only during the last five months. Why do you think this has become an important issue now?

Ask when certain people noticed this issue.
This issue has gotten the attention of a number of people. Who was the first to notice this issue? Who was the last to notice this issue?

Place

Explore where people talk about this issue.
You've said that many people in the community are talking about the need to have additional recreational services. Where are people talking about this issue?

Who's there

Focus on who is presently involved with the situation.
You've said that several people have been involved in conversations about drug resistance programs. Who specifically has been involved?

Ask people who else needs to be involved with the situation.
You identified several people who have been involved with these conversations regarding recreational facilities for kids. Who else needs to be involved with these conversations who has not been so far?
Who else needs to be invited to participate in these talks?

Encourage parties to speak from personal experience.
You've talked about how other people would like to see how city government works. Tim, I'm curious about what your personal hopes are for how the city government will work in the future.

Explore other people's perspectives on the situation.
How do you think youth in the Waco area would perceive this situation?

(Continued)

Table 8.1 (Continued)

What they do together

Explore the timeline (keep time alive).
I would appreciate it if you would talk about the situation.
When did it begin? What happened first? What happened next?

Focus on behaviors.
Jake, you said that you felt mistreated by this group. How did they show their
disrespect to you?

Hope for the future

Invite a search for shared concerns and futures.
People who disagree often have the same basic concerns. I want to take a few
minutes to explore this possibility here. Could you each take a minute or two to talk
about what you think your shared concerns might be?

Move past the problem.
You talked about how much you appreciated the efforts of the people involved with
the youth theatre program. And those people have said they also felt they were
appreciated then. I'm wondering what would need to change for that former level of
appreciation to return? If it did return, what would be different for you both?

Ask questions about the positive.
What was it about the Neighborhood Association that attracted you? I'm curious
about what you really loved about the Neighborhood Association then.

Focus on the future.
It would be very helpful, I think, if each of you could talk for a few minutes about
the kind of crime prevention program you would like to see developed here.

When questioning, we explore stories about *situations*, at a particular *time*, occurring in a specific *place*, involving people *who are there*, *what they do*, and their *hopes for the future*.

Another method of inviting personal stories comes from John Winslade and Gerald Monk. Searching for an innovative approach to conflict management, they have developed a process called Narrative Mediation. In contexts where conflict is being explored, this type of process privileges stories that create reality rather than report on the accurateness of that reality (Winslade & Monk, 2000). The participants' stories are not viewed as either true or false accounts of an objective reality, but rather as the way in which people have organized their experiences in story form. A tightly woven story is one where judgment and accusation are so intertwined around the parties to a conflict that there does not seem to be any space for other descriptions. A person interested in constructing an environment that honors face will "open up spaces" in the tightly woven stories (Winslade & Monk, 2000, p. 5). One method we use to move participants past their tightly woven stories is to ask dialogical questions. These questions invite people to move past negative and accusatory stories to discussions of positive resources and possibilities for the relationships. The following dialogical questions can offer forward movement and positive face implications (Domenici & Littlejohn, 2005).

- Invite the parties to speak only for themselves.

Ron, you've been referring a lot to what the doctors want. I wonder how your personal view might differ from those of other members of the medical staff on this issue. What personal experiences of yours might be different from those of the other members of the family?

- Encourage parties to speak from personal experience.

Tim, what is it like to work in this office?

- Encourage parties to speak directly to one another.

Joanne, what would you like to ask Robert about where he stands right now? Could you ask him directly? And Robert, I'm hoping you might take a few moments to answer her question the best you can.

- Invite a search for shared concerns.

People who disagree often have the same basic concerns. I want to take a few minutes to explore this possibility here. Could you each take a minute or two to talk about what you think your shared concerns might be?

- Ask parties to reveal their uncertainties, gray areas, dilemmas, and doubts.

We've spent quite a bit of time exploring your feelings about this issue, and it's clear that you feel strongly about it. I don't want us to forget those feelings, but for the moment, I would like to shift gears a little and ask each of you to think about your uncertainties and gray areas—you know, your doubts. What aspects of this issue are not so clear for you?

- Elicit parties' true curiosities, rather than posturings.

I'd like to suggest a little session here that is sometimes helpful. I would like each of you to think about what the others have been saying and what you'd like to ask them about. Here's what's different. We're going to have a rule that you can't ask questions to make a point, but you have to ask questions out of true curiosity, to really understand more about where the other person is coming from. What do you think? Would you like to give this a try?

- Uncover complexities and help the parties become less polarized.

George, you've said that you're interested in keeping your full-time job and working evenings and weekends to build your ceramics business. I wonder if you could talk a little more about how your week would go and what your schedule would look like with this plan.

- Elicit creative thinking rather than standard arguments.

Margaret, you have been really clear about the reasons you want a private office. I wonder if you have a few ideas about how the office as a whole might be arranged.

A final example of artisans comes to us from the far north, from the organized village of Kake, Alaska (American Indian Report, 2004). In 1999, the village re-established its traditional method of dispute resolution, which brings together victims, wrongdoers, families, religious leaders, and social service providers in a forum that restores relationships and community harmony. *Kake Circle Peacemaking* has worked both to support victims and to rehabilitate offenders. The program is based on establishing a support system for both victims and perpetrators. The outcomes have been overwhelming. The recidivism (repeating the offending behavior) rate of the 65 circles that have been held in the past 6 years is nearly zero. Before instituting the Peacemaking Circles, the rate was more than 50%. The strength of the Circles is that they pull community together to form a network of support. Mr. Rogers would be proud.

❖ DOING FACEWORK THAT MATTERS

In this small volume we have explored many ways in which people affect their personal, relational, and community identities in communication. Facework is not an incidental or ancillary goal of communication. It is central to all human social interaction. In the social construction of reality, building identity is omnipresent. Once we realize this, we think differently about communication. In addition to accomplishing whatever instrumental goals we want to achieve, effective communication creates a sense of who we are individually and together. This is surely an outcome worthy of careful consideration as we relate both to ourselves and to others.

References

Adler, P. S. (2003). Unintentional excellence: An exploration of mastery and incompetence. In D. Bowling & D. Hoffman (Eds.), *Bringing peace into the room* (pp. 57–77). San Francisco: Jossey-Bass.

Adler, P. S., & Birkhoff, J. E. (2002). *When knowledge from "here" meets knowledge from "away."* Portland, OR: National Policy Consensus Center.

Agne, R. R., & White, C. H. (2004). The nature of facework in discussion of everyday problems between friends. *Southern Communication Journal, 70*, 2–14.

Albrecht, T. L., Burleson, B. R., & Goldsmith, D. (1994). Supportive communication. In M. L. Knapp & G. R. Miller (Eds.), *Handbook of interpersonal communication* (2nd ed., pp. 419–449). Thousand Oaks, CA: Sage.

Altman, I. (1993). Dialectics, physical environments, and personal relationships. *Communication Monographs, 60*, 26–34.

Altman, I., & Taylor, D. (1973). *Social penetration: The development of interpersonal relationships.* New York: Holt, Rinehart and Winston.

American Indian Report. (2004). *Kake circle peacemaking.* Fairfax, VA: Falmouth Institute.

Applegate, J. L. (1982). The impact of construct system development on communication and impression formation in persuasive messages. *Communication Monographs, 49*, 277–289.

Arnett, R. C., & Arneson, P. (1999). *Dialogic civility in a cynical age.* New York: SUNY.

Asher, W. (1986). The moralism of attitudes supporting intergroup violence. *Political Psychology, 7*, 403–425.

Avruch, K. (2004). *Culture and conflict resolution.* Washington, DC: United States Institute of Peace.

Barge, J. K. (2001). Creating healthy communities through affirmative conflict communication. *Conflict Resolution Quarterly, 19*, 89–102.

Barge, J. K., & Craig, R. T. (in press). Practical theory. In L. R. Frey & K. N. Cissna (Eds.), *Handbook of applied communication.* Mahwah, NJ: Lawrence Erlbaum.

Bateson, M. D. (1990). *Composing a life.* New York: Plume.

Baxter, L. (1993). The social side of personal relationships: A dialectical perspective. In S. Duck (Ed.), *Social context and relationships: Understanding relationship processes* (pp. 139–169). Newbury Park, CA: Sage.

Bochner, A. P. (2002). Perspectives on inquiry: III. The moral of stories. In M. Knapp & J. Daly (Eds.), *Handbook of interpersonal communication* (3rd ed., pp. 73–101). Thousand Oaks, CA: Sage.

Bourdieu, P. (1991). *The logic of practice.* Cambridge, UK: Polity.

Brown, P., & Levinson, S. (1987). *Politeness: Some universals in language usage.* Cambridge, UK: Cambridge University Press.

Buber, M. (1947). *Between man and man.* New York: Macmillan.

Burgoon, J. K., & Bacue, A. E. (2003). Nonverbal communication skills. In J. O. Greene & B. R. Burleson (Eds.), *Handbook of social interaction skills* (pp. 179–220). Mahwah, NJ: Lawrence Erlbaum.

Burleson, B. R. (2003). Emotional support skills. In J. O. Greene & B. R. Burleson (Eds.), *Handbook of communication and social interaction skills* (pp. 551–594). Mahwah, NJ: Lawrence Erlbaum.

Burleson, B. R., & Goldsmith, D. J. (1998). How the comforting process works: Alleviating emotional distress through conversationally induced reappraisals. In P. A. Andersen & L. K. Guerrero (Eds.), *Handbook of communication and emotion: Research, theory, applications, and contexts* (pp. 245–280). San Diego, CA: Academic Press.

Cameron, D. (2001). *Working with spoken discourse.* London: Sage.

Capra, F. (1996). *The web of life.* New York: Anchor Books.

Carbaugh, D. (Ed.). (1990). *Cultural communication and intercultural contact.* Hillsdale, NJ: Lawrence Erlbaum.

Carson, C. L., & Cupach, W. R. (2000). Facing corrections in the workplace: The influence of perceived face threat on the consequences of managerial reproaches. *Journal of Applied Communication Research, 28,* 215–234.

Carstensen, L. L., Gottman, J. M., & Levenson, R. W. (1995). Emotional behavior in long-term marriage. *Psychology and Aging, 10,* 140–149.

Carter, J. (1993). *Talking peace: A vision for the next generation.* New York: Penguin.

Carter, J. (1998). *Living faith.* New York: Three Rivers Press.

Chelune, G. J., et al. (1979). *Self-disclosure: Origins, patterns, and implications of openness in interpersonal relationships.* San Francisco: Jossey-Bass.

CNN.com/Entertainment. (2005, March 16). *Mr. Rogers dies at age 74.* Retrieved March 16, 2005, from http://www.cnn.com/2003/SHOWBIZ/TV/02/27/rogers.obit/

Collier, M. J. (1991). Conflict competence within African, Mexican, and Anglo-American friendships. In S. Ting-Toomey & F. Korzenny (Eds.), *Cross-cultural interpersonal communication* (pp. 132–154). Newbury Park, CA: Sage.

Conlon, D. E., & Ross, W. H. (1997). Appearances do count: The effects of outcomes and explanations on disputant fairness judgments and supervisory evaluations. *International Journal of Conflict Management, 8,* 5–31.

Cooley, C. H. (1902). *Human nature and the social order.* New York: Scribner.

Covey, S. (1990). *The 7 habits of highly effective people: Powerful lessons in personal change.* London: Simon & Schuster.

Covey, S. R. (1991). *Principled-centered leadership.* New York: Simon & Schuster.

Craig, R. T. (1999). Communication theory as a field. *Communication Theory, 9,* 119–161.

Craig, R. T., & Tracy, K. (1995). Grounded practical theory: The case of intellectual discussion. *Communication Theory, 5,* 248–272.

Cronen, V. E. (2001). Practical theory, practical art, and the pragmatic-systemic account of inquiry. *Communication Theory, 11,* 14–35.

Cronen, V. E., Pearce, W. B., & Snavely, L. (1979). A theory of rule structure and forms of episodes, and a study of unwanted repetitive patterns (URPs). In D. Nimmo (Ed.), *Communication yearbook 3* (pp. 225–240). New Brunswick, NJ: Transaction Press.

Crum, T. F. (1987). *The magic of conflict.* New York: Simon & Schuster.

Cupach, W. R., & Metts, S. (1994). *Facework.* Thousand Oaks, CA: Sage.

Daniels, S. E., & Walker, G. B. (1996). Collaborative learning: Improving public deliberation in ecosystem-based management. *Environmental Impact Assessment Review, 16,* 71–102.

Daniels, S. E., & Walker, G. B. (2001). *Working through environmental conflict: The collaborative learning approach.* Westport, CT: Praeger.

Delia, J. G., Kline, S. L., & Burleson, B. R. (1979). The development of persuasive communication strategies in kindergartners through twelfth-graders. *Communication Monographs, 46,* 241–256.

Dickens, C. (2005). BookRags book notes on *A Christmas Carol. BookRags.* Stave 1, pg. 71. Retrieved May 3, 2005, from http://www.bookrags.com/notes/xmas/

Domenici, K., & Littlejohn, S. W. (2001). *Mediation: Empowerment in conflict resolution.* Prospect Heights, IL: Waveland.

Domenici, K., & Littlejohn, S. W. (2005). *Facilitators' toolkit.* Unpublished document. Albuquerque, NM.

Donohue, W. A., & Kolt, R. (1992). *Managing interpersonal conflict.* Newbury Park, CA: Sage.

Duck, S. (1994). *Meaningful relationships: Talking, sense, and relating.* Thousand Oaks, CA: Sage.

Ellis, D. G. (1999). *From language to communication.* Mahwah, NJ: Lawrence Erlbaum.

Emmers-Sommer, T. M. (2003). When partners falter: Repair after a transgression. In D. J. Canary & M. Dainton (Eds.), *Maintaining relationships through communication: Relational, contextual, and cultural variations* (pp. 185–205). Mahwah, NJ: Lawrence Erlbaum.

Estes, H. E. (2004, March/April). Advanced practice registered nurses: Current problems and new solutions. *NC Medical Journal, 65*(2).

Faber, A., & Mazlish, E. (1999). *How to talk so kids will listen and listen so kids will talk.* New York: HarperCollins.

Faure, G. (2002). International negotiation: The cultural dimension. In V. A. Kremenyuk (Ed.), *International negotiation: Analysis, approaches, issues* (pp. 392–415). San Francisco: Jossey-Bass.

Feeney, J. (1999). Adult attachment, emotional control, and martial satisfaction. *Personal Relationships, 6,* 169–185.

Ferdig, M. A. S. (2001). *Exploring the social construction of complex self-organizing change: A study of emerging change in the regulation of nuclear power.* Doctoral dissertation, Benedictine University, Lisle, IL.

Fincham, F. D. (2004). Communication in marriage. In A. L. Vangelisti (Ed.), *Handbook of family communication* (pp. 83–104). Mahwah, NJ: Lawrence Erlbaum.

Fine, M. G. (1995). *Building successful multicultural organizations: Challenges and opportunities.* Westport, CT: Quorum.

Fisher, R., & Ury, W. (1991). *Getting to yes: Negotiating agreement without giving in.* New York: Penguin.

Fitness, J. (2001). Betrayal, rejection, revenge, and forgiveness: An interpersonal script approach. In M. R. Leary (Ed.), *Interpersonal rejection* (pp. 73–103). New York: Oxford University Press.

Fitness, J., & Duffield, J. (2004). Emotion and communication in families. In A. L. Vangelisti (Ed.), *Handbook of family communication* (pp. 473–494). Mahwah, NJ: Lawrence Erlbaum.

Fontaine, G. (1993). The experience of a sense of presence in intercultural and international encounters. *Presence: Teleoperators and Virtual Environments, 1,* 1–9.

Foss, S. K., & Foss, K. A. (2003). *Inviting transformation: Presentational speaking to a changing world.* Prospect Heights, IL: Waveland.

Foss, S. K., & Griffin, C. L. (1995). Beyond persuasion: A proposal for an invitational rhetoric. *Communication Monographs, 62,* 2–18.

French, J. P. R., Jr., & Raven, B. (1960). The bases of social power. In D. Cartwright & A. Zander (Eds.), *Group dynamics* (pp. 607–623). New York: Harper & Row.

Gardner, K. A., & Cutrona, C. E. (2004). Social support communication in families. In A. L. Vangelisti (Ed.), *Handbook of family communication* (pp. 495–512). Mahwah, NJ: Lawrence Erlbaum.

Gastil, J. (2000). *By popular demand: Revitalizing representative democracy through deliberative elections.* Berkeley: University of California Press.

Gergen, K. J. (1999). *An invitation to social construction.* Thousand Oaks, CA: Sage.

Giddens, A. (1977). *Studies in social and political theory.* New York: Basic Books.

Giddens, A. (2003). *Runaway world: How globalization is reshaping our lives.* New York: Routledge.

Gibb, J. R. (1961). Defensive communication. *Journal of Communication, 11,* 141–148.

Goffman, E. (1959). *The presentation of self in everyday life.* New York: Overlook.

Goffman, E. (1967). *Interaction ritual: Essays on face-to-face behavior.* New York: Pantheon.

Goldsmith, D. J. (1994). The role of facework in supportive communication. In B. R. Burleson, T. L. Lalbrecht, & I. G. Sarason (Eds.), *Communication of social support: Messages, interactions, relationships, and community* (pp. 29–49). Thousand Oaks, CA: Sage.

Goldsmith, D. J. (1995). The communicative microdynamics of support. In B. Burleson (Ed.), *Communication yearbook 19* (pp. 414–433). Thousand Oaks, CA: Sage.

Goldsmith, D. J., & MacGeorge, E. L. (2000). The impact of politeness and relationships on perceived quality of advice about a problem. *Human Communication Research, 26,* 234–263.

Goodall, J. (1986). *The chimpanzees of Gombe: Patterns of behavior.* Cambridge, MA: Belknap Press.

Grice, H. P. (1975). Logic and conversation. In P. Cole & J. Morgan (Eds.), *Syntax and semantics* (Vol. 3, pp. 41–58). New York: Academic Press.

Gross, E., & Stone, G. P. (1964). Embarrassment and the analysis of role requirements. *American Journal of Sociology, 70,* 1–15.

Hajek, C., & Giles, H. (2003). New directions in intercultural communication competence: The process model. In J. O. Greene & B. R. Burleson (Eds.), *Handbook of communication and social interaction skills* (pp. 935–958). Mahwah, NJ: Lawrence Erlbaum.

Hale, C. (1980). Cognitive complexity-simplicity as a determinant of communication effectiveness. *Communication Monographs, 47,* 304–311.

Hall, E. T. (1959). *The silent language.* Garden City, NY: Doubleday.

Hall, E. T. (1966). *The hidden dimension.* New York: Random House.

Hall, E. T. (1976). *Beyond culture.* Garden City, NY: Anchor.

Harré, R. (1984). *Personal being: A theory for individual psychology.* Cambridge, MA: Harvard University Press.

Hecht, M. L. (1993). A research odyssey: Towards the development of a communication theory of identity. *Communication Monographs, 60,* 76–82.

Hecht, M. L., Collier, M. J., & Ribeau, S. A. (1993). *African American communication: Ethnic identity and cultural interpretation.* Beverly Hills, CA: Sage.

Hecht, M. L., Jackson, R. L., & Ribeau, S. A. (2003). *African American communication: Exploring identity and culture.* Mahwah, NJ: Lawrence Erlbaum.

Hecht, M. L., Ribeau, S., & Alberts, J. K. (1989). An Afro-American perspective on interethnic communication. *Communication Monographs, 56,* 385-410.

Heydenberk, R., & Heydenberk, W. (2004, Fall). Sticks and stones may break my bones but words will bruise my brain. *ACResolution,* pp. 21–25.

Ho, D. (1976). On the concept of face. *American Journal of Sociology, 81,* 867–884.

Hofstede, G. (1991). *Cultures and organizations: Software of the mind.* London: McGraw-Hill.

Hu, H. C. (1944). The Chinese concept of "face." *American Anthropologist, 46,* 45–64.

Huston, T., & Houts, R. (1998). The psychological infrastructure of courtship and marriage: The role of personality and compatibility in romantic relationships. In T. Bradbury (Ed.), *The developmental course of marital dysfunction* (pp. 114–151). New York: Cambridge University Press.

Husserl, E. (1969). *Ideas: General introduction to pure phenomenology.* London: Collier Books.

Institute of Cultural Affairs International (2005). A global strategy for human development: The work of the Institute of Cultural Affairs. Retrieved February 20, 2005 from http://www.ica-international.org/

Irizarry, C. A. (2004). Face and the female professional: A thematic analysis of face-threatening communication in the workplace. *Qualitative Research Reports in Communication, 5,* 15–21.

Jabusch, D. M., & Littlejohn, S. W. (1995). *Elements of speech communication.* San Diego, CA: Collegiate.

Jameson, J. K. (2004). Negotiating autonomy and connection through politeness: A dialectical approach to organizational conflict management. *Western Journal of Communication, 68,* 257–277.

Johnson, F. L. (2000). *Speaking culturally: Language diversity in the United States.* Thousand Oaks, CA: Sage.

Jones, E. E., & Pittman, T. S. (1982). Toward a general theory of strategic self-presentation. In J. Suls (Ed.), *Psychological perspectives on the self* (pp. 231–263). Hillsdale, NJ: Lawrence Erlbaum.

Jones, W., & Hughes, S. H. (2003). Complexity, conflict resolution, and how the mind works. *Conflict Resolution Quarterly, 20,* 485–494.

Jones, W. H., Kugler, K., & Adams, P. (1995). You always hurt the one you love: Guilt and transgressions against relationship partners. In J. P. Tangney & K. W. Fischer (Eds.), *Self-conscious emotions: The psychology of shame, guilt, embarrassment, and pride* (pp. 301–321). New York: Guilford.

Jones, W. H., Moore, D. S., Schratter, A., & Negel, L. A. (2001). Interpersonal transgressions and betrayals. In R. M. Kowalski (Ed.), *Behaving badly: Aversive behavior in interpersonal relationships* (pp. 233–255). Washington, DC: American Psychological Association.

Jorgenson, J., & Bochner, A. P. (2004). Imagining families through stories and rituals. In A. L. Vangelisti (Ed.), *Handbook of family communication* (pp. 513–538). Mahwah, NJ: Lawrence Erlbaum.

Jung, E., & Hecht, M. L. (2004). Elaborating the communication theory of identity: Identity gaps and communication outcomes. *Communication Quarterly, 52,* 265–283.

Keltner, J. W. (1994). *The management of struggle: Elements of dispute resolution through negotiation, mediation, and arbitration.* Cresskill, NJ: Hampton.

Kerssen-Griep, J. (2001). Teacher communication activities relevant to student motivation: Classroom facework and instructional communication competence. *Communication Education, 50,* 256–273.

Kilmann R., & Thomas, K. (1977). Interpersonal conflict-handling behavior as reflections of Jungian personality dimensions. *Psychological Reports, 37,* 971–980.

Kim, M. (1993). Culture-based interactive constraints in explaining intercultural strategic competence. In R. Wiseman & J. Koester (Eds.), *Intercultural communication competence* (pp. 132–150). Newbury Park, CA: Sage.

Kochman, T. (1981). *Black and white styles in conflict.* Chicago: University of Chicago Press.

Kochman, T. (1990). Force fields in black and white communication. In D. Carbaugh (Ed.), *Cultural communication and intercultural contact* (pp. 193–217). Hillsdale, NJ: Lawrence Erlbaum.

Kraslow, D., & Loory, S. H. (1968). *The secret search for peace in Vietnam.* New York: Random House.

Kritek, P. B. (1994). *Negotiating at an uneven table: Developing moral courage in resolving our conflicts.* San Francisco: Jossey-Bass.

Krugman, P. (1996). *Pop internationalism.* Cambridge: MIT Press.

Kuhn, M. H., & McPartland, T. S. (1954). An experimental investigation of self-attitudes. *American Sociological Review, 3,* 68–76.

Lacey, M. (2005, April 18). Atrocity victims in Uganda choose to forgive [Electronic version]. *New York Times.* Retrieved May 3, 2005, from http://www.globalpolicy.org/intljustice/icc/2005/0418forgive.htm

Laing, R. D. (1971). *The politics of the family.* New York: Vintage.

Langer, E. J. (1989). *Mindfulness.* Reading, MA: Addison-Wesley.

Lebra, T. S. (1976). *Japanese patterns of behavior.* New York: Oxford University Press.

Lederach, J. P. (2005). *The moral imagination: The art and soul of building peace.* Oxford, UK: Oxford University Press.

Lim, T. S. (1994). Facework and interpersonal relationships. In S. Ting-Toomey (Ed.), *The challenge of facework: Cross-cultural and interpersonal issues* (pp. 209–229). Albany: State University of New York Press.

Lim, T., & Bowers, J. (1991). Face-work: Solidarity, approbation, and tact. *Human Communication Research, 17,* 415–450.

Littlejohn, S. W. (2004). The Transcendent Communication Project: Searching for a praxis of dialogue. *Conflict Resolution Quarterly, 21,* 337–359.

Littlejohn, S. W., & Domenici, K. (2001). *Engaging communication in conflict: Systemic practice.* Thousand Oaks, CA: Sage.

Littlejohn, S. W., & Foss, K. A. (2005). *Theories of human communication.* Belmont, CA: Wadsworth.

Lumsden, G., & Lumsden, D. (1993). *Communicating in groups and teams: Sharing leadership.* Belmont, CA: Wadsworth.

Mayer, B. S. (2004). *Beyond neutrality: Confronting the crisis in conflict resolution.* San Francisco: Jossey-Bass.

MacGeorge, E. L., Lichtman, R. M., & Pressey, L. C. (2002). The evaluation of advice in supportive interactions: Facework and contextual factors. *Human Communication Research, 28,* 451–463.

McCullough, M. E., Hoyt, W. T., & Rachal, K. C. (2000). What we know (and need to know) about assessing forgiveness constructs. In M. E. McCullough, K. I. Pargament, & C. E. Thoresen (Eds.), *Forgiveness: Theory, research, and practice* (pp. 65–88). New York: Guilford.

McNamara, R. S., Blight, J. G., & Brigham, R. K. (1999). *Argument without end: In search of answers to the Vietnam tragedy.* New York: Public Affairs Books.

McNamee, S., & Gergen, K. J. (1999). *Relational responsibility: Resources for sustainable dialogue.* Thousand Oaks, CA: Sage.

McPhail, M. L. (2004). Race and the (im)possibility of dialogue. In R. Anderson, L. A. Baxter, & K. N. Cissna (Eds.), *Dialogue: Theorizing difference in communication studies* (pp. 209–224). Thousand Oaks, CA: Sage.

Mead, G. H. (1934). *Mind, self, and society.* Chicago: University of Chicago Press.

Mehrabian, A. (1972). *Nonverbal communication.* Chicago: Aldine/Atherton.

Metts, S. (1994). Relational transgressions. In W. R. Cupach & B. H. Spitzberg (Eds.), *The dark side of interpersonal communication* (pp. 217–239). Hillsdale, NJ: Lawrence Erlbaum.

Metts, S., & Grohskopf, E. (2003). Impression management: Goals, strategies, and skills. In J. O. Greene & B. R. Burleson (Eds.), *Handbook of communication and social interaction skills* (pp. 357–402). Mahwah, NJ: Lawrence Erlbaum.

Millar, F. E., & Rogers, L. E. (1987). Relational dimensions of interpersonal dynamics. In M. E. Roloff & G. R. Miller (Eds.), *Interpersonal processes: New directions in communication research* (pp. 117–139). Newbury Park, CA: Sage.

Milne, A. L. (2004). Mediation and domestic abuse. In J. Folberg, A. L. Milne, & P. Salem (Eds.), *Divorce and family mediation* (pp. 304–335). New York: Guilford.

Minnesota Indian Affairs Commission. (1999). *Minnesota Indian Affairs Council.* Retrieved December 28, 2005, from http://www.cri-bsu.org/IA_web/htdocs/protocol.html

Montgomery, B. M. (1998). Dialogism and relational dialectics. In B. Montgomery & L. Baxter (Eds.), *Dialectical approaches to studying personal relationships* (pp. 155–183). Mahwah, NJ: Lawrence Erlbaum.

Montgomery, B., & Baxter, L. (Eds.). (1998). *Dialectical approaches to studying personal relationships.* Mahwah, NJ: Lawrence Erlbaum.

Moore, L. (2001, Fall). Higher ground. *ACResolution,* pp. 26–27.

Mr. Rogers' Neighborhood. (2005, March 16). Retrieved March 16, 2005, from http://pbskids.org/rogers/all_ages/thoughts4.htm

Noller, P., & Roberts, N. (2002). The communication of couples in violent and nonviolent relationships: Temporal associations with own and partners' anxiety/arousal and behavior. In P. Noller & J. Feeney (Eds.), *Understanding marriage: Developments in the study of couple interaction* (pp. 348–380). New York: Cambridge University Press.

Oetzel, J. G., Ting-Toomey, S., Yokochi, Y., Masumoto, T., & Takai, J. (2000). A typology of facework behaviors in conflicts with best friends and relative strangers. *Communication Quarterly, 48,* 397–419.

O'Hair, D., & Friederich, G. W. (1992). *Strategic communication in business and professions.* Boston: Houghton Mifflin.

O'Keefe, B. J. (1988). The logic of message design: Individual differences in reasoning about communication. *Communication Monographs, 55,* 80–103.

Our community. (2001). Our Community Pty Ltd, retrieved February 25, 2005, from http://www.ourcommunity.com.au

Pearce, W. B. (1989). *Communication and the human condition.* Carbondale: Southern Illinois University Press.

Pearce, W. B. (1994). *Interpersonal communication: Making social worlds.* New York: HarperCollins.

Pearce, W. B. (1995). Bringing news of difference: Participation in systemic social constructionist communication. In L. R. Frey (Ed.), *Innovations in group facilitation* (pp. 94–116). Cresskill, NJ: Hampton.

Pearce, W. B. (2005). The coordinated management of meaning (CMM). In W. B. Gudykunst (Ed.), *Theorizing about intercultural communication* (pp. 35–54). Thousand Oaks, CA: Sage.

Pearce, W. B., & Cronen, V. E. (1980). *Communication, action, and meaning.* New York: Praeger.

Pearce, W. B., & Kearney, J. (2004). Coordinated management of meaning: Extensions and applications [Special issue]. *Human Systems: Journal of Systemic Consultation and Management, 15,* 1–208.

Pearce, W. B., & Littlejohn, S. W. (1997). *Moral conflict: When social worlds collide.* Thousand Oaks, CA: Sage.

Penman, R. (1990). Facework and politeness: Multiple goals in courtroom discourse. *Journal of Language and Social Psychology, 9,* 15–38.

Penman, R. (1994). Facework in communication: Conceptual and moral challenges. In S. Ting-Toomey (Ed.), *The challenge of facework: Cross-cultural and interpersonal issues* (pp. 15–46). Albany: State University of New York Press.

Petronio, S. (2000). *Balancing the secrets of private disclosures.* Mahwah, NJ: Lawrence Erlbaum.

Petronio, S. (2002). *Boundaries of privacy: Dialectics of disclosure.* Albany: State University of New York Press.

Philipsen, G. (1987). The prospect for cultural communication. In D. L. Kincaid (Ed.), *Communication theory: Eastern and Western perspectives* (pp. 245–254). New York: Academic Press.

Pilotta, J. (2001). *Communication and social action research.* Cresskill, NJ: Hampton.

Pollock, D. C., & Van Reken, R. E. (2001). *Third culture kids: The experience of growing up among worlds.* Yarmouth, ME: Intercultural Press.

Public Conversations Project. (1999). *PCP dialogue toolbox: Other exercises and tools for mulling.* Cambridge, MA: Author.

Public Conversations Project. (2003). *Constructive conversations about challenging times: A guide to community dialogue.* Cambridge, MA: Author.

Rawlins, W. K. (1992). *Friendship matters: Communication, dialectics, and the life course.* Hawthorne, NY: Aldine.

Robins, L. S., & Wolf, F. M. (1988). Confrontation and politeness strategies in physician-patient interactions. *Social Science and Medicine, 27,* 217–221.

Roloff, M. E. (1981). *Interpersonal communication: The social exchange approach.* Beverly Hills, CA: Sage.

Roloff, M. E., & Cloven, D. H. (1994). When partners transgress: Maintaining violated relationships. In D. J. Canary & L. Stafford (Eds.), *Communication and relational maintenance* (pp. 23–43). San Diego, CA: Academic Press.

Roloff, M. E., Soule, K. P., & Carey, C. M. (2001). Reasons for remaining in a relationship and responses to relational transgressions. *Journal of Social and Personal Relationships, 18,* 362–385.

Ruggie, J. G. (1998). *Constructing the world polity.* London: Routledge.

Rusbult, C. E., Bissonnette, V., Arriaga, X. B., & Cox, C. (1998). Accommodation processes during the early years of marriage. In T. Bradbury (Ed.), *The developmental course of marital dysfunction* (pp. 74–113). New York: Cambridge University Press.

Schlenker, B. R. (1980). *Impression management: The self-concept, social identity, and interpersonal relations.* Monterey, CA: Brooks/Cole.

Scholtes, P. R., Joiner, B. L., & Streibel, B. J. (2003). *The team handbook* (3rd ed.). Madison, WI: Oriel.

Schonbach, P. (1990). *Account episodes: The management or escalation of conflict.* Cambridge, UK: Cambridge University Press.

Schutz, W. (1958). *A three-dimensional theory of interpersonal behavior.* New York: Rinehart.

Searle, J. (1969). *Speech acts: An essay in the philosophy of language.* Cambridge, UK: Cambridge University Press.

Seldman, C. (2004, January 2). Do we re-gift that dreadful present or grin and bear it? *Albuquerque Tribune,* p. C8.

Shimanoff, S. (1988). Degree of emotional expressiveness as a function of face-needs, gender and interpersonal relationship. *Communication Reports, 1,* 43–53.

Shotter, J. (1989). Social accountability and the social construction of "you." In J. Shotter & K. J. Gergen (Eds.), *Texts of identity* (pp. 133–151). London: Sage.

Sillars, A., Canary, D. J., & Tafoya, M. (2004). Communication, conflict, and the quality of family relationships. In A. L. Vangelisti (Ed.), *Handbook of family communication* (pp. 413–446). Mahwah, NJ: Lawrence Erlbaum.

Snow, C. P. (1964). *The two cultures and a second look.* Cambridge, UK: Cambridge University Press.

Spano, S. (2001). *Public dialogue and participatory democracy: The Cupertino Community Project.* Cresskill, NJ: Hampton.

Stewart, J., & Thomas, M. (1990). Dialogic listening: Sculpting mutual meanings. In J. Stewart (Ed.), *Bridges, not walls* (pp. 192–210). New York: McGraw-Hill.

Stiglitz, J. E. (2003). *Globalization and its discontents.* New York: W. W. Norton.

Stohl, C. (1986). The role of memorable messages in the process of organizational socialization. *Communication Quarterly, 34,* 231–249.

Stone, E. (1988). *Black sheep and kissing cousins: How our family stories shape us.* New York: Penguin.

Sundarajan, N., & Spano, S. (2004). CMM and the co-construction of domestic violence. *Human Systems: The Journal of Systemic Consultation & Management, 15,* 45–58.

Sunwolf. (2004). *Gift giving unwrapped: Relational strategies and stresses during the giving or receiving of gifts.* Unpublished paper presented to the Western States Communication Association Annual Convention, Albuquerque, NM.

Ting-Toomey, S. (1985). Toward a theory of conflict and culture. In W. B. Gudykunst, L. Stewart, & S. Ting-Toomey (Eds.), *Communication, culture, and organizational processes* (pp. 71–86). Beverly Hills, CA: Sage.

Ting-Toomey, S. (1986). Conflict communication styles in Black and White subjective cultures. In Y. Y. Kim (Ed.), *Interethnic communication: Current research* (pp. 75-95). Newbury Park, CA: Sage.

Ting-Toomey, S. (1988). Intercultural conflict styles: Face-negotiation theory. In Y. Y. Kim & W. Gudykunst (Eds.), *Theories in intercultural communication* (pp. 213–235). Newbury Park, CA: Sage.

Ting-Toomey, S. (1994). Face and facework: An introduction. In S. Ting-Toomey (Ed.), *The challenge of facework: Cross-cultural and interpersonal issues* (pp. 1–14). Albany: State University of New York Press.

Ting-Toomey, S. (1999). *Communicating across cultures.* New York: Guilford.

Ting-Toomey, S., & Cocroft, B. (1994). Face and facework: Theoretical and research issues. In S. Ting-Toomey (Ed.), *The challenge of facework: Cross-cultural and interpersonal issues* (pp. 287–306). Albany: State University of New York Press.

Ting-Toomey, S., & Kurogi, A. (1998). Facework competence in intercultural conflict: An updated face-negotiation theory. *International Journal of Intercultural Relations, 22,* 187–225.

Ting-Toomey, S., & Oetzel, J. G. (2001). *Managing intercultural conflict effectively.* Thousand Oaks, CA: Sage.

Tomkins, S. (1979). Script theory: Differential magnification of affects. In H. E. Howe & R. A. Dienstbier (Eds.), *Nebraska Symposium on Motivation: Vol. 26* (pp. 201–236). Lincoln: University of Nebraska Press.

Tracy, K. (2002). *Everyday talk: Building and reflecting identities.* New York: Guilford.

Tracy, K., & Tracy, S. J. (1998). Rudeness at 911: Reconceptualizing face and face attack. *Human Communication Research, 25,* 225–251.

Tracy, S. J., & Trethewey, A. (2005). Fracturing the real-self↔fake-self dichotomy: Moving toward "crystallized" organizational discourses and identities. *Communication Theory, 15,* 168–195.

Trees, A. R., & Manusov, V. (1998). Managing face concerns in criticism: Integrating nonverbal behaviors as a dimension of politeness in female friendship dyads. *Human Communication Research, 24,* 564–583.

Triandis, H. C. (1995). *Individualism and collectivism.* Boulder, CO: Westview.

Umpleby, S., & Oyler, A. (2005). *A global strategy for human development: The work of the Institute of Cultural Affairs.* Retrieved December 12, 2005, from http://www.ica-international.org/history_2.htm

Van de Vliert, E., & Euwema, M. C. (1994). Agreeableness and activeness as components of conflict behaviors. *Journal of Personality and Social Psychology, 66,* 674–687.

Verderber, R. F., & Verderber, K. S. (1992). *Inter-act: Using interpersonal communication skills.* Belmont, CA: Wadsworth.

Wagoner, R., & Waldron, V. R. (1999). How supervisors convey routine bad news: Facework at UPS. *Southern Communication Journal, 64,* 193–209.

Waldron, V. R. (1991). Achieving communication goals in superior-subordinate relationships: The multi-functionality of upward maintenance tactics. *Communication Monographs, 58,* 289–306.

Walz, K. (2005, April 26). Suppressing dissent popular, but deadly. *Albuquerque Journal*, p. A7.

Watzlawick, P., Beavin, J., & Jackson, D. (1967). *The pragmatics of human communication*. New York: W. W. Norton.

Wendt, A. (1999). *Social theory of international politics*. Cambridge, UK: Cambridge University Press.

Wenzhong, H., & Grove, C. L. (1991). *Encountering the Chinese: A guide for Americans*. Yarmouth, ME: Intercultural Press.

Werner, C. M., & Baxter, L. A. (1994). Temporal qualities of relationships: Organismic, transactional, and dialectical views. In M. L. Knapp & G. R. Miller (Eds.), *Handbook of interpersonal communication* (pp. 323–379). Thousand Oaks, CA: Sage.

Wheatley, M. J. (2002). *Turning to one another: Simple conversations to restore hope to the future*. San Francisco: Berrett-Koehler.

Windt, T. O. (1972). The diatribe: Last resort for protest. *Quarterly Journal of Speech, 58*, 7–8.

Winslade, J., & Monk, G. (2000). *Narrative mediation: A new approach to conflict resolution*. San Francisco: Jossey-Bass.

Wolin, S. J., & Bennett, L. A. (1984). Family rituals. *Family Process, 23*, 401–420.

Woodward, B. (2004). *Plan of attack*. New York: Simon & Schuster.

Yankelovich, D. (1999). *The magic of dialogue: Transforming conflict into cooperation*. New York: Simon & Schuster.

Index

About the Authors

Kathy Domenici and Stephen W. Littlejohn work with individuals, groups, organizations, and communities throughout the United States as well as abroad to promote constructive communication and effective planning. Dedicated to improving human relationships and organizational effectiveness, they use a systems approach in their work. They have written two books about their experience: *Engaging Communication in Conflict: Systemic Practice* (Sage, 2001) and *Mediation: Empowerment in Conflict Management* (2001). A third book, *Communication, Conflict, and the Management of Difference,* is scheduled to appear in 2006.

Kathy Domenici is a partner in Domenici Littlejohn, Inc., and a project consultant for the Public Dialogue Consortium. A consultant since 1990, she is a conflict-management specialist, mediator, facilitator, and trainer. She founded the Mediation Clinic at the University of New Mexico and now specializes in designing high-level strategy and leadership processes. She has worked on behalf of such clients as Eastman Kodak, The President's Commission on Critical Infrastructure, Sandia National Laboratories, Lockheed Martin, and the Kellogg Foundation.

Stephen W. Littlejohn is a conflict management consultant, mediator, facilitator, and trainer. He is consultant for the Public Dialogue Consortium and a partner in Domenici Littlejohn, Inc. He is a co-author of *Moral Conflict: When Social Worlds Collide* (Sage, 1997) and has written numerous other books and articles on communication and conflict. He was a professor of communication at Humboldt State University in California and is currently Adjunct Professor of Communication and Journalism at the University of New Mexico. He has done research on mediation and conflict management for 19 years and has been an active mediator for 8 years. He has been a consultant for such clients as the Waco Youth Summit, the Alliance for Constructive Communication, the City of Cupertino, Columbia Basin College, and Washington State University.